Educating for Service

Educating for Service

PACIFIC LUTHERAN UNIVERSITY

1890-1990

Philip A. Nordquist

PACIFIC LUTHERAN UNIVERSITY PRESS

TACOMA, WASHINGTON

CONTENTS

FOREWORD

THE CENTENNIAL YEAR is a time to celebrate beginnings, to review achievements, to set directions for the future, and generally to enjoy the relationships that make up the Pacific Lutheran Academy/College/University community. To set the background for such celebration, Dr. Philip Nordquist, professor of history, was commissioned to write a history of our one hundred years as an educational institution of the Lutheran church. Perhaps no one is more qualified to write such a record than Dr. Nordquist. Having been associated with the school for thirty-seven years, he offers a unique insight from the perspectives of student (1952–56), faculty member (since 1963), and researcher. Dr. Nordquist was on sabbatical leave for academic year 1986–87 to prepare the publication. The result is a comprehensive, lively, and very human record of the events that framed the character of the institution from its founding in 1890 to the centennial year. Like all good histories, the account is interpretive, bearing a viewpoint specific to the writer. It is a chronicle of progress that is both informative and appealing.

Reading the chapters, one is reassured that the mission of the university has been sustained throughout the years. The title of the book, and the theme of the centennial—"Educating for Service"—describes the motivation and mission that set PLU apart from many other schools. Its Norwegian Lutheran founders set as their task equipping students to make their way in the frontier Northwest. Along with teaching skills and language, developing faith became a natural partner of education. Through growth and change, from academy to college to university, an increasingly wide array of courses and facilities were added to meet needs. Leaders continued to affirm that service to others was the noblest goal of the educated person. As we approach the next century, contemporary society places ever-greater demands on students to help solve the awesome problems that are part of everyday living. The idea of service—service given from a base of knowledge and as a response to God's redeeming love— remains an integral part of the total educational experience at PLU.

To walk about the campus is to be made aware of the importance of individuals in our history. Many persons who have made lasting differences are remembered by the names seen every day on our buildings: Harstad, Hong, Hinderlie, Kreidler, Pflueger, Foss, Stuen, Ordal, Tingelstad, Ramstad, and Xavier halls; Eastvold and Olson auditoriums; Hauge Administration Building; Mortvedt Library; Rieke Science and Names Fitness centers; Blomquist, Haavik, Knorr, and Nesvig houses. These serve as constant reminders of those who have kept the school alive by their love and their efforts. Their names prompt recollections of personalities, of encounters, and of shared experiences. They and those who served with them marked the institution with their particular gifts. They are not forgotten, and our centennial will evoke renewed appreciation of their lives. In the same way, the 26,500 or more alumnae and alumni, who serve in all areas of the globe, have been influenced by PLU. Through their achievements, leadership, and involvement in their communities and homes, they reflect the kind of education that is the hallmark of the university. We are grateful for their choosing PLU and confident that the degrees from their *alma mater* serve them well.

"Educating for Service—Century II." May God grant us continued grace as we enter a new and exciting era!

William O. Rieke, M.D.
President, Pacific Lutheran University
(Class of 1953)

ACKNOWLEDGEMENTS

IT SEEMS like I have been surrounded by PLU's history since I first arrived in Parkland as a freshman football player in September 1952. During my undergraduate years I lived in the home of J. P. Pflueger, one of PLC's most important and beloved faculty members. I learned much from him. Long-time coach and athletic director Cliff Olson lived next door, and pioneer faculty member J. U. Xavier lived just down the street. I played football and basketball for Marv Harshman. Milt Nesvig soon became a friend, and I became a student of Walter Schnackenberg, who came to PLC as a student in 1935—when Oscar Tingelstad was president—and devoted most of his academic career to understanding and shaping the institution and strength-ening its liberal arts emphasis. By 1965, when Snack wrote *The Lamp and the Cross*, the seventy-five-year history of PLU, I was a member of the history department, and we spent many hours talking about the meaning of that history and the appropriate role of a Lutheran university in the Pacific Northwest. *The Lamp and the Cross* and Snack's doctoral dissertation, which dealt with Norwegian Lutheran higher education in the Northwest, have been very helpful in my own work.

With that background, I was happy to accept President William Rieke's suggestion (seconded by the centennial committee) that I should write the centennial history of PLU. The task took longer and was more complicated than I first anticipated, but it was also more gratifying. I hope the reader experiences some of the pleasure and discovery I felt as I worked on the book.

The writing of an institutional history is inevitably a cooperative ven-ture; I want to thank the many people who assisted me. President Rieke (and his office staff, executive associate Lucille Giroux and secretaries Anne Lucky and Roberta Marsh) provided financial support, technical as-sistance, information, access to university records, and complete freedom. I appreciated the freedom very much. The alumni association has been warmly supportive and among other things has subsidized research trips to Palo Alto, California, and Northfield, Minnesota. The archivists at Stan-ford University and the Norwegian-American Historical Association, located at St. Olaf College, were very helpful. Librarian John Heussman energetically gathered together materials about Lutheranism and Lutheran higher education in North America. Vice presidents Perry Hendricks and Don Sturgill gathered the financial data that appear in appendices B and C. Milt Nesvig answered dozens of questions, opened his own files, and helped me find my way into the university archives. His knowledge of

PLU's history is legendary. Loleta Espeseth gathered much of the academic information that is included in the appendices. For the photographs I am indebted to the PLU Archives and the university's photo services office. Many of the photographs were taken by Ken Dunmire; others are from the Edmond Richards collection in the university archives.

More than thirty people agreed to be interviewed about their roles in— or memories of—PLU's history. The book was enriched by their contributions. Many of those interviews are preserved on tape and are located in the university archives. A number of individuals responded by letter or telephone to questions I posed. The endnotes supply a record of those responses. Several colleagues provided various kinds of artistic and technical assistance. Among them are Ken Dunmire, Jim Peterson, Kris Ringdahl, and David Swanson. Eight colleagues helped me resolve questions of accuracy, appropriateness, and style by reading chapters at various stages of preparation. If inaccuracies and infelicities remain, they are my responsibility. The eight are: George Arbaugh, Chris Browning, Wayne Carp, Ken Christopherson, Don Farmer, Bill Giddings, Jim Hushagen, and Erv Severtson. Lisa Shannon and Susan Young prepared the final draft that was electronically sent to the typesetter, Susan Morrison read the page proofs, and the index was prepared by Sandy Faye Cassio.

Three people require special thanks. Kay Hirst turned my smudged drafts into neat and orderly pages. She deserved combat pay. Moreover, she compiled the list of faculty members included as appendix F. Confused records made that task an arduous one. Paul Porter handled technical questions related to graphics, typesetting, printing, and book design. He is wonderfully competent. Finally, and most important, Megan Benton with her cheerful manner and her extensive knowledge of publishing, editing, and typography served as editor, copy editor, and book designer. The book has been much improved because of her skill and taste.

The book is dedicated to my wife. The reasons for that are myriad, as all who know me understand.

Philip A. Nordquist

For Helen

Educating for Service

1

Athens and Jerusalem

THE HISTORY of Pacific Lutheran University—an institution founded by Norwegian Lutherans that has retained a strong connection to the Lutheran church—really began two thousand, not one hundred, years ago with the birth of the Christian religion and its strong commitment to education. That commitment has been expressed in a rich variety of ways over the centuries, and its impact on Western history has been profound. The story of PLU has to be placed within that context if it is to be fully comprehended; PLU's educational philosophy has always been shaped by its Christian orientation and its specifically Lutheran character.

Christianity first emerged within the culture of the Roman Empire and all of its configurations. Christian leaders had to come to terms with that culture in order to communicate with their world. In the process the new religion absorbed the visions of the mystery cults, ancient science, and large amounts of Roman law, organization, rhetoric, and philosophy. The church battled to keep the fundamental message of Christ's Incarnation intact, uncorrupted, and—its defenders argued—compromised only in those areas that were not basic to the Christian faith. It was a difficult enterprise and there were critics.

Tertullian (150–230) was the most famous early critic. A member of the puritan wing of the North African church, he was a lawyer and a convert to Christianity. He saw the radical distinction between Greco-Roman and Judeo-Christian traditions and asked: "What has Jerusalem to do with Athens, the Church with the Academy, the Christian with the heretic?... I have no use for a Stoic or a Platonic or a dialectical Christianity. After Jesus Christ we have no need of speculation, after the Gospel no need of research."[1]

Tertullian argued with all the passion of a North African Christian and the honed intelligence of a superbly trained Roman rhetorician and lawyer. By the time of his death, however, the church had committed itself to Greco-Roman intellectual categories and educational forms while trying to keep clear the distinction between Athens and Jerusalem. There were, of course, already strong emphases on teaching and learning within the Christian community. Jesus was a teacher, and that he chose and trained disciples was a very important precedent for the future. That he called those disciples friends was more important still. Again and again in

Western history, significant intellectual advances have resulted when groups of friends talk. As one contemporary scholar has observed, "this inseparable bond between truth and personal relationship is worth remembering as we enter the computer age."[2] Truth is mediated through personality. That is the hallmark of Christian education.

St. Augustine (354–430) completed the unification of secular and Christian themes and gave the mixture an enduring form that is still recognizable. His times were badly out of joint as the classical world painfully turned into the medieval world. Augustine merged classical culture and Christianity, and he served as a gateway between the two worlds. In the process he hammered out the doctrines that became orthodox norms for the church for the next thousand years. He also insisted that the church could absorb the world without losing its identity, because that identity was based on the objective promise of God worked out in history and in the sacraments.

Late in his career Augustine authorized and justified the use of force against opponents when he concluded that more than spiritual pressure was needed to avoid evil. The church would use force to accomplish its ends with some regularity—often with Augustinian arguments—from this time on. Force would sometimes be used by its educational institutions as well, especially when puritanical groups got the upper hand. They also would rely on Augustinian arguments.

After Augustine's death the classical world slowly disappeared and the forms of the Middle Ages began to appear. Education and classical learning almost completely disappeared; they were saved only in the libraries and copying rooms of the Benedictine monasteries. European civilization depended on the efforts of the monks, who saved at least a fragment of the earlier culture and produced what little literacy there was between the sixth and the twelfth centuries. Such learning explored within a pattern of community would remain basic to subsequent Christian education.

By the eleventh and twelfth centuries rapid and complex change began to take place. Growing confidence pushed along by an expanding population, a healthy economy, and the emergence of cities required broader literacy and more and better schools. The conservative monasteries, whose main activity was the pursuit of salvation, were too limited for this dynamic and growing enterprise, so new educational institutions began to emerge. At first cathedrals responded to the expanding demands for education, but when cathedral schools proved too small and conservative, a new and distinctive educational institution emerged—the university. Universities appeared first in Paris and the Italian cities, next in Oxford, and then more slowly throughout the rest of Europe.

Universities were present in Germany by the mid-fourteenth century.

The Protestant Reformation would begin in the sixteenth century at a German university, and universities dominated by Reformation thought (Wittenberg, Geneva, Cambridge) have influenced Protestant and Lutheran education ever since. The basic elements out of which a Lutheran philosophy of education would be formed include the Reformation experience, but they also stretch back to include Christian humanism, the curriculum and practices of medieval universities, St. Augustine, the church fathers, classical definitions of the liberal arts, and the extended conversation—and sometimes accommodation—that took place between Athens and Jerusalem. It is a long story. It can be ignored only at great peril because the community that ignores or repudiates its history will end up in bondage to the recent past.

Martin Luther

Martin Luther was born in the easternmost part of Germany in 1483. He left Germany only once and he never escaped from his medieval roots, but—from his position as a professor in a small new university in a tiny and colorless town—he changed the course of history. The story of the Reformation and Lutheranism cannot be separated from the story of universities. The Reformation began as an academic movement within a university.

Martin Luther was an excellent student. He studied in Latin schools and then matriculated at the University of Erfurt in 1501. Founded in 1392, it was the most famous—and probably the best—university in Germany. The curriculum featured the liberal arts. For the B.A. degree Luther studied grammar, rhetoric, and logic, known as the trivium. He took that degree in 1502 and continued on to study music, astronomy, geometry, and arithmetic—the quadrivium. This earned him the M.A. degree in 1505, which allowed him to teach.

That year Luther began law school at Erfurt and studied for a term before leaving to join the Augustinian order of hermits and concentrate his intellect and will on the pursuit of salvation. He was very exercised by the apparent uncertainty of that quest, as were many in the sixteenth century. He was ordained in 1507 and then directed to the study of theology. In 1508–09 he taught ethics at the University of Wittenberg and took two theological degrees while there. He continued his theological study the next year at Erfurt, visited Rome in 1510–11, and in 1512 returned to Wittenberg as a professor of Bible, where he remained the rest of his life.

Luther received the doctorate in October 1512 and began his new career. He was a bright scholar with impeccable academic credentials who turned out to be an excellent teacher. The sparks that set off the Reformation came from the frictions caused when his severe spiritual anxiety, lecture preparation, and up-to-date Renaissance-influenced, language-oriented scholarship came together. Luther remained committed to language study and the liberal arts, as has the Lutheran educational tradition he inspired.

Luther was a dedicated teacher. He frequently grumbled that students were not sufficiently attentive to their studies. Some were able and diligent, but they did not have adequate financial aid. "There are many godly and gifted students who live all year on bread and water and endure frost and cold in order that they may study the Holy Scripture and the Word of God."[3] At the university there were also inevitable problems of marriage and romance that had to be settled. The canon law of marriage and betrothal practices of the day sometimes created traps, and students needed champions. "Your son John is attached by a great love to an honorable girl here . . . I am unwilling to see his hope turn to ashes. It . . . behooves you as a loving mother to give your consent," Luther urged one reluctant parent. The use and abuse of recreational time further prompted concerns. Luther thought that students, like most Germans, often drank too much. That was unfortunate; while physical exercise, such as swimming and playing ball, was appropriate for students, excessive drinking was not. Even dancing was appropriate under the right conditions. Students could attend dances "for the sake of honest discipline" and to "learn reverence and modesty in conversation and deportment." But there were limits. "We should severely punish those who foolishly cause disturbances at such gatherings, and especially those who are immodest in their dancing and lead girls in gyrations beyond the common harmony of modest dancing." Luther maintained, however, that eating, drinking, and dancing were not solely to blame. "Go ahead and dance. Faith and love are lost neither by dancing nor by sitting out the dance, provided you do what you do with decency and moderation." The Pacific Lutheran University governors would dispute this until 1963.

LUTHER'S EDUCATIONAL PHILOSOPHY

Luther's dynamic and paradoxical—or dialectical—theology crept into virtually all aspects of his work, including education. He juxtaposed and wrote of the tensions, but also of the connections, between law and gospel, faith and works, the Kingdom of God and the worldly kingdom, the spiritual realm and the secular realm, the sword and the Word of God, and *simul justus et peccator* (at the same time justified and sinner).[4]

One of the basic themes in Luther's theology is called the doctrine of the two kingdoms. This notion is complex and sometimes controversial; some Luther scholars suggest that it would be better to describe it as the two "ways" or "modes" through which God works. St. Augustine contrasted the city of man (the earthly city where alien residents lived and moved as pilgrims toward God) and its opposite, the City of God. The two kingdoms Luther described are both of God—one is the right hand and the other the left. They are "two modes of his love."[5]

One of these modes—the right hand—is the "spiritual" realm of God's activity, which Luther says is the "proper" work of God and is expressed most powerfully in Jesus Christ, then in the proclamation of the Gospel and the administration of the sacraments. Salvation is the work of the right hand. The other mode, the left hand, where God is "hidden," is the "secular" realm that includes all human work—government, law, art, intellectual activity, family life, social and economic structures, and much else. This is no less a part of God's activity even though the mode is different. The mode or realm of the left hand is to be taken with the utmost seriousness and concern. Each mode bears its own integrity. Each is part of God's creation.[6] The Lutheran Church in America spelled this out in a 1976 statement:

> As we live and work with others, we discern the outlines of this design. We are set in families; we establish governments; we take our place in the structures of commerce and industry; we form organizations—colleges among them—to promote the public good. The creator does not intend us to make a lonely way through life; he has provided us with companions and colleagues. It is his will that we ally ourselves with all who are moved by reason and conscience to respond, even if unawares to his law written in their hearts, as they seek to advance and improve the human condition. This association is God-given, this cooperation in the secular is God-pleasing. For the term secular means non-redemptive; it does not mean God-forsaken.[7]

This means that education has an integrity and purpose grounded in the first article of the Apostles' Creed, concerning creation. In Lutheran theology God is ambidextrous: the right hand works for salvation and the left hand for justice and fulfillment in creation.[8]

One of the first tasks addressed as a result of Luther's new understanding of faith, grace, and the "two modes" was the reform of the University of Wittenberg and its curriculum. Lectures on the Bible and St. Augustine and careful instruction in languages replaced the medieval preoccupation with Aristotelian logic and metaphysics. Regular instruction in the classical and biblical languages was introduced. As a result Wittenberg became the first German university where Latin, Greek, and Hebrew were all taught. It thus became the first university in Germany to adopt a curriculum corresponding to the educational program of Christian humanism. It was much imitated.

Luther also addressed the education of children. At first he thought they could be taught at home by parents, and he prepared manuals for family use. The publication of *The Small Catechism* in 1529 had a profound religious and educational influence throughout the next four centuries. This family-oriented education was inadequate for the enormity of the tasks at hand, however, and instead Luther, pushed strongly by unruly events, soon addressed the role of society and rulers in education. The shift can be seen in his 1524 recommendation "To the Councilmen of All Cities in Germany That They Establish and Maintain Christian Schools." Forcefully written and programmatic, it advocated universal compulsory education under the direction of civil authorities. This shift of emphasis was of seminal importance for the development and spread of universal education in the Western world.[9]

Luther was soon concerned that leaders in Germany were not taking up the educational responsibilities that the new theology pointed to.

> For it is a grave and important matter, and one which is of vital concern both to Christ and the world at large, that we take steps to help the youth. . . . My dear sirs, if we have to spend such large sums every year on guns, roads, bridges, dams, and countless similar items to insure the temporal peace and prosperity of a city, why should not much more be devoted to the poor neglected youth—at least enough to engage one or two competent men to teach school?[10]

Parents cannot take up the task of education in an adequate way, Luther argued. Most are not fitted for the job and, in any case, they are too busy. Therefore, public school teachers would have to be hired. Languages should be a major part of the curriculum because the Gospel comes through the medium of languages: "The languages are the sheath in which the sword of the spirit is contained."[11]

What, according to Luther, was the purpose of education? Pleasure, satisfaction, the thrill of discovery, and the sheer joy of learning were all certainly important, but Luther made it clear that what really counted was "education for citizenship, for responsible service to one's city and country."[12]

> Here we are excelled and put to shame by the pagans of old, especially the Romans and Greeks. Although they had no idea of whether this estate were pleasing to God or not, they were so earnest and diligent in educating and training their young boys and girls to fit them for the task, that when I call it to mind I am forced to blush for us Christians, and especially for us Germans. We are such utter beasts and blockheads. . . .[13]

If education were handled in a responsible, thoughtful, and informed way, Luther was convinced, people would no longer be such beasts and blockheads, and the world might be made better. Education would not bring salvation, but it could bring important benefits.

In addition to reforming the Wittenberg curriculum and redirecting education, Luther recognized the integrity and autonomy of the various academic disciplines. He defended academic freedom, which he understood as the right of each discipline to pursue its own goals, with its own methods and categories, without interference from other disciplines, including Christian theology.[14]

The evangelical breakthrough of Martin Luther rearranged the nature of life and thought for many in the sixteenth century. Developments in the world of educational thought and institutions stemming from his ideas still influence Western education, and are present in varying ways in Lutheran higher education in North America.[15] One does not have to dig very deep—or look very hard—to encounter them. The most basic, and perhaps controversial, Lutheran theme is the foundation role of dialectical theology and the two kingdoms. David Lotz has argued convincingly that "the Lutheran doctrine of the two kingdoms . . . affords a supple, serviceable, and sophisticated theological foundation for higher education in the church-related college and university."[16] Luther's own experiences with liberal education and the enthusiasm he felt for language study helped lead to the curricular reforms at the University of Wittenberg and gave an enduring stamp of approval to liberal education and linguistic study at Protestant—and certainly Lutheran—colleges, universities, and seminaries. Those emphases continue to the present day.

By the mid-1520s Luther advocated universal compulsory education. This Reformation notion, more fully developed in later centuries, has been fundamentally important in Western history. Another tenet of Luther's philosophy was that education should enhance qualities of citizenship and service. This notion, too, has had a lively and influential life. (The 1990–91 centennial theme selected for Pacific Lutheran University, "Educating for Service—Century II," was selected in deliberate recognition of this tradition.) Further, Luther's insistence on academic freedom established a dominant motif in the development of the modern university and the intellectual discoveries of the modern world. This principle would be more fully developed in German universities in the eighteenth and nineteenth centuries.

THREE TRADITIONS

The University of Wittenberg best illustrated these various themes or motifs for a time, but then other Lutheran universities were founded—Jena, Marburg, Königsberg—that also embraced the programs of Lutheran theology and Christian humanism. When Philipp Melanchthon, one of Luther's coworkers, helped reform still other educational institutions in Germany, the Reformation's influence could not be dislodged.

The Lutheran educational enterprise split into at least three traditions around the end of the sixteenth century. Those traditions sprang out of the Reformation, but remained more or less distinct even though they influenced each other fairly substantially during the long course of post-Reformation history. All three are authentically Lutheran, and no single tradition by itself exhausts all the possibilities inherent in the Lutheran educational legacy. The late Sydney Ahlstrom called these traditions the scholastic (or orthodoxist), the pietistic, and the critical. Each has enjoyed considerable prominence and vitality in both Europe and America.[17]

The scholastic tradition emerged out of the fierce intra- and extramural debates of Lutheranism beginning in the late sixteenth century. It was a nasty time politically and religiously as battles raged within Lutheranism and between Lutherans and Roman Catholics, on the one hand, and between Lutherans and the followers of John Calvin, on the other. The theological structure that emerged rested on two pillars: "The first of these was an almost unbelievably great confidence in the infallibility and total sufficiency of the received biblical text. The second was a whole-hearted adoption of Aristotelian metaphysics. . . . The result was a precise but extremely intellectualized theoretic exposition of Lutheran doctrine."[18]

The scholastic tradition acquired new life and direction in the nineteenth century, as did tenets of the Lutheran Confessions. This was in part a reaction against nineteenth-century philosophical and historical study, with its implications for biblical scholarship. Much important scholastic doctrinal research and publication took place, but at a heavy price; as Ahlstrom noted, "Lutheran Orthodoxy tended to disengage itself from many of the 19th century's achievements, and became more reactionary than it had ever been before."[19] The Norwegian Synod—the branch of Norwegian Lutheranism that founded PLU—was deeply influenced by the scholastic tradition.

The pietistic tradition emerged primarily during the seventeenth and eighteenth centuries. It focused on the inner life and the doing of good works. It reacted strongly against the formalism and intellectualization of orthodoxy. Its "pervasiveness and vitality" made a deep impression on education; the "Bible and prayer circles entered the university sanctuaries of scholasticism, undermining formalistic views of worship, making personal evangelism a part of the academic scene, and deprecating the significance of doctrinal precisianism."[20] Pietism—in its eighteenth- and nineteenth-century German and Scandinavian varieties—is scattered all through Lutheran education.

The critical tradition appeared most clearly in the nineteenth century's resurgent interest in science and philosophy. It was and is dominated by a willingness to question the received understanding of things. It owes an important debt to Luther, since such openness was at least part of what shaped his evangelical breakthrough. The critical tradition came to terms with modern science and did not think of scientific inquiry as an enemy of religion. It also undertook a serious investigation of the whole historical world, and this involved critical scholarly work in the history of the Scriptures, in the churches and their various doctrines (including the Lutheran Confessions), and in other world religions. As a result, Lutheran scholars have done far more than their share in modern religious scholarship.[21]

This critical tradition with its readiness to reexamine produced extraordinary results in nineteenth-century European scholarship, but had little impact—except perhaps negatively—in North America. That would have to wait until the twentieth century, when it would join forces with post-World War I neo-orthodox theology and advances in Luther scholarship (the "Luther Renaissance") to affect powerfully American Lutherans and Lutheran higher education. Its influence would not hit PLU in any significant way until the 1950s, but when it hit, it hit with considerable impact.

2

Ethnicity, Theology, and Education

M<small>ANY OF THE</small> theological and educational traditions and concerns that led to the establishment of Pacific Lutheran University originated in nineteenth-century Norway. Luther's educational views and the traditions that developed in Germany provided an important foundation, but the social, economic, political, educational, intellectual, and religious patterns in Norway added dynamic complexity to the situation. They came together to produce several varieties of Norwegian-American Lutheranism and Lutheran higher education in North America.

By the beginning of the nineteenth century, Denmark and Norway had shared the same ruler since 1380, but with the advent of nationalism that relationship was strongly opposed by the Norwegian people. In 1814 representatives of the Norwegian people met and drew up a national constitution that provided for a very democratic government. Deeply buried conservative structures in society, however, would be at odds with the constitution for a long time. Norway did not gain complete independence even with this; it had to align itself with Sweden and, while the Norwegian constitution was recognized, Norway was clearly the junior partner in the relationship. This was not resolved until 1905 when Norway and Sweden finally separated completely. In a century of ferocious nationalism this ongoing relationship chafed, which was apparent in many aspects of Norwegian life.

A cultural renaissance—tied to romanticism and nationalism—accompanied the political changes that took place after 1814. This brought a deep look into Norway's past to find its true history and authentic character. The discovery of folk music and folk tales, a burst of literary activity and history writing, and the development of a national university in 1811 (the University of Christiania) were by-products of this renaissance. The Lutheran church became a state church in 1814, with a formal structure of bishops and clergy. The laity had to play second fiddle.

In the midst of these changes, the social-economic cleavages, strong class distinctions, and as-yet-unredeemed promises of the new constitution produced a volatile situation. The rationalism and formalism of the state church had made it a target for reformers as well. The two sets of problems came together in the powerful folk movement, led at first by the redoubtable Hans Nielsen Hauge (1771–1824), that fought for social justice and a revived, evangelical, and lay-oriented Christianity.

Hauge came from peasant stock. In 1796 he had a religious experience that inspired him for the rest of his life; he became a traveling preacher and led a national revival between 1796 and 1804. He emphasized law and repentance—but also grace. He was critical of the state church, but he never separated from it. Hauge emphasized conversion, Bible reading, small group meetings (conventicles), lay preaching, and moral rigorism. Political and religious opposition was quick to rise to this challenge, and Hauge spent about ten years in prison, where his health was broken but not his spirit. Political, social, and economic reforms would result from Hauge's revival, and Norwegian church life would be reshaped. Pietism influenced by Hauge and others became very widespread, though never official, in Norway. It traveled to America and was very influential there as well. Especially in the Midwest, the moral rigor brought from Europe— Sunday observance and opposition to alcoholic beverages, dancing, card playing, and the theater—was reinforced by the puritanical and revivalist tendencies present in much of American Protestantism in the latter part of the nineteenth century.[1]

Pietism in Norway continued under the leadership of Gisle Johnson (1822–94), a theology professor and leader of ongoing revivals. He combined pietism and orthodoxy in a way that became quite typical of Norwegian and Norwegian-American Lutheranism. Virtually all latter nineteenth-century Norwegian Lutheran pastors were influenced by Johnson. Later in the century, some of the weaknesses of pietism also began to appear—its censoriousness, emotionalism, pettiness, and somberness.[2] Whatever the face of pietism, however, it deeply influenced religious life and education in America and among Norwegian-Americans.

Emigration from Norway to America began in 1825, when the first boatload arrived on the sloop *Restaurationen*. Three-quarters of a million emigrants would follow, most after 1865. The motivation for coming to America was mostly economic, but nearly all were Lutherans who brought their interpretations of what that meant into the new country, where freedom of religion ruled and where society and culture were only partly formed. Church leaders faced the task of transforming and adapting a state church tradition with its formalism and clerical domination into a lively, free church system based on voluntary organization and financial support from members.[3] Thus, the religious passions and concerns in Norway were translated into a number of interpretations of Lutheranism in America. Colleges and seminaries were often formed to help maintain and transmit those interpretations, but the chief vehicle was the synod, a form of polity or organization that fused together ethnically similar and theologically like-minded Lutherans.

SYNODS

The first Norwegian Lutheran synod established in America was the Eielsen Synod (1846), which was organized by the followers of the itinerant lay preacher Elling Eielsen (1804–84). He introduced the Haugean lay movement to America with great energy, stressing repentance, conversion, and lay activity. He disliked formality, rules, systems, vestments, and liturgy. "One-sided and prejudiced, individualistic in character and disposition, Eielsen was withal an earnest trail-blazer for the Church among Norwegian-Americans."[4] The new synod was based on loose, individualistic ties with little formal organization. From the beginning the Eielsen Synod led a very precarious existence; it was plagued with splits, theological dissension, disagreements, and a constant lack of organization. Three times—in 1848, 1856, and 1876—groups separated from Eielsen and went their own way. The almost complete absence of structure frustrated many—even those committed Haugeans who wanted relatively little organization—and bred disagreement. The 1876 split led to the creation of the Hauge Synod, which produced a new constitution to provide some additional structure and order. The new synod regarded itself a legitimate continuation of the older body with authentic connections back to Norway. It continued the pietistic emphasis that to some degree had made its way into all the Norwegian-American churches by the 1870s.[5]

The Eielsen Synod—tiny and perversely stubborn though it was after 1876—continued to exist into the late 1980s. The Hauge Synod continued until 1917, when it became part of the newly merged Norwegian Lutheran Church of America. Two PLU presidents—Seth Clarence Eastvold and Robert A. L. Mortvedt—had roots in the Hauge Synod: both their fathers were pastors in the synod. In addition, Eastvold was educated at the Hauge Synod's Red Wing College and Seminary, and his father was the synod's last president.

The Norwegian Evangelical Lutheran Church in America (usually referred to as the Norwegian Synod) was founded in 1853. It was the synod that founded PLU in 1890. With its formalism and liturgical emphasis it closely resembled the state church in Norway, and it was guided by a group of doctrinally minded, university-educated clergymen who were intent on orthodoxy.[6] Such men as J.W.C. Dietrichson, A. C. Preus, H. A. Preus, H. A. Stub, and U. V. Koren were among its pioneers. They were "orthodox to the finger-tips."[7]

> Within a free-church framework the Norwegian Synod retained as many of the state-church principles as possible. It adopted the ritual of the Church of Norway and its ecclesiastical garments, defended the Augsburg Confession's ban against lay preaching, was dogmatic in its teachings, and asserted churchly authority in all questions of doctrine. The Synod was to an

unusual extent preoccupied with doctrine, with determining what were the Bible's true teachings.[8]

In matters of theology the Norwegian Synod had a great deal of sympathy for the German-American Missouri Synod, which also thought of itself as a champion of orthodoxy. This attitude quite often resulted in a "dogmatic censoriousness" that was resented by other Lutheran groups.[9] It certainly separated the Norwegian Synod, with its doctrinal and liturgical tradition, from the frontier anticlericalism of the Eielsen and Hauge synods, both of which emphasized experiential religion, conversion, moral rigorism, and lay involvement.[10] In fact, the Hauge Synod and the Norwegian Synod were the two extremes of the Norwegian-American Lutheran spectrum.

The Norwegian Synod tradition was frequently criticized as too intellectualized and dogmatic, but it was intent on keeping learning, orthodoxy, and piety alive in the frontier conditions of America. As long as that dream seemed possible, the Norwegian Synod combined faith and learning in such a way as to produce piety and service.[11] When most of the Norwegian Lutherans merged into a single body in 1917 it was in "no small measure" indebted to the Norwegian Synod for its theological vitality. The first six presidents and most of the early faculty at PLU came from the Norwegian Synod.[12]

Women also played an important role in the Norwegian Synod. Sigurd Ylvisaker appealed to a long synod tradition in his response to criticisms from the Missouri and Wisconsin synods about using women as teachers: "Why, we always knew how important the women were. Maybe that's why they [the German pastors] are so uncouth. They've been shortchanged in their educations."[13]

Swedish Lutherans (along with a small number of Norwegians and Danes) organized in 1860 as the Augustana Synod. They managed to keep pietism and some degree of formalism and liturgical emphasis balanced reasonably well. The Swedes did not split over organization and theology as the Norwegians did. The name Augustana (the Latinized form of Augsburg) suggests their enthusiasm for the Augsburg Confession, that important Reformation creed (1530) that reemerged with such power in the nineteenth century.

In 1870 Danish and Norwegian members split off from the Augustana Synod and formed two new bodies: the Norwegian Augustana Synod and the Conference for the Norwegian-Danish Evangelical Lutheran Church. These two groups tried to stay in the middle of Norwegian-American Lutheranism in a mediating position. The Norwegian Augustana Synod attempted to maintain its Haugean heritage, frequently in opposition to the Norwegian Synod. The Conference tried to occupy a position between the Norwegian Synod and low church pietists, but was regularly critical of the synod's "blind adulation of Missourianism."[14]

Each synod's relationship with the Missouri Synod became paramount by 1880 when the most divisive of the theological arguments that rocked midwestern Lutheranism emerged. It was about predestination. Remarks of the Missouri leader C.F.W. Walther seemed unduly Calvinistic to some, who responded vigorously. The Norwegian Synod was sympathetic to Missouri's position, but many other Lutheran groups reacted very negatively. The German-American Ohio Synod, which had been quite friendly to the Missouri Synod, broke with it over predestination; the two new synods that seceded from the Augustana Synod in 1870 continued in their opposition to Missouri's theology; and after 1883 even the Norwegian Synod distanced itself from Missouri. A new group emerged out of this controversy as well, the Anti-Missouri Brotherhood, formed in 1887. Its leaders did not like the negative tone of the name, but because they could not tolerate some of Missouri's theology, they accepted the name and devoted much energy to mediation and merger activity. They organized their educational activity at St. Olaf College.

Three of these groups—the Norwegian Augustana Synod, the Conference, and the Anti-Missouri Brotherhood—merged in 1890 to form the United Norwegian Lutheran Church in America, commonly known as the United Church. It was inclusive and devoted to mission; it was also the largest of the Norwegian Lutheran synods.[15] St. Olaf College consequently became the school of the new United Church. It was a coeducational liberal arts college, unlike the classically oriented institutions for preseminary training established by other synods. One group could not go along with the United Church's educational commitment to St. Olaf College, however, and separated in 1893, calling itself the "Friends of Augsburg." This group preferred an educational institution (Augsburg College and Seminary) that prepared ministers from high school through seminary with an integrated curriculum. This group became the Lutheran Free Church in 1897. The United Church and the Lutheran Free Church both founded educational institutions in the state of Washington, the former in Everett and Spokane, and the latter in Poulsbo and Everett.

The 1890 merger that produced the United Church was a major event in the movement toward Norwegian Lutheran and American Lutheran unity. Merger discussions among the three large remaining Norwegian groups began almost immediately after 1890. The breakthrough came in 1912 with the Madison Agreement, which acknowledged that both sides of the argument about election or predestination that had plagued Lutheranism since the 1880s were legitimate: the Missouri position of "election unto faith" and the more broadly based view of election in view of foreseen faith. C. J. Eastvold, the last president of the Hauge Synod and the father of PLU president S. C. Eastvold, was an "active and interested" member of the committee on union who favored union. But as his son recalled: "He was heart and soul in favor of union, but not at the expense of yielding a single essential point of truth, as he saw it."[16]

The Norwegian Lutheran merger was made possible by the 1912 agreement. Events transpired quickly after 1912, and the merger took place in 1917 on the four hundredth anniversary of the beginning of the Reformation. As church historian E. Clifford Nelson described it: "In a huge, enthusiastic convention in St. Paul, which combined Norwegian religious and cultural elements in a way not always easily distinguishable, over 92 percent of Norwegian Lutherans, comprising 30 percent of all Norwegians in America, combined to form the Norwegian Lutheran Church of America."[17]

Not all joined. The Eielsen Synod, the Lutheran Free Church, and the Lutheran Brethren (another Haugean group) stayed out, and some loyal Norwegian Synod members, led by thirteen pastors who could not stomach the 1912 agreement because of its odor of compromise, separated in 1918. That year they formed a new body—the Norwegian Synod of the American Evangelical Lutheran Church—which they believed preserved the tenets of the old.[18] The "Little Norwegian Synod," as it came to be called, elected the Reverend Bjug Harstad, the founder of PLU, as its first president. Norwegian Lutherans continued to take theology and education very seriously.

One other Lutheran group would participate in the early operation of PLU—the German-American Joint Synod of Ohio. Formed in 1818, it established Capital University as its college and seminary. The Joint Synod was quite theologically conservative, and it maintained an ongoing and sometimes enthusiastic sympathy with the Missouri Synod until a controversy over predestination severed that relationship. The Joint Synod engaged quite early in missionary and educational activity in the Northwest: in Portland, in Tacoma (where a preparatory school was organized in 1889), and east of the Cascade Mountains. (One early missionary it sent there was the Reverend Henry Rieke, grandfather of the future PLU president.) The Joint Synod also established the first Lutheran theological seminary on the Pacific Coast in Olympia in 1907. It was closed in 1910, but in 1914 the United Norwegian College in Spokane invited Joint Synod students to come there. The invitation was accepted, and by 1922 a Joint Synod professor taught in Spokane. In 1927 a subsidy was extended to Spokane College by the Joint Synod; this pioneering intersynodical Lutheran cooperation continued in Parkland in 1929 when Spokane College merged with Pacific Lutheran College.

The Joint Synod of Ohio and three other synods (the Iowa, Texas, and Buffalo synods, founded in 1854, 1851, and 1845, respectively) merged in

1930 to create the American Lutheran Church. It continued the cooperation in Parkland begun by the Joint Synod of Ohio.

LUTHERANS IN THE PACIFIC NORTHWEST

The first Lutheran to enter the Pacific Northwest may have been a
member of the Lewis and Clark expedition in 1805–06.[19] The migration
began along the Oregon Trail in the 1840s, and by the 1860s and 1870s
fairly sizeable numbers of Lutherans were entering the region. With the
completion of the Northern Pacific Railroad to Seattle in 1883, settlers,
many of them immigrants, came in droves. After Washington became a
state in 1889, there was a fourfold growth in population by 1910. Half a
million Americans of foreign extraction lived in the state by 1910; 123,701
of them were Scandinavian. Most newcomers settled around Puget Sound,
although some settled in Spokane, in Portland, and in the Willamette
Valley. Germans, who became the largest contingent of foreign-born in
Oregon, migrated to the Northwest also, often settling around Portland.
Many of these Germans and most of the Scandinavians were Lutheran,
even though only a small percentage ended up associating with Lutheran
churches.

The first Lutheran congregation on the Pacific Coast was in Sitka,
Alaska.[20] Worship there began in 1840 and continued until 1867. The same
year a short-lived Lutheran congregation began in Portland. The next
church was established in 1871, also in Portland, and thereafter half a
dozen synods began serious missionary work in the area. By 1890, after
twenty years of hard, lonely, and sometimes terribly disappointing labor,
the Lutheran church—in its various synodical expressions—was firmly
established in the Northwest. There were sixty-seven congregations,
forty-seven ordained clergy, and 6,055 members. The Augustana Synod
had sixteen congregations, the United Norwegian Church had fifteen, and
the Joint Synod of Ohio had nine. The Norwegian Synod, which founded
PLU, had five congregations, two ordained pastors, and 250 adult members.[21]

Almost as soon as churches were established, pastors and lay members
turned their attention to founding charitable and educational institutions.
Leaders had to be educated, English had to be learned, and people needed
jobs. Between 1890 and 1910 four Norwegian Lutheran colleges, one
Swedish Lutheran college, one German Lutheran college, and two theological seminaries were founded in the Northwest. The first and ultimately
most successful of these institutions was Pacific Lutheran University.[22]

3

The Founding of
Pacific Lutheran University

In 1861 the Norwegian Synod established Luther College in Decorah, Iowa, to prepare young men for theological study. A linguistic curriculum based on the study of Latin, Greek, German, and Norwegian was established, which was not significantly reformed until the 1930s. Because the school was originally intended for pretheological training, it did not become coeducational until 1936.

As the first Norwegian Lutheran college to grant baccalaureate degrees and to send its graduates into both graduate and theological education, Luther College provided important leadership for other Norwegian Lutheran educational institutions. It educated the first two presidents and most of the early faculty of St. Olaf College, the first president of Concordia College, and the first six presidents as well as most of the early faculty of Pacific Lutheran University.[1] Luther College was an important role model for PLU for a long time, even though PLU was coeducational and its curriculum was from the beginning much broader.

By the early 1870s Norwegian Lutherans led by the Norwegian Synod launched an "academy movement" that resulted in the establishment of seventy-five secondary and normal schools in the Midwest, Canada, and the Pacific Northwest. The purpose of these schools was quite different from that of the classical schools that prepared men for theological study, yet they too embodied the "education for citizenship and service" tradition established by Martin Luther. Several present-day Scandinavian Lutheran colleges—Gustavus Adolphus, St. Olaf, Bethany, Concordia, Pacific Lutheran, and Upsala—were founded as church academies during this movement.[2]

Interest in education began quite early among Scandinavian Lutherans in the Northwest. One of their first leaders was the Reverend Christian Joergensen, who came in 1878 to the rich agricultural land of Stanwood in Washington's Stillaguamish Valley, which, as one real estate broker's stationery boasted, was "as fertile as the Nile." Many Norwegians had settled in that area, and Joergensen wanted a school there. Several sites were explored, but nothing came from these preliminary explorations until a young Seattle real estate agent by the name of Louis Evenson acquired some lots in Tacoma. He spoke with the Reverend Peter O. Langseth about the possibility of a school there. The two of them then went to see real estate developer Ward T. Smith, who had lots for sale in

Parkland, about eight miles south of Tacoma, and a scheme—illustrated by maps and charts on the walls of his office—that had set aside a plat for a college. There had been some talk of an "Eastern interest" in establishing a college at the site, but that had not materialized.

Pastor Langseth explained that Norwegian Lutherans might be interested in building a school in Parkland, but that they had no money. Smith then proposed that some money from the sale of lots could help finance the new school. This was a fairly typical method of developing real estate and building colleges in the late nineteenth century. Langseth, excited by this, wrote to the synod pastors meeting in Decorah, Iowa, about the pressing need for a Lutheran school in the Northwest, the appropriateness of Parkland as a site, and the development plans that Smith had proposed.[3]

On 14 October 1890—"Founder's Day" at Luther College—the synod decided to try to initiate some educational activity on the Pacific Coast. The following resolution was passed:

> The conference deems the establishing of a Lutheran High School on the West Coast as very timely, yes, necessary, and wishes to encourage the brethren on the Coast to proceed with the erection of such a High School. Without in any way whatever making the Synod responsible, the conference recommends that the brethren here support the school with donations, and further, that Rev. B. Harstad, if possible together with another pastor of practical bent, take a trip to the Coast to assist in starting the work in the proper manner.[4]

By November the Reverend Bjug Harstad, president of the Minnesota District, had arrived in Seattle. He set to work at once with the seriousness and energy that marked his career.

BJUG HARSTAD

Bjug Aanodson was born on 17 December 1848 on a farm named Harstad near Valle, Setesdal, Norway. (A granite monument was dedicated to him there on 26 June 1983. It was given by the community of Valle to honor the native son who became an important pastor and educator in the United States. A number of PLU officials—including President William Rieke—were present at the dedication.) Of ten children in the family, Bjug was the youngest boy. The family was very poor. Young Bjug worked on the family farm and as a shepherd in the mountains in the summers. One summer he received only a pair of shoes and a firkin of barley as wages. In 1861 the family immigrated to America on a three-masted schooner, following the lead of the oldest son, Kittel, who came in 1854. Harstad wrote later that "the emigrants provided their own food, but during a storm or heavy seas it was impossible to cook anything. . . . Fortunately, nearly all the passengers were from Setesdal and were well supplied with flat bread."[5]

From 1865 to 1871 Harstad was a student at Luther College, where he chose to use the name of Harstad rather than Aanodson upon the suggestion of Professor Laurentius Larsen, the longtime president of Luther College.[6] From 1871 to 1874 he studied theology in St. Louis at Concordia Seminary. Dr. C.F.W. Walther made the "greatest impression" on him, and Harstad consequently admired the Missouri Synod and Concordia's serious approach to theological education for the rest of his life.[7]

Harstad married Guro Svensdaughter Omlid in 1877. From 1879 to 1891 he was pastor and missionary in Mayville, North Dakota, and the Red River Valley; founder of seventeen congregations; president of the Minnesota District (1884–92); and founder of three academies: Franklin School (1878), Gran Boarding School (1880), and the Bruflat Academy (1889), all in North Dakota. Harstad was an intellectually able, theologically conservative pastor dedicated to the Norwegian Synod's doctrinal and educational views.[8] The synod could not have chosen a better person for the educational enterprise envisioned in the Northwest, but the task would sorely test Harstad's courage, strength, and determination.

Harstad met with pastors in Seattle soon after he arrived, but nothing came of that first meeting; the Seattle pastors were not ready to commit themselves. By 11 December 1890, however, a corporation called "The Pacific Lutheran University Associates" was formed, with Bjug Harstad, Peter Langseth, Ole Storaasli, Carl Hordness, and Louis Evenson as the original incorporators. The association held its first meeting in the real estate office of Ward T. Smith, where Harstad was elected president and an agreement with Smith was reached.

The agreement stipulated that Smith would give the association one hundred acres of land in the "Parkland Addition" as soon as it had invested fifteen thousand dollars in building there. Smith also promised that 10 percent of his income from the sale of the four thousand lots that he owned—presumably sold over a five-year period—would go to the association. According to the agreement, when the first thousand lots had been sold and paid for, the association would receive ten thousand dollars, and it would receive another ten thousand after twenty-five hundred lots had been sold.[9] Thus the Lutheran university was to be built in Parkland, helped along by a land development scheme.

PARKLAND

Parkland was mostly uninhabited in 1890, consisting of only a few scattered houses and farms. When the glaciers retreated about fifteen thousand years earlier they left outwash and till of sand, gravel, silt, and clay in Parkland, making agriculture marginal at best. The area was covered with grasses, bracken fern, Douglas fir, Oregon oak, cedar, hemlock, and a great deal of scotch broom (brought by English pioneers at Fort Nisqually). The weather was mild and the area parklike.[10] On a clear day Mt. Rainier loomed over the flat Parkland prairies. A steam railway traveled from Tacoma through Parkland on C Street to Spanaway Park twice a day. Clover Creek, which ran through the campus below a rather steep hill, was a year-round source of water for both Parkland and Tacoma. It was thought to be an important asset of the area. The weather was gray in the winter and it did rain a bit, but that was seen as a positive feature by at least some commentators: rainfall was a calming, soothing, refreshing influence, credited in part for the moderate tone of the region and its already existing colleges.[11] The first PLU catalog announced:

> Persons wishing a healthy and pretty place with the climate of the Pacific Coast can hardly find a more desirable place than right here. . . . Yet cold and heat are not so extreme and distressing as for instance in Wisconsin or Iowa. . . . The climate is healthy. The water [is] clear and in wells and springs as well as in the rivers soft as rain water. . . . The pungent smell of fir needles is grateful to weak lungs.[12]

The climate reputedly helped people with rheumatism and weak nerves.

By March 1891 the association was working furiously on building plans to honor its agreement with Smith. In April it began to publish the *Lutheran University Herald*, not only to inform Scandinavians about the new school but also to keep Lutherans in the area informed about church activities. The first issue of the paper had a sketch of the proposed university building on the first page. It was a large and imposing masonry building that appeared to be about two hundred feet long and six stories high. It was never built as presented in the sketch, but the drawing suggests the association's seriousness: the university was to be a "first-rank school."[13] The first *Herald* also reported:

> Lutheran University will give instruction on a Christian foundation. The school shall be conducted in the Christian spirit and be Evangelical Lutheran in its confession and activity. . . . But the school shall also give instruction in all practical courses that our young people need to have knowledge of, each in his own situation. The school will educate and bring up good Christians and good citizens.[14]

Not everyone was pleased, however. From Stanwood came a protest at what was transpiring in Parkland. It expressed Pastor Joergensen's unhappiness that Utsallady on Camano Island was not chosen for the school's location; there were not enough Scandinavians in Tacoma, and the Parkland site was "barren and unfruitful."[15]

Nonetheless excavation work was underway by May 1891. The June issue of the *Herald* included a sketch of the building that was actually to be constructed. Scaled down a bit from the original planned structure, it was still quite impressive. Harstad traveled to the Midwest looking for financial assistance during the summer (he remained president of the Minnesota District until 1892). He was welcomed with enthusiasm, but received no actual promises of money. While he was gone the excavation was completed and twenty thousand feet of lumber were received as a gift. The building committee also got word of a good deal on bricks at a very low price.

The cornerstone was laid on 4 October 1891. The occasion was a grand success. Pastor O. N. Gronsberg from San Francisco gave the main address and two other pastors also spoke, one in Norwegian and one in English. The president of the Norwegian Synod, the Reverend H. G. Stub, sent greetings and his hope that the undertaking would succeed. Debt, however, was piling up—over sixteen thousand dollars by November— and various financial schemes were launched to help provide the necessary cash.[16] A loan of twenty thousand dollars was sought early in 1892, at about the same time that the bricks—not available at bargain prices as it turned out—were being laid. The rush of building activity also led to "booming expansion" in Parkland as houses were built and stores opened.[17]

By spring the basement and first floor had been roughed in, and everyone seemed to like the look of the new building. About 350 apple, pear, cherry, and plum trees were planted along Clover Creek; within a few years the fruit would be canned by Parkland Lutheran women to help reduce the costs of food service. Bonds were issued and an additional loan, backed by university property, was taken to ensure completion of the building. It was confidently thought school could open in the fall of 1892: teachers were hired (the first was a Tacoma pastor, the energetic musician Carlo Sperati), and a catalog committee was appointed.

By the end of the summer it became apparent that such an opening date was optimistic; building activity had slowed almost to a stop during the summer. Rain had stalled brickmaking, and the local sawmill went bankrupt. The association eventually purchased the sawmill, but wet conditions slowed its operations also. Pastor Joergensen and his church in Stanwood recovered from their unhappiness and provided two hundred thousand cedar shingles for the roof, but opening was still impossible. That would have to wait another year.[18]

Money became a more agonizing problem. The *Herald* reported in January 1893 that the workers were not being paid fully and that there were unpaid debts. By 20 January an eight-thousand-dollar debt was due. The *Herald* pleaded, "Even if you have to borrow money in order to send us a contribution, will you not do it?"[19] In April it reported that the collection of funds was going slowly. University-owned property was to be marketed in the Midwest, but sales there went slowly too. In June the *Herald* asked plaintively: "Where shall the necessary monies come from? Not easy to answer . . . [but] if you think this school is God-pleasing then don't hold back because you are not rich. . . ."[20] The financial difficulties were compounded by the savage impact of the economic crash and panic of 1893. Money was short, real estate values declined precipitously, and people became angry about the methods employed by agents in the sale of lots. Harstad traveled in the Midwest during the summer searching for contributions. It was strenuous and frustrating work, and only moderately successful.

There were also a few positive signs and actions, fortunately. Harstad was elected president of the university, and the Norwegian Synod formed a new Pacific District in June 1893. Harstad had resigned his position as president of the Minnesota District, but he quickly acquired additional responsibilities by being elected president of the new district. He would soon have to be on the road much of the time supervising the new far-flung district and raising money for the university.

Also encouraging was the possibility of cooperation from the Missouri Synod Lutherans in California. Parkland was far north, they mused, but closer than the Midwest; their children could get home once in a while. The *Herald* reported:

> Pastor Buehler, the president of the German Lutheran Church on the Coast, visited Tacoma recently and also the place where the PLU is to be built. Pastor Buehler lives in San Francisco and is highly regarded in the large church body he belongs to—Missouri Synod. The location of the school was very pleasing to him as well as the building plans. It is now the plan of the German Lutherans to get a German pro-seminar added to Lutheran University. It stands without doubt that the Germans in such case will establish a thorough school and place teachers there who can give our University a good reputation from the very beginning.[21]

Nothing came of this, however. The Missouri Synod would establish its own colleges, both named Concordia, in Portland (1905) and in Oakland (1907). Meanwhile, construction work in Tacoma continued through the summer and fall, but by December 1893 the opening was postponed still another year. This meant additional disappointment for many, but since not even half the building was finished, there was nothing else to do.

The Reverend Tobias Larson joined the staff at this time, as the faithful and hard-working Peter Langseth left to teach in the normal school in Sioux Falls, South Dakota. Larson, already sixty-five, had married the Harstads in Harmony, Minnesota, in 1877; he would work tirelessly for the next ten years in Parkland for the university and the children's home he established nearby. He brought administrative ability and common sense, and his skills and leadership would complement Harstad's very nicely.

In April 1894 it was decided that the dedication of PLU should finally take place on 14 October, "if God wills." Two meetings were held to consider whether the school could be opened and dedicated: "Good attendance at both meetings. The answer was YES."[22]

Plans had to be mounted for both the dedication and the beginning of the school year. That meant arranging a program and finding speakers, acquiring all the necessary supplies, finding a faculty, and organizing courses and programs of study. Harstad, Larson, and others were even busier than usual. How about the furnace? Would there be electric lights? Where would the beds and mattresses come from? How many students could be expected? At least they knew that the curriculum should be like that of Luther College. Pacific Lutheran University in Parkland was to be a Norwegian Synod school, but educational needs were different in the individualistic and extensively urbanized but still raw Pacific Northwest.

The religious situation was different too. People seemed to have forgotten strong religious and community structures like those in the Midwest after they moved west. In 1885 Reverend N. G. Nilsen reported from Portland that "the Norwegians out here . . . have fallen into disrepute because of their pronounced ungodliness. . . . It is not easy for me to comprehend why the people here, more than elsewhere in America, should be spiritually depraved and indifferent to God's Word and the Sacraments and more given to the service of Mammon."[23] Despite the rhetorical excess, the problem Nilsen described was acute. Even today, Washington and Oregon are the two least-churched states in the nation, and the Pacific Coast remains the least-churched region in the United States.[24]

The courageous, determined leaders who had labored so mightily to launch the new university hoped that people would like what they saw when they came to the dedication. Although the discouragements had been almost overwhelming, they hoped to establish a great institution of learning that might become a rallying point for Lutheranism in the West and the spiritual and cultural center for all Scandinavians in the region. As Charles M. Gates, in his centennial history of the University of Washington, noted:

> It was the common experience of those who migrated to the American West to "grow with the country" that their dreams far outdistanced the possibilities of fulfillment. One lived imaginatively in a kind of never-never land, always reaching out toward goals that lay beyond the grasp. . . . A frontier population of necessity proclaimed its purposes long before it achieved

them, and held up symbols of culture and learning even when they were little more than tokens of good intention.[25]

The symbols of culture, learning, and religion were to be raised at last in Parkland.

DEDICATION AND OPENING

On 14 October 1894, as planned, a large tent was rigged for the dedication ceremonies. At least two thousand people were present. The weather was perfect. The Reverend Carlo Sperati organized a band for the occasion and led the singing of "A Mighty Fortress Is Our God." It was sung simultaneously in English, German, and Norwegian. Harstad gave the invocation and welcoming speech. The Reverend Ole Ottersen of Eureka, California, delivered the principal address in English, synod president U. V. Koren gave the dedicatory address in Norwegian, and the Reverend Tobias Larson pronounced the benediction. The ladies' aid served dinner in shifts to more than one thousand people. In the afternoon the band played, a choir sang, and more speeches were heard. In the evening the electric lights were turned on for the first time and, to the delight of all, they worked. Finally, just as most people were about to leave, the choir assembled on the roof and provided still more song. Nearly three hundred dollars was collected in the offering; it was a wonderful day for all concerned.

The school opened for classes on 25 October, welcoming thirty students. (This was a respectable number; in 1890 the University of Washington had just 273 students.[26]) They were welcomed by President Harstad, who led a short devotion and encouraged them to do their best. The catalog listed four courses of study—normal, commercial, literary, and scientific—and explained that "the aim and objective of this school is by thorough instruction and Christian discipline to prepare boys and girls for some useful work in life."[27] Tuition was one dollar a week. The faculty consisted of Professor Meyer Brandvig, a graduate of Iowa State College, who would teach Greek, German, English, and literature; Professor Sophie Peterson, who had a Bachelor of Science degree from Valparaiso University and who would teach grammar, mathematics, and art (PLU was coeducational and had women teachers from the beginning); Professor W. Shahan, a graduate of Roanoke College in Virginia, who would teach the "commercial" or business subjects; and Pastor Carlo Sperati, who would teach music. The first extracurricular activities at the university involved the bands and choirs he organized and directed.

CARLO SPERATI

Carlo Sperati is one of the most interesting figures in the university's early history. He firmly established the importance of music at the new school and significantly influenced music education and performance at other Lutheran colleges as well. His father, Paolo Agostino Sperati, brought Italian opera to Denmark. The elder Sperati spent nine years at the court theater in Copenhagen and married a Danish woman. In 1850 he accepted a position as orchestra conductor at the Christiania Theater, and for the next thirty-five years he was a leading figure in Norway's musical life. He was one of the teachers of Edvard Grieg. Carlo was born in 1860 and baptized a Catholic, but he was raised a Lutheran and thought of himself as a Norwegian. At the age of six Carlo appeared before royalty at Tivoli as a drum virtuoso. The snare drum was his solo instrument, although he also played the viola, violin, and piano. He also sang.

The young Sperati went to sea when he was seventeen. While ashore in Brooklyn, New York, he was encouraged at the Norwegian Seamen's Mission to go to Luther College and prepare for the ministry. In 1884 he did so and quickly made a musical impact on that institution. He went to Luther Seminary in 1888, was ordained in 1891, and took his first parish in Whatcom County, Washington. By 1894 he was serving a church in Tacoma and teaching all the music classes at the new university. He organized an "oratorio club" as well as various choirs and bands in Tacoma and at PLU. In 1896 he led a band in playing "A Mighty Fortress Is Our God" at the ten-thousand-foot level of Mt. Rainier. Sperati clearly made an important contribution to music in the Puget Sound area as well as at PLU.[28]

In 1905 he was called to become professor of music and religion at Luther College, where he remained for the rest of his life. In 1934 he received an honorary Doctor of Music degree from St. Olaf College.[29] Sperati was one of the Luther College teachers of Gunnar Malmin, long-time Choir of the West director at PLU.

CAMPUS LIFE

The 1894-95 academic year went by relatively smoothly. There were seventy-three students by Christmas and a small budget surplus at the end of the year. The students seemed to like the new school. There was, however, a debt of $37,442.12, and it was not at all clear how that was going to be paid. There were also no systems of internal governance for either the faculty or the students. Those would have to emerge, often as situations required them.

The system of faculty governance that was pragmatically worked out was a quite democratic committee of the whole. President Harstad partici-pated in the discussions but did not dominate them. In fact, he sometimes came out on the short end of the vote. His position on student behavior was a moderate and thoughtful one, reflecting years of observing and counseling people. Pastor Tobias Larson typically voted as Harstad did, but the lay people on the faculty took a harder stand on disciplinary matters. They wanted the institution to be firm. Pastor Carlo Sperati, the fiery professor of music, was also on the side of firmness. Sophie Peterson, the only woman faculty member, was moderate and tried to find middle ground in the discussions.

It was decided in November that students could not attend dances, although President Harstad questioned the absolute prohibition. Major disciplinary problems emerged in January, however, when about ten students were accused of disorderly conduct on New Year's Eve. They had tarried around the kitchen after hours, loitered in the stairwells, and made unnecessary noise A few had even visited members of the opposite sex in their rooms. New rules about room and kitchen visitation were promptly discussed on 3 January.

An even bigger scandal took place on 7 January, and almost daily faculty meetings the rest of the month were needed to resolve it. On that day, John Risland and Iver Johnson organized a prank that consisted of telling Minnie Kraabel that a Mr. Linbak wanted to see her in his room. She went to the room with Christina Larson, opened the door, and saw Linbak in his underwear. Of course this was all witnessed by the gang of boys present in the room.

What should be done? The social structure was obviously too loose. Harstad lamented that depravity and roguery were common among all people; virtue and goodness were rare. This was a trivial offense, however, and should be forgotten. No laws had been broken, and proof was too difficult to establish. It was better to let ten guilty parties escape, he concluded, than to punish one innocent person. Pastor Larson agreed. Meyer Brandvig and Carlo Sperati did not agree. Rigorous rules were needed for the school, they insisted; both moral and civil law as well as the sixth commandment had been violated by the "indecent conduct and suggestiveness." The faculty was locked in disagreement.

The matter worsened on 10 January when John Risland showed "great disrespect" toward Sperati "while being advised in a friendly manner, and according to the Word of God, of certain mistakes in his conduct." Risland refused to apologize for his part in the escapade. Sperati told him he was "stiff-necked and obstinate and lacking in courage." Risland snapped back that "he did not do like the Italians, who stab a man in the back." Professor Shahan reported rather ponderously: "This no doubt was intended to reflect on Professor Sperati's nationality."

The underwear affair dragged on. Ultimately, all parties were forced to apologize and Risland was censured—he had violated the rules of gentle-manly behavior, it was decided—though it is not clear whether the censure was made public in chapel. Sperati apologized to the faculty for his heat in debate. He was interested in the school's welfare, which had seemed threatened, he explained; he wanted it to be a fine school.

The school's first comprehensive set of rules for student conduct were quickly established. They were posted by the middle of January as follows:

1. Boys can't go in girls' rooms and vice versa.
2. No loafing in the kitchen.
3. No loitering in the halls and stairwells.
4. Study hours have to be spent in your own room.
5. No smoking by those under 17 and no smoking or chewing in the building.[30]

The pressure on Harstad remained great, and he was very busy. He added even more responsibilities by initiating some formal religious instruction with Bible lectures; previous religion instruction had been informal and devotional. The board decided to call a theologian to the faculty to assist with this part of the work. Harstad was certainly competent to teach religion, but with his manifold duties at the university, in the district synod, in the Parkland church, and elsewhere, he simply did not have enough time. Help was needed. Calls went out to two men to serve as principal and professor. They did not accept the calls. Then a letter of call (university positions were understood to be like calls to churches) was sent to the Reverend O. N. Gronsberg, the San Francisco pastor who had delivered the main address at PLU's cornerstone-laying ceremonies in 1891, to be president. (The board had decided that "president" sounded better than "principal.") The salary was six hundred dollars a year, and he was offered living quarters in the Old Main building. Within a month he accepted the call.

Gronsberg was a Luther College graduate. He had studied theology at Concordia Seminary in St. Louis and since 1880 had been a pastor in San Francisco. He was installed as PLU's second president on 3 October 1895. Harstad said some words of farewell, and it was clear to all that he would be missed. Gronsberg thanked Harstad for the confidence that had been shown him and asked for patience while he figured out what needed to be done and what he could do.[31]

Meanwhile, some agreeable activities had been organized for the 107 students now enrolled, but there was also considerable griping about the food (the bread and butter were not acceptable), and jokes were often played at night after the lights were turned off. Some hall lights were left on to counteract this. Other disciplinary measures included mandatory evening study hours and the need to secure presidential permission to travel to Tacoma. Further, males and females were not to be out together after dark.

The 1896–97 catalog listed five faculty members: President Gronsberg, who taught religion, history, Norwegian, and Latin; professors Peterson and Sperati, who still taught their subjects; Professor J. L. Jensen, who taught natural history, physiology, and hygiene; and Professor Hannah Jahr, who directed the primary department. There were now six courses of study—preparatory, collegiate, commercial, musical, normal, and primary—a structure that would remain fairly constant for the next twenty-five years. All students were required to be present for daily chapel and to attend Sunday services. The catalog ended with a stern warning: "The government of the school may be characterized as parental. Patience and forbearance toward the weak and erring will not hinder the swift justice to the willful wrongdoer."[32]

Harstad, after leaving the presidency of PLU, devoted himself to church responsibilities. They required constant travel, but he enjoyed that and it seemed to challenge and refresh him. In July 1895 he traveled almost nine hundred miles through the Willamette Valley on a horse named Flyer at a total cost of $11.25. He was engaged in mission work, searching out and ministering to churchless Norwegians. He found many Norwegians and much irreligion and indifference. He then stayed in San Francisco from October 1895 to May 1896, serving the congregation that Gronsberg had left, which had some difficulty securing a new pastor.

Meanwhile, debt remained the agonizing and unanswered problem for the Parkland school. Harstad, in particular, was sick at the thought that he had been a party to a land development scheme that had caused many people to lose money, and he continued to work with the greatest determination to resolve that unfortunate situation. He and others fervently hoped that the synod would decide to take over the debt and ownership of the institution during its general meeting in the summer of 1896. If not, the problems might be terminal. Harstad was to attend the meeting and plead the case, but with a debt of thirty-seven-thousand dollars in question, it would not be easy. The matter, however, would be a major item on the agenda.

Synod president U. V. Koren addressed the problem in his annual speech at the meeting. He admitted that there were problems, mostly financial, at PLU, and that land had lost much value, largely as a result of the panic of 1893. That was unfortunate. But could anybody have done better? He argued that the church should take over the property and the debt. "We must not leave here before we have done all in our power, whether by gifts or by loans or by whatever means with God's help to prevent the school's sinking."[33]

The synod appointed a committee to consider the matter, and after long discussion it proposed that a special time should be set aside during the convention to consider the financial status of PLU. This would not be an official meeting; the problem would be handled on an "informal" basis. At the meeting a number of pastors and parishes agreed to subscribe as much as they could for the cause. By the time the session was over thirteen thousand dollars had been subscribed and the rest was to be secured as soon as possible. The Pacific District agreed to raise ten thousand dollars for the cause. If the money pledged could be raised, the problem of debt would be reduced. Time would tell; perhaps McKinley's "Good Times" would help restore national prosperity, and with it the prospects of the new university.[34]

In April 1897 President Gronsberg, who had admitted that he came to PLU not because he was experienced but because he was called, resigned. The position of president was very trying, too trying, he conceded, and he went back to California as a traveling missionary. Harstad was elected president again and served for the next year.

In May the board decided to call a young man named Nils J. Hong to the faculty. He seemed able. He was a Luther College graduate who had taught for several years at the Willmar Academy in Minnesota.[35] He accepted the call, thus launching—although no one knew it until much later—a new and vital period in the institution's history. Hong, through patience, good sense, determination, high standards, honesty, and an astonishing attention to detail, would leave an enduring stamp on the new school. Under his leadership PLU would acquire substance and form. Hong also taught generations of reluctant students the patterns of English grammar (it was to be done correctly!), was socially sensitive, read widely, translated hymns, and wrote poetry. Nils Hong was not showy, but he was a man of many parts.

4

Pacific Lutheran Academy and Business College

Nils Joseph Hong graduated from Luther College in 1895. A man of many interests and concerns, he had worked for the Scandinavian Association for Total Abstinence in Minnesota. He also studied socialism and, with some energy, trusts. He was interested in horticulture (he corresponded with Luther Burbank about cacti) and cultivated a large garden. But he was mostly a dedicated and demanding teacher: "I chose . . . the profession of teaching. I have on the whole found it pleasant, but not always profitable from a financial point of view."[1]

Hong taught at least a dozen subjects at PLU before he retired in 1938, but he was primarily a teacher of language and literature. That teaching was undoubtedly enhanced by his translations from the classical and Scandinavian languages, which included at least thirty-six hymns and a large number of poems, some later set to music by Gunnar Malmin. He was a demanding teacher of grammar and rhetoric. The student literary publication discussing class bequests in 1912 said: "We give, devise and bequest to our honored Mr. N. J. Hong, one small spoon with which he can dish out English to his scholars and thereby prevent them from choking on it."[2]

Hong knew that conditions in the Northwest were a little "rough and frontier-like" and that the work would be "hard," but the adventure of the frontier and the promise of the school, perched so unsteadily there, were exciting. Conditions would improve, he wrote to John Xavier: "It is the work of the moral pioneer to *make* them improve. As far as the school is concerned I believe it has a promising future."[3]

Fundraising along the Yukon

A little money had come in from the pledges made in the summer of 1896, but debt continued to threaten that promising future. Bjug Harstad was haunted by the problem. He was physically exhausted and deeply concerned that investors might feel cheated and blame him.

> It was not my idea that a school should be built on the West Coast nor was it my decision that I should have anything to do with the matter. . . . I am intensely sorry that those who have bought property on account of the school cannot now sell and get their money back. . . . I do not believe the

disappointments can be as bitter and humiliating for anyone as they have been for us.[4]

Could anything be done? Perhaps. By 1898 gold had been discovered in Alaska, and both Harstad and the sober board of trustees were excited by the prospects of finding a fortune there. Debt could be eliminated, the school could be adequately financed, and guilt could be assuaged: "the merciful Father will not permit us to become swindlers in your sight." The board, after a long discussion, granted Harstad permission to travel to Alaska to search for gold, and it gave Mrs. Harstad the use of the farm and cows in his absence.

On 6 January 1898 the Parkland Help Society was formed to search for gold in Alaska (in an "honorable and God-fearing manner"). If gold were found half the profits would go to the members and half to the school. In February the fifty-year-old Harstad and Otis Larson, each paying his own way, left for Alaska on the SS *City of Seattle*. The boat was so jammed with eight hundred people that they had to stand to eat. Manners were oafish. An extraordinary adventure followed: Harstad and Larson landed in Dyea, Alaska, and lived in a tent in subzero weather. They dragged their three thousand pounds of gear by sleigh and pack over Chilkoot Pass and by handmade boat through a series of lakes. "Our work is so heavy," Harstad wrote, "that in spite of the cold we perspire all day. Up gentler slopes we haul a hundred pounds on a sled each trip, but on the steepest slopes we use a block and tackle." They eventually staked out a claim at Dawson.

The two men encountered adventure, cold, mud, irreligion, and human vagaries in the next year and a half, but not gold. "Unfortunately, the school has not yet received any financial help from my trip. The reason is the Lord has not seen fit to give us any of the gold in Klondike." Harstad reported his health was restored, however: "At my departure both my body and mind were so worn out, enfeebled and exhausted that it seemed impossible that I could hold out long." Strength and courage returned with physical exertion. He later recalled, "That year-and-a-half was the easiest and least worrisome time I have had since I have come to the Pacific Coast."

One gift did come to the university as a result of this adventure. While moose hunting up the Klondike River, a Dr. Lee, a dentist from La Crosse, Wisconsin, "shot a large buck . . . and was so kind as to present the horns to the Lutheran University. It is an exceptionally large pair of horns with a spread of over five feet and fourteen points."[5]

The Norwegian Synod's Pacific District members, meeting in Silverton, Oregon, in July 1898, were not thrilled that Harstad—the district president—had gone off without first getting district permission. The pastors and lay people assembled there grumbled a bit, but decided to wait until he returned to pursue the matter further. The question was raised at the meeting whether the district should take over ownership of the school now that it was clear that the synod would not. After long deliberation a resolution was passed by the assembly that specified that the district had— and wanted—no legal right in the governance of the school, but it did want to exercise influence over the work done there and so organized an inspection committee for that purpose. The district officially declined any fiscal or legal responsibility for the operation of the university in Parkland.

Hong acted as university president in Harstad's absence and seemed to do well. In March Pastor M. Borge of Iowa reported that the congregations in the Midwest had subscribed over 90 percent of the thirty thousand dollars they had promised to raise. If that money were paid and if the Pacific District could raise the ten thousand dollars it was responsible for, the problem of debt would be significantly reduced.[6] There were lots of "ifs." Hong tried to help the financial situation by proposing a "tuition plan": the school would operate on tuition income, adding only five hundred dollars to the budget for advertising and catalog costs.

The first class was graduated in June 1898. There were two candidates: Ettie C. Kraabel of the normal course and Amanda Swan of the preparatory course. The graduation program consisted of music by the band, orchestra, and glee club, a piano duet, and orations by the two graduates. The following fall, the 1898–99 academic year began with Hong as president and principal, officially replacing Harstad. The institution also changed its name to correspond a little more closely to reality; it was now called the Pacific Lutheran Academy and Business College.

THE ACADEMY

The 1899–1900 catalog listed annual costs to students of $104.50 and announced five hundred bound volumes in the library. (Most were from old pastors' libraries, though; only three or four dozen were of much use to the students.) Regulations remained strict: "Students who participate in dancing or cardplaying, or visit saloons or gambling-houses, do thereby sever their connection with the school."[7] These strict regulations—which were typical of most educational institutions in the late nineteenth century—were influenced by Norwegian pietism, but they also had a fundamental religious and educational importance that was deeply ingrained in American history and widely accepted. The regulations were inextricably tied to the understanding of how educational institutions should operate. The acquisition of knowlege was of secondary importance; character building and preparation for citizenship were what counted. Restrictive and demanding campus rules were thought essential in shaping character and producing individuals who would serve the community. Radical changes in the philosophy and purpose of higher education would undercut this educational philosophy in the first decades of the twentieth century, and professionalism, specialization, research, and precise knowledge would become new norms. The new age, professional and utilitarian, would ultimately take over most of American higher education, but the older vision of service still persists at PLU; its restrictive rules would survive long after the educational philosophy that gave coherence to their existence had been pushed aside.

In June 1900 the corporation sold some land to Pastor Tobias Larson as a nearby site for the Parkland Children's Home (on the corner of 124th and A Streets), and additional land was later given to the home by individuals. In fall 1902 the home was dedicated, fulfilling a dream Pastor Larson had pursued since coming to Parkland. Larson's retirement was an active and productive one: he helped found the university, preached at least twice a month for ten years, and founded the Parkland Children's Home. When he died of influenza in 1903, the Rev. L. C. Foss replaced him on the academy's board.

ACADEMIC DEVELOPMENT

The academy and its curriculum became a little more substantial each year. In 1901 the preparatory—or high school—course took three years. The normal—or teacher-training—course, requiring a high school background, took two. There were three slightly different college preparatory courses—the classical, the English-scientific, and the Luther College course—and each took three years. The college preparatory courses included three years of Latin, two years of Greek, and two years of either German or Norwegian. All students took religion courses: Bible history in the first year, Luther's *Catechism* in the second, and either another Bible course or one studying the Augsburg Confession in the third. Religion was thus the first "core curriculum" requirement at the institution. Physical education—gymnastics—was the second, and English composition was the third. Other courses were taken as part of a program sequence; there were very few electives. The curriculum did not change appreciably until the 1920s.

The commercial—or business education—branch took one year and included commercial arithmetic, bookkeeping, parliamentary law, business writing, business law, rapid calculation, and, if desired, shorthand and typewriting. Courses in music (piano, organ, voice) and art, directed by the talented painter F. Mason Holmes, were available on demand. Swedish educational gymnastics was taught "to train the different organs of the body in such a way as to increase the efficiency of the heart and lungs and to render the voluntary muscles the obedient and ready servants of the will."[8] There was a Lyceum—a literary society that met twice a month— and two debating societies, one in English, the other in Norwegian. In addition to the band and orchestra, athletic competition was popular, perhaps too popular. The catalog warned: "under no circumstances will athletics be allowed to encroach upon the regular school work or become an end in itself."[9] Days and nights must have been full for the 103 students and the half dozen faculty members.

The next year several new faculty members arrived: Anna Tenwick, a 1900 PLA graduate who would later go to China as a missionary, was hired to teach history, reading, and mathematics; Elizabeth Sihler came as the new preceptress as well as professor of language, music, and physical culture; and the Reverend J. U. Xavier was hired to teach religion, history, Latin, and Greek. Hong wrote that the school "has spared no effort to secure teachers of moral and Christian character with intellectual and educational qualifications of a high order."[10] Sihler, for instance, had studied at the Victoria Lyceum in Berlin. As the school's publication to constituents boasted, she "speaks German, French, and Italian. She taught six years in Mount Holyoke College . . . a school of fine spirit and reputation, from which she has the very best testimonials with respect both to ability and character."[11]

J. U. XAVIER

J. U. Xavier was hired at an annual salary of $650 to be the resident theologian. Hong described him "as a very thorough, faithful student and also as a man of noble, Christian character and a very loveable disposition."[12] The years would bear this out; he taught in Parkland until 1942.

Xavier was born in Norway and educated at Luther College and Luther Seminary, then taught several years at the Lutheran Ladies' Seminary in Red Wing, Minnesota. He took an M.A. degree at the University of Washington in 1929. Upon his arrival in Parkland he became the school's librarian. He learned something of the Dewey decimal system, then began classifying the library collection, newly housed in the library room that was provided that year. During the next forty years he would teach, at one time or another, courses in history, Bible, the Augsburg Confession, Latin, Greek, rudiments of nutrition, library science, botany, and zoology. He also served as a pastor all over the Northwest and was acting president of the school in 1920–21. His wife, Signe Skattebol, was the first women's basketball coach.

Xavier's fifteen hundred pages of notes for Bible courses, written in an almost unreadable, microscopic hand, indicate very painstaking lecture preparation. His theology was clearly within the dogmatic and biblical traditions of nineteenth-century Lutheranism and the Norwegian Synod (what Sydney Ahlstrom called the "scholastic" tradition), but he was sympathetic to science—a bugbear to many pastors and biblical scholars—and his literary training and active intellect jumped out in unpredictable and surprising ways. His scholarship and approach to biblical interpretation cannot be classified in any simplistic way. Einstein and relativity theory, the different uses of language in different settings, the refraction of light, Frederick Nietzsche, and the Roman writer Ovid all appear in his lecture notes on miracles.[13] Xavier, like all the PLA teachers, was vastly overworked, but that never extinguished his stubborn determination or his lively intelligence.

Two other important people came on the scene in the first years of the new century. Ludvig Larson, who had entered as a student for the first time in 1896, reentered in 1901 and graduated from the academy in 1903. He would later serve the institution for many years in the business office and as business manager. His father, P. T. Larson, came west in 1908 to serve as manager of the children's home.

Ole Johnson Stuen, who was born in Oppdal, Norway, and attended Trondheim Cathedral School, entered the academy in 1902 to learn English. He graduated from the University of Washington in 1912, took an M.A. degree in 1913, and joined the PLA faculty that year. Stuen was thus the first faculty member with a graduate degree. He taught German, Norwegian, mathematics, and science. In addition he coached, built the first tennis courts, advised the *Mooring Mast* and *Saga*, and administered the alumni association for a time. After Xavier retired, Stuen became librarian until his own retirement in 1952. Stuen was a genial, affirmative, and determined man who was a stubborn fighter for causes he believed in, as more than one president discovered. In 1914 he married Agnes Hougen, who had come as preceptress in 1912. Shortly before the marriage she wrote a very touching letter to Hong wondering if she could continue as preceptress "as a married woman."[14]

STUDENT LIFE

Life for students in the new academy was full of activities as well as academic responsibilities. Students had many questions about life and vocation, but they were also filled with fun and, quite quickly, school spirit. Hong counseled, guided, and recruited students, and he corresponded with their parents. For example, he told a young man in 1901 that "there is a crying need for devoted and consecrated ministers of the Gospel . . . I think you ought to continue your schooling here and afterward take up . . . the study of theology. It may seem pretty hard for a poor boy to accomplish all this but by God's help it can be done."[15] That same year he wrote to a concerned Arlington merchant, N. K. Tvete, that "we shall be pleased to receive your daughter Alfield and give her every advantage in our power. We shall give her a nice front room on the first floor. . . . She will have the use of our best piano, a Ludwig piano. I shall try to get her a good steady girl for a roommate."[16] The capable Alfield Tvete would later marry the future PLC president Oscar Tingelstad.

The students, especially the Lyceum members, began publishing the *Hurricane*, a literary magazine and student newspaper, in 1901. It would continue, with gaps, until 1915. It was full of campus news, humor, literary exercises, opinions, descriptions of athletic competition, and much else. It provides a wonderful glimpse into academy life in the early years of the twentieth century. The first editor was Oscar Tingelstad, under whose editorship there was a strong literary emphasis and plenty of jokes about the inadequacies of some student translations from Greek, Latin, and Norwegian. (No doubt his translations were always correctly done; his love letters to his wife were written in Latin.)

The 30 November 1901 issue of the magazine-newspaper described the first PLA basketball game against the Tacoma YMCA's fearsome Skookum Club: "The PLA people sent a goodly-sized delegation to witness it, only to see our boys defeated by a score of 33–10." The *Hurricane* promised a "different story" when the return game would be played.[17] It also announced that the Lyceum had organized a "Grand Entertainment" for 12 December, featuring instrumental and vocal solos, three recitations, an instrumental duet and trio, a play in Norwegian, a play in English, and a piano solo by Carlo Sperati. Admission was twenty-five cents for adults.

In the 11 January 1902 issue the debate topic was announced: "Resolved, that a miser is more injurious than a spendthrift." The issue—as were most—was full of humorous advertisements and execrable jokes: "*Boils, Carbuncles & Co.* have established a branch office at the office of Tenwick, Vieg & Co. in Room 305. Boils and carbuncles delivered free to any part of the body. Good specimens on display." In the 1 March 1902 issue the editor confessed that there had been no *Hurricane* for five weeks. The reason was athletic enthusiasm: "The athletic club has over-shadowed the Lyceum." The PLA team had again been defeated in basketball by the Skookum Club, but "the playing was a credit to both teams." The orchestra had also played "well" at the last concert.

In the 1 March game with the University of Washington "the hats came off for the P.L.A. for the score was 12–15 in their favor." This was the school's first basketball victory. The game was preceded by a Lyceum lecture on *The Merchant of Venice*. The team's next victory, over the Skookum Club, caused such elation on campus that it was celebrated by a six-verse poem in the *Hurricane*. The second verse sang:

> Sweet Parkland! loveliest village
>   of the plains;
> To cultivate their rudimental brains
>   'Tis there the western sons and
>   daughters go
> And study till their craniums
>   overflow.

Bed-dumping was apparently a popular activity, music flourished, and basketball and baseball continued to be popular. Not all liked basketball, however. In 1905 one boy who had "got saved" protested that basketball was cultivated more than Christianity. Prayer meetings should be held on Saturday nights, he thought. A *Hurricane* editorial lamented the Athletic Club's decision to "let a basketball game take prominence over an athletic entertainment." Making a distinction between sports and athletics, it argued that basketball players stumble into each other and raise dust, while the athlete (one who systematically performs exercises) is much more appealing and gains something a ballplayer never attains: "an erect and healthy body." This salutary warning notwithstanding, basketball flourished, and the 1905–06 team won the unofficial regional championship.

"Girlology" was taken up by a number of male students in 1906: "Sophus, Victor, and Nestor will be able to graduate from this course next spring." The League of Courtesy was born that year also, and nineteen students were enrolled in the International Prohibition Association. The lack of school spirit and ignorance of yells were attacked editorially in 1908. Girls began playing organized basketball that same year. In 1909 the boys played a team from Whitworth College (then located in Tacoma) for the first time and defeated them 37–11, "in spite of their playing one of the roughest games that ever was played." One clever reporter wrote, "The band is rising rapidly. It played upon the top of the building last Sunday afternoon."

The fourth alumni reunion was held on 10–11 February 1912. Earlier reunions, beginning in 1902, had gone well, but this one topped them all. Hong was the organizer and orchestrator. The event included a basketball game, which the "old boys" won, and a banquet with music and lots of toasts ("Our Heritage," "Our Church," "Miss PLA," "The PLA Boy"). The alumni decided a new gymnasium was essential. A tiny crackerbox built for ninety dollars had served for more than a decade, but it was too small and decrepit for the games and entertainments held there. Students had complained about its inadequacies almost from the beginning. The enthusiastic alumni pledged forty-three hundred dollars for the new building, which was promptly built on the brow of the hill south of Old Main, where the present University Center now stands. It had a basement, a stage on the west end, and a seven-foot gallery around the whole building that could be used as a running track. This gymnasium was used steadily until it burned in 1946.

Baseball was also very popular at PLA. The 1912 team lost only one game. The stars of this era were pitcher Theander Harstad and catcher Anton (Tony) Brottem. Both later played in the major leagues, Harstad for Cleveland and Brottem for Washington and Pittsburgh. It was a formidable battery for schoolboy competition; Harstad would regularly strike out more than twenty in a game. He turned professional in 1912 and, after a 13–2 season in 1914 with Vancouver, B.C., was sold to Cleveland for three thousand dollars. The first major league batter he faced was Ty Cobb, and his first victory was against Walter Johnson.

The April 1912 issue of the *Hurricane* described Governor M. E. Hay's visit to the campus, remarking, "We were struck by the Governor's democratic ways." The issue also included a long editorial denouncing dancing: "It is the intoxicating cup of sensualism, the destroyer of virtue, and blunting hammer of the finer and higher sensibilities, and, eventually, the curse of body and soul, and the destroyer of homes and happiness." The editorial reported a total of six hundred thousand prostitutes in the United States, adding that "about eighty percent of this number say that the first step was the dance hall, then the ice cream parlors, and so on." Dancing would be controversial in Parkland for a long time.

PROBLEMS

There were ongoing problems, of course. Not all students liked the moral regulations. Faculty meetings frequently dealt with disciplinary cases. Some students had to be disciplined for playing cards, drinking, smoking, or dancing, and a few had to be expelled. One young woman "began receiving attention from young men and attended variety theaters. This seemed to have turned her head entirely. She now says the manager of one of these has offered her a position. . . . That this would lead to her ruin is almost certain."[18] Hong carried on a long correspondence with her guardian about what should be done. And in 1909 one faculty member was found to have used "stimulants and narcotics, by which he has been rendered unfit for his work." This brought a sharply stated resolution of censure from the faculty to the board of trustees, which the faculty thought then moved very slowly. "We consider his example and influence extremely pernicious and calculated to bring upon the school disrepute and eventual ruin," the faculty wrote.[19] Standards were taken seriously: "Our country needs today . . . men and women who do right because it is right."[20]

Proper sewage disposal was also a problem by 1904. The cesspool on the hillside was draining into Clover Creek and threatening the purity of local drinking water. The city of Tacoma objected and asked that something be done immediately. Nonetheless, the problem would persist.

The major problem, however, remained the school's debt. All kinds of schemes were tried and enormous effort was expended to solve this seemingly intractable problem. Some monies pledged continued to come in. Synod president U. V. Koren tried to help, Hong persisted in his fundraising labors, and Mr. T. C. Satra had some success raising money in the Northwest. In 1912 the outstanding pledges were brought together and paid off through the Luther College Endowment Fund and other private sources. For the first time the debt was well financed and some of the pressure was removed, but considerable debt remained—$25,760 in 1914—which could never be forgotten.

ACCOMPLISHMENTS

By 1914, after twenty years of educational activity, there had been accomplishments as well as perennial problems. The greatest accomplishment, of course, was survival. Gritty effort, dedication, and sacrifice had been required to found the institution and bring it through its first quarter century. PLA had also developed a strong sense of community, which would continue to be important. Hong, Xavier, and Stuen were influential in shaping that sense of community. Xavier commented shortly before his death: "I may add that at no other school have I found such a fine school spirit as at this, and I hope it will continue through the years of the Pacific Lutheran University."[21]

In 1907 Oscar Tingelstad spoke at graduation and, in a formal and somewhat flowery speech, tried to summarize what was best and most important about the academy. The speech was perceptive and moving, not least of all because Tingelstad would become an important Lutheran educational leader for forty years. Themes with which he would work the rest of his life emerged in the speech:

> I have not been in any institution where this honesty in work has had such a prominent place as in this institution. They do not seek to fill your head with facts, but endeavor to help you develop your own powers. . . . They teach you a spirit of faithfulness even in the minutest detail. They say examinations are hard here, that they are difficult to pass [but] . . . I can assure you that if you have passed these examinations . . . no examinations . . . will offer you any difficulty. The highest ideals are held up for the students; the students are under the influence of the Word of God. . . . It has been said by some that within five years this Pacific Lutheran Academy will be the Pacific Lutheran College. I do not consider this impossible.[22]

Tingelstad thought it possible that as much as one hundred thousand dollars might be raised in the near future for an endowment.

In 1914 full accreditation came to the academy from the University of Washington, completing a process that stretched back to the late nineteenth century.[23] Students could now transfer to the university with no loss of credits. The State Agricultural College in Pullman had already placed PLA on an accredited list, and for a long time Luther College had granted PLA students advanced standing when they transferred.[24] By 1914 there were four thousand volumes in the library and 207 students.

Pacific Lutheran Academy had also made sizeable cultural and educational, but also practical, contributions to the Parkland community. The Parkland Light and Water Company was created in 1914, with Nils Hong playing a major role in its inception and continuing operation. It was the first and is now the oldest operating nonprofit public utility in the United States. Hong drafted its original articles of incorporation and served continuously on its board until 1938, mostly as secretary but also as president. Ole Stuen served on the board for thirty-six years and was treasurer for twenty.

By 1914 more than two hundred students had graduated since 1898: twenty from the normal course (including two missionaries to China); ninety-five from the commercial course (bookkeepers, contractors, farmers, merchants, and one lawyer); fifty-three from the stenographic course; and thirty-nine from the college preparatory course (three pastors, one missionary, one lawyer, and many teachers).[25] Education at PLA was certainly for "citizenship and service," and it had a clearly articulated religious point of view and a strong moral emphasis.

Music remained important. "The Pacific Lutheran Academy recognizes the great importance of music as a means of culture and refinement, and aims to furnish high-grade instruction at a very moderate price."[26] There were courses in piano (one-fourth of the student body took lessons in 1914), organ, voice, and the history of music. Since Sperati's departure in 1905 the instruction in music, especially violin, was handled by Professor Olof Bull, "an artist of more than ordinary ability and well known all over the Pacific Coast." Bull had studied in Europe under "the famous Wienawaski."[27]

At the twenty-fifth annual meeting of the corporation on 8 December 1915, President Hong described the past year as the best in the history of the institution. The budget and debt were under control, he announced, the institution's graduates had assumed important roles in society, and the enrollment was over two hundred. He expressed hope that collegiate status might soon be achieved. A tempered optimism briefly prevailed but, ironically and unfortunately, quickly faded.

Hong warned that the terrible war raging in Europe might produce problems for the American people and the academy in the near future. He was correct. Enrollment soon declined rather sharply and the high inflation that accompanied the war brought severe financial problems. Debt rose almost ten thousand dollars in the next two years, despite very careful husbanding. The Norwegian Synod could not help; it was preoccupied with the manifold activities leading to the merger of the Norwegian Synod, the United Church, and the Hauge Synod and with plans for the celebration of the four hundredth anniversary of the Reformation, both in 1917. For the time being no other fundraising could compete with the great jubilee campaign planned to subsidize those events.

The merger would bring under one umbrella three competing colleges in the Northwest. It was not at all evident how the new Norwegian Lutheran Church would deal with those educational rivalries, even though three schools were clearly too many. Something would have to be done, but criteria for making those difficult decisions were not clear. Uncertainty seemed to rule. In 1917 Hong wrote, perhaps a little naively, "We are looking forward to the coming union, trusting that it will be the beginning of a better era for our school."[28] In retrospect it was, but three very trying and combative years would pass before the issues were resolved. Hong felt constrained to resign in the process. Harstad refused to join the new Norwegian Lutheran Church, thus formally separating himself from the school he had founded, and Pacific Lutheran Academy was forced to close down operations for two years. Only the most generous optimist could have thought this was the dawn of a new and better era.

COLLEGIATE RIVALS

Six Lutheran colleges were established in the Northwest between 1890 and 1910, one by Swedes, one by Germans, and four by Norwegians. The region could perhaps have supported one Lutheran college adequately. The multiplicity of activity divided resources and loyalty badly. Rivalry was intense. The Norwegian groups found it particularly difficult to communicate and cooperate.[29] The fates of those Norwegian Lutheran schools were intertwined very tightly from 1917 to 1920.

The Lutheran Free Church had established an academy in Poulsbo in 1894. The next year the institution took the name Bethania College. It closed in 1896, but leaders of the Lutheran Free Church remained interested in education. In 1903 the city of Everett offered free land and a grant of about nine thousand dollars to build a school there. Bethania College was reborn. A large frame building was purchased and the institution opened in October 1904. There was only one teacher that first year,

Professor Peter J. Bardon, but enrollment and faculty grew a bit in the next few years, despite severe financial difficulties. When a United Lutheran college was built in Everett in 1909, Professor Bardon proposed cooperation. When this did not happen he left Bethania and joined the faculty of PLA, where he served with distinction until 1938. Bardon's move was a blow from which Bethania could not recover.[30] Faculty and enrollment there diminished while debt grew, and Bethania College closed in 1917. The building was used as an apartment house for a time, but since 1931 it has housed the Bethany Home for the Aged.

The United Norwegian Lutheran Church—since 1890 the largest of the Norwegian Lutheran synods—also entered the educational race in the Northwest. In 1903, after some preliminary studies, it decided to establish colleges both east and west of the Cascades: Spokane College was founded in 1907, and Columbia College was established in Everett in 1909. The Everett location—a forested hill with a view of Port Gardner Bay and both the Olympic and Cascade mountains—was strikingly beautiful. Money was a constant problem in Everett, however; it went a little better in Spokane, at least initially.

A large and substantial building was constructed in Everett, and the school opened in 1909. Debt skyrocketed (it was soon ten times greater than Bethania's) until the Reverend Rasmus Bogstad arrived on the scene. He had been a professor and president at Concordia College in Minnesota, and in 1910 he had become president of the board of trustees of the United Church. He brought experience, influence, and energy, which was quickly apparent. He became a forceful champion of United Norwegian Lutheran education in the Northwest. Bogstad served as president of both the Spokane and Columbia colleges in 1913–14, and thereafter only at Columbia in Everett.

In 1914 the United Church decided that Columbia College should be turned into a hospital, but local resistance brought a reversal the following year. The college was restored and the synod implicitly agreed to take on much of the accumulated debt. By 1916 it promised to pay twenty-four thousand dollars of the school's debts by diverting money from the jubilee funds being raised in anticipation of the 1917 merger. This put Columbia College in fairly sound financial shape, certainly better than PLA; what would happen next would be up to the new church body.

> The leaders all realized that either Columbia College at Everett or Pacific Lutheran in Parkland would eventually be selected as the only school of the Norwegian Lutheran Church on the coast. None at this date knew which one it would be. Bogstad, however—aggressive, energetic, and optimistic as he was—felt sure it would be Columbia College.[31]

Spokane College began with considerable local and financial support. In

1907 a three-story brick building was constructed on 29th Street just east of Grand Avenue, and 108 students and 24 faculty members launched the first year. P. M. Glasoe of St. Olaf College was the first president. There were seven academic units: liberal arts, commercial studies, law, normal studies, music, art, and the academy. The law school and commercial studies program were particularly appealing to the Spokane business community, and a wide range of majors existed. A major fundraising campaign, designed to raise two hundred thousand dollars for an endowment fund, was underway by 1909. That same year the Spokane Public Library placed a branch library near the college, making an ample supply of books available to faculty and students. Up to that point everything had gone well, but then problems began to emerge.

A new United Lutheran church (Manitou United Norwegian Lutheran Church) was built near the college to serve the faculty and students, but this brought disagreement and competition with an older church (Our Savior's) that had provided much of the early leadership and support for the college. When Our Savior's withdrew most of its financial and leadership support, some civic leaders wanted to make the institution into a nondenominational—but still "positively Christian in character"—institution, a sort of city college. The church would neither sell the college nor give up control, however, so civic support began to fade. Spokane College was soon "securely impaled upon the horns of a dilemma": Should it be a civic or a United Norwegian Lutheran college?[32]

The United Church was determined that Spokane College would continue to operate, and it paid $33,888 on the school's debts in 1916. Its officials soon realized, however, that there were relatively few Lutherans in the Inland Empire, which made it difficult to maintain a large, comprehensive, and vigorous institution. The last trustees' report of the United Church observed: "Had the Church taken this into consideration when they years ago began the school, they would have escaped a great deal of expense."[33] Enrollment fell sharply, and in the 1920s Spokane College functioned mostly as an academy. The Joint Synod of Ohio began sending some students to the college in 1914, thus launching the first educational cooperation among Lutherans in the Northwest. That was a positive sign in an otherwise bleak and debt-ridden situation.

5

Pacific Lutheran College

HONG'S OPTIMISM of 1915 was sorely tested by the events of the next three years. The war brought inflation, a severe drop in enrollment, and nationwide antiforeign feelings that became quite savage. The Norwegian Lutheran merger and the 1917 celebration of the Reformation's anniversary made it difficult for the national church to focus on educational problems in the far Northwest. The celebration fundraising made it next to impossible to raise money locally. Disrepair became a problem and debt mounted. In 1914 the debts of PLA were $27,271; by 1917 they had mounted to $37,192. Hong, reporting this, said: "I write this with a very heavy heart feeling sorry that our debt has increased. Yet we have done our best to keep it down."[1] He hoped the coming merger would bring some solution to the manifold problems. Meanwhile, Columbia College was also having a very difficult time; it was not at all clear whether either school could open for the 1917–18 academic year.

THE MERGER

The Norwegian Lutheran Church of America (NLCA) convention in Minneapolis in the summer of 1917 finally determined that Pacific Lutheran Academy should be its only school west of the Cascades. Columbia College was ordered to merge with PLA, a decision helped along by the Tacoma Commercial Club's promise to help secure twenty-five thousand dollars to keep the institution in Tacoma.[2]

This should have been the end of it, but it was not. The NLCA also made clear that the Parkland institution should be under its control. This was aimed at the Reverend Bjug Harstad and his supporters. Harstad had not been happy with the 1917 synod merger, believing it to be built on a theologically unacceptable compromise. In 1918, consequently, he would help form a new church body. Harstad, the much-beloved pastor of the Parkland congregation, was still influential at the school and a member of its controlling corporation. If the NLCA was to support the school, it had to control it; and Harstad would have to be dealt out. If those problems could be settled, money from the jubilee fund would be available to help with financial difficulties.[3] But at this point the NLCA decided its earlier decision had been premature and turned the educational difficulties over to the joint boards of trustees and education for resolution. Hong was told that it was a good idea to open school in the fall, but that he would have to act on his own. There would be no help from church headquarters.

On 13 August Hong wrote to the NLCA board of trustees secretary Lars W. Boe, the future St. Olaf president, about the matter. Hong assured Boe that the payment of the debt had been guaranteed, that the Tacoma Commercial Club had been approached about the money they had promised, and that the school corporation had agreed to transfer ownership to the new church, but still the church had not responded. If PLA was to open in the fall it had to know where it stood, Hong pleaded. "Kindly let us know how the matter stands."[4]

Boe responded on 21 August that the synod did not know PLU was waiting for a response. He thought that the Tacoma Commercial Club's promise did not comply with the convention's wishes, and he did not think it was advisable for the church to own the Parkland property.

> What the Church wishes to know, as far as I can understand, is that it shall be entirely within the control—the unquestionable control—of the people belonging to the Norwegian Lutheran Church of America. . . . Another matter which undoubtedly will cut a big figure in the settlement of the school question out West, is the question whether the Parkland Academy is to have at its front door a church fight that will hinder the work that the school otherwise could do.[5]

Columbia College would be closed, Boe said; perhaps you can use some of its teachers. What you do next year is up to you, he told Hong; "the Church has not assumed any other responsibility towards Parkland as yet, than it has heretofore."

The PLA board decided to open school on 15 October. In September Hong met with representatives from Columbia College and presented his view about merging faculty, students, and boards in Parkland. It was not accepted.[6] Soon there were two competing schools again, rather than one consolidated school, because the indomitable Rasmus Bogstad in Everett had used the confusing situation to bring that institution back to life again, arguing that the joint institution should be located there. Hong was aggrieved. It seemed that no progress had been made toward solving the Norwegian Lutheran educational disagreements in the Northwest after all.

By November Hong did not think PLA could hang on for a second term. Debt loomed larger and larger, and the enrollment was down to forty-five. The Parkland congregation was still divided between those who accepted the merger and those who did not—who were led by Bjug Harstad. No monies, no clear advice, and certainly no resolutions of problems had come from church leadership in Minneapolis. What should be done? Boe's answer from Minneapolis was, we cannot do much for you, but hang on: "it would be bad policy to close down the school now that you have started.... The times are out of joint, and no one knows what the future has in store. I hope that you will find it possible in some way to continue your school year."[7] Five hundred dollars was sent to help with the most pressing debts even though, it was somewhat archly pointed out, the correct forms had not yet been submitted.

The PLA corporation met on 12 December, and Hong described what had happened in the past several months. The corporation decided the church had given its moral support and wanted them to continue to operate, so that is what they should do, despite the frequently mixed messages and the obvious problems. Hong reported to Boe: "The discussion centered mainly on determining the exact status of the school as to ownership and responsibility which, it must be conceded, is a somewhat puzzling and anomalous one."[8] He also wrote that "towards the close of the session Rev. Harstad, Mr. T. C. Satra, and six other 'Minority' men resigned as members of the Corporation and withdrew from the meeting, leaving the 'Majority' in absolute control."[9] Hong regretted "exceedingly" that these men felt obliged to separate from the corporation and the school, but it seemed necessary. The separation would undoubtedly make future actions and decisions easier.

Pacific Lutheran Academy limped through the 1918 spring term. There were 60 students that February, compared to 134 in February 1917 and 214 in 1916. Hong did not think drastic steps would be taken to unseat Harstad in the Parkland congregation; that would be counterproductive. Moderation would heal wounds, Hong believed.[10] There had been heated biblical, theological, organizational, and legal discussion in the Parkland congregation, but without resolution. The congregation remained evenly divided.[11] By April only forty-two students remained at the academy, and Hong was criticized for failing to lead the fight to unseat Harstad.[12] The sum of ten thousand dollars was received from the jubilee fund, which helped pay some long overdue debts and string things out a little longer.

Four days after the term ended Hong resigned as president. He told the board that he could not lead a fight against Harstad—who was his pastor and friend—but he knew that was not satisfactory to the board or to Minneapolis.[13] He also thought the Everett and Parkland institutions, when they merged, should have new leadership and a new name, Pacific Lutheran College. There should be a fresh beginning, he urged. Columbia College and its aggressive president, Rasmus Bogstad, were not very cooperative, however. They resisted the new name and refused to give up their local sovereignty to the new Pacific District's joint committee, hoping they could keep things going in Everett. Hong was angry and upset, convinced that attempts to resolve problems had been met with "quibbling, subterfuges, and evasions." He could not work under those conditions. All of the problems made an impossible setting for a new college.[14]

Pacific Lutheran Academy was then closed for two years. The Old Main building was used by the children's home. Hong ended his twenty-one years of devoted service to the school and joined the faculty at Lincoln High School in Tacoma. This may have been the darkest moment in the history of the institution.

The Pacific District at its June 1918 meeting decided that the two institutions should merge; it did not care where. A decision came from Minneapolis that it should be in Everett, so a 1918–19 academic year was organized in Everett at what was now called Pacific College. Fewer than one hundred students showed up. This new name did not mean that consolidation had taken place; no teachers and few, if any, students came from Parkland. Neither had a psychological shift occurred. Some Norwegian Lutheran pastors began objecting to the move and what it suggested about the future, and PLA's alumni association, claiming to be three thousand strong, organized a campaign to undo the damage and reestablish their alma mater.[15] These pressures seemed to have some influence.

The tortuous enterprise groaned on for another year without resolution. Finally, in 1920, after flip-flopping district meetings, four joint board meetings, and seemingly endless maneuvering, the issue was resolved. Everett was to organize a hospital association and turn its building into a hospital. (Eventually the children's home moved north and occupied the sturdy Columbia College building, even though for decades it was still called the Parkland Children's Home.) A new Pacific District College Association was formed by the NLCA, and it was decided the college should be located in Parkland. Some financial responsibilities were assigned, but it was made absolutely clear that the national church should have no financial responsibility for operating the school. The national church accepted these proposals at its biennial meeting in 1920, and they went into effect immediately.

It had been a long, hard, and perhaps understandable struggle in a church body that took education and theology very seriously. But at last it was over; the college was to be in Parkland where it had started, and all parties were eager to get on with the work.[16] Even Rasmus Bogstad worked hard for the new college and was an invaluable source of advice and encouragement in the years ahead.

THE ROARING TWENTIES

By 1920 the world had changed quite dramatically. Four years of world war had helped to unleash social, political, cultural, and intellectual forces that had been dammed up for decades. Ten million combatants had been killed on the battlefields. The young had been sent off to die by the hordes, and those who survived were often openly rebellious. The three empires of central Europe were gone. America had become the dominant world power, but the Soviet Union was waiting in the wings. National economic control became widespread, not to test theories of socialism but to organize and control wartime industries. Technology and total war mentalities became dominant facts of life. Women agitated for the right to vote, social experimentation was very widespread, and peace movements appeared left and right.

By the twenties, culture and patterns of thought, now free from nineteenth-century restraints, swirled along as well. The shock of the new seemed to be the order of the day. Bourgeois culture and the static structures of formalism were attacked by painters, poets, composers, and philosophers, just as a generation earlier the structure of Newtonian space and time had been assaulted and rearranged by a cluster of stunning thinkers. The picture of the physical universe had changed, and the cultural and intellectual universe was changing too. What would replace the older forms was not very clear. This situation produced searching and excitement, but also frustration and fear. The new forces and approaches, which textbooks typically label "modernism," produced dazzling insights as well as tentative and disposable solutions. Models and heuristic devices appeared. Truth—like space and time—was relative, students were increasingly told. Modernism would not disappear. Nietzsche's slightly earlier diagnosis of Western civilization seemed appropriate: "Perhaps never before in history did such an open sea exist."

The Lutheran churches (and Lutheran theology and education), like all churches, were forced to address the changes and complexities of the period. It was a daunting task, and many of the first responses were understandably negative. Critical study of the Bible—the so-called higher criticism—evolution, and historicism were thought to be the principal enemies. One response was to grasp more firmly the orthodox and scholastic pillars of the past and to deny that there could be development in doctrine or any substance in these new concepts and approaches. That certainly was the NLCA's response, which assumed that any concession to evolution would lead to the relativizing of the Christian faith. The new biblical studies raised warning flags (and brought heresy trials in other denominations) all through the twenties. Church leaders and theologians responded in various ways; one way was to invoke the nineteenth-century notion of inerrancy: "Total inerrancy seemed to be the basis of all doctrinal integrity and a particularly pertinent doctrine amidst the infidelity of the twenties."[17] Some Lutheran synods tied themselves very closely to this interpretive view. It was a defensive weapon that meant retreat into biblical and theological bunkers, and it ignored the previous century's scholarship, but it seemed safe and appropriate. It was the Word of God that was being defended, after all. The persisting problem would eventually hit theological seminaries, bother religion departments in Lutheran colleges, and influence Lutheran mergers in the early 1960s and late 1980s.

Not all the responses and developments were negative and fearful, however. Lutherans in America began to play a larger role in American life by 1920. The years between 1915 and 1920 constitute an important watershed in American Lutheran history. The 1917 Reformation anniversary celebration achieved enough Lutheran cooperation to make it a turning point. Never before had Lutherans in America been so visible. The 1917 Norwegian Lutheran merger and the 1918 merger of mostly East Coast Lutherans into the United Lutheran Church in America added to the impact and growing confidence. "These actions signaled that a multilingual European Lutheranism was moving to assert its identity as a confessional community in the midst of the religious pluralism of America."[18]

Lutheran higher education had to live in the midst of this complexity, debate the theological questions, struggle with modernism, grapple with advances in Luther scholarship, build buildings, raise endowment monies, and satisfy accreditation agencies. It would take several decades to address and work through the questions and problems that became explicit in the roaring twenties.[19]

THE NEW COLLEGE

In the summer of 1920 the Pacific District of the NLCA decided to institutionalize the educational decisions that had just been made locally and nationally. They did this by incorporating the Pacific Lutheran College Association with the State of Washington.[20] The original articles of incorporation (1890) were not invalidated by this action, however, so two sets of articles existed until 1959, when studies leading to the achievement of university status rectified the situation. The new college was formed by the merger of Columbia College and Pacific Lutheran Academy. It claimed to be a college, but it would take a little time to work that out.

Professor J. U. Xavier was tapped as president because he was the oldest and most experienced faculty member. The board assumed he would serve; he was not asked. "Speak about headaches!" Xavier recalled. "Had it not been for the loyalty of the teachers, I don't know how it would have ended. . . . I was never present at a trustee meeting, nor was I asked to be, and I was not even told what they met about or what resolutions, if any, had been passed. I was, as far as I know, simply on my own."[21]

Only eighteen students arrived for the first day, but the number grew to sixty-eight by the end of the year. The curriculum was almost identical to what had been offered before closure in 1918. The stigma the German language had acquired during the war was reflected in the 1921 catalog: "German has been more or less taboo since the war, and it will be some time before it will become a regular course in our schools again." German science and literature were too important to be ignored, however. "Besides, it was not the German language or literature or science we fought in the World War, but Kaiserism."[22] The library housed fifty-five hundred books, the Bible would be taught according to the teachings of the Lutheran church, and students were required to attend chapel daily, the catalog explained. Rules remained stringent. The college's fundamental aim as declared that year was to prepare young people for some useful work in life. A new ecumenical note appeared in its publications: "While especially adapted for students of Lutheran faith and antecedents, it welcomes those of other denominations as well." The college intended to provide individual attention and be "democratic to the core."[23]

Most of the old teachers returned—Hong was the major exception— and some new faculty entered the scene as well. The most notable was a young man named Philip E. Hauge, who had just graduated from St. Olaf College. Intending to teach a few years before continuing on to law school, he served the school steadily until his retirement in 1968. Hauge taught psychology, education, government, civics, and English that first year; he also served as dean of men. The next year he was appointed registrar. He became dean of the college in 1925. Hauge would have an incalculable influence on the institution in the years ahead, especially on teacher education. Also in 1920 Lora Bradford Kreidler began her long career as dean of women and professor of art. She was related to the New England Bradfords and was a member of the Mayflower descendants' association.

A chapel building was constructed in 1920 on the north side of Old Main. Those two buildings, along with the gymnasium, formed the campus facade that would remain until the 1940s. The chapel, a square, gabled, wooden structure, was built to provide a place for the PLC community to gather for public events and worship, but it also served as a church building for the members of the NLCA who lived in Parkland, since the Parkland congregation, which dated back to the 1890s, had finally split. The Reverend Carl Foss ('08) came as pastor in 1921 to serve the new NLCA church, called Trinity Lutheran. The "Little Norwegian Synod" members and Pastor Harstad retained the old church building for their congregation—Parkland Lutheran. The cemetery was divided between the two churches. Controversy over the merger had been difficult and finally proved divisive.

Xavier's interim service as president ended in 1921 when the trustees selected the Reverend Ola J. Ordal, pastor of Our Savior's Lutheran

Church in Tacoma, as president. He had been educated in the grammar schools of South Dakota, attended the Lutheran Normal School in Sioux Falls, taught in the public schools in Iowa, and graduated from Luther College (1898) and Luther Seminary (1901). He had served parishes in Minnesota and Washington and had been a PLA and PLC trustee.

The long-dreamed-of collegiate status was soon articulated under the leadership of Ordal and Hauge. The junior college took shape with both liberal arts and normal departments. A high school, business department, stenographic course, beginner's English course, and music instruction existed alongside the collegiate structure. The published justification for the junior college was that it could keep young people under the influence of the church for a longer period of time, "before they came under the dissolving influences of our irreligious state institutions."[24] In 1922 the faculty petitioned the board to approve a system of rules to govern their appointment, salaries, and promotion. The proposed system, quite lengthy and carefully constructed, was taken under consideration. Collegiate structure was pushed a little further in 1923 with the establishment of an elaborate committee system; nine committees were established for the ten full-time faculty members. Meanwhile, several musical activities at the school resumed, as did basketball teams, and there was brief mention in 1923 of a school paper called the *Sparkplug*.

Its successor, the *Mooring Mast*, was born in the fall of 1924, named in honor of the large mooring structure that had been built near Fort Lewis for the famed dirigible *Shenandoah*. Palma Heimdahl was the first editor. There are great needs, she wrote, that must be met with "enthusiasm and determination." The first issue reported that the Debating Club's mock presidential election had been won by the Republicans.[25]

Early issues of the *Mooring Mast* provide rare glimpses of the everyday concerns and interests on campus. The 12 November 1924 issue reported that Professor Hauge had earned an M.A. degree in education at the University of Washington. Fittingly, his thesis was "The Elements Which Constitute a School Grade"; he would deal with those elements for more than forty years as registrar and dean. The 26 November issue reported that Burton Kreidler had won the state Women's Christian Temperance Union essay contest with an essay entitled "Dope Addiction." In December the paper reported that debate on the question, "Resolved: That bobbed hair is desirable," by the PLC Debating Society drew a larger audience than any other fall program. The 15 April 1925 issue described the visit of the Reverend William Schoeler of Aurora, Oregon, who lectured on evolution. Schoeler told the crowd that evolutionists had to be met on their own ground. "The evolutionists cannot account for the origin of life, so therefore the very first rung on their ladder is missing." That particular battle would go on for a long time.

In 1925 the normal department was accredited by the state, an achievement met with rejoicing on campus. Across the country throughout the 1920s there was both rapid physical expansion of colleges and a consequent growing concern for the content and quality of their educational programs. The accreditation movement, which began in the late nineteenth century, was an important goad and measuring device for progress.[26] Over the years PLC would continue to work hard for appropriate accreditation. This quest would add to the cost of running the school, something that became painfully obvious in the decades ahead.

Two important additions to the faculty arrived in 1925. Joseph O. Edwards took up the work in music. He had attended St. Olaf College for three years before earning his B.M. degree from the University of Washington. At St. Olaf he had sung under the direction of the internationally famous conductor, F. Melius Christiansen. Edwards brought the tradition he had learned there—great choral music with religious texts sung a capella—with him to Parkland. He wanted to organize a choir that would tour the Northwest, help advertise the school, and give pleasure. That was first accomplished in 1927, and thereafter the choir traveled every year. It acquired the name Choir of the West on a trip to the Great Lakes region in 1931. Edwards's lively wife, Ardy, was also very active on campus, organizing and directing dramatic presentations.

The other noteworthy faculty addition in 1925 was Anders Ramstad, a Minnesota farm boy with an amiable disposition, myriad interests, a capacious memory, and a gift for languages. He was educated at St. Olaf College (1914) and Luther Seminary (1918) and served parishes in Seattle and Bremerton from 1918 to 1925. He was elected to the PLC board of trustees in 1920 and was called to the faculty in 1925 as vice president, dean of men, purchasing agent, and coach, as well as professor of mathematics, science, religion, and Norwegian. A little chemistry had been taught before 1925, but it was Ramstad who really established the teaching of chemistry at PLC. He built the first chemistry laboratory in a converted men's washroom on the third floor of Old Main. The laboratory was later shifted to the basement of the gymnasium, then in 1947 to the new science building that was ultimately named Ramstad Hall in his honor.

In 1926 Ramstad also established the first football team at PLC (he had played football at St. Olaf). He found one boy on campus who had played football before coming to PLC, convinced others to play, found equipment, practiced with the boys, and helped organize a junior college league in the state. The teams were first called the Greyhounds and then the Gladiators, the name that would survive officially until 1960. One of the players on that first team, Carl Coltom, had a son, Ronald, and two grandsons, David and Donald, who also played football for PLC and PLU.[27]

The women's basketball teams continued to be popular and were remarkably successful from 1925 to 1927. They compiled a 22–2–1 record during that time. The outstanding player was Polly Langlow, who scored 270 points in twelve games in 1926, setting a national basketball scoring record for women. Bloomers were replaced by shorts the next year, which undoubtedly speeded up play. Ramstad was the women's basketball coach.

Anders Ramstad and his gifted wife, Emma, were delighted to be at the new junior college, but there were costs. They lost the house they were purchasing in Bremerton and had to cancel insurance policies. Emma later recalled:

> I guess we had not realized just how tight things were. There were no paydays, so to speak, but when the first of the month came, the little money that was in the treasury would be divided among faculty and staff and the most urgent bills. . . . Sometimes it would amount to fifteen dollars. But the advantages of being here so far outweighed the disadvantages that there was not much complaint. We knew for a certainty that this school had a promising future, and we wanted very much to be a part of it.[28]

In 1926 the first Ph.D. joined the faculty. He was Hans Jacob Jules Hoff, a 1901 graduate of Bethany College in Kansas. Hoff had studied philology in Berlin and traveled extensively in Russia between 1901 and 1903. He completed his doctorate at the University of Illinois in 1908, then taught at the University of Washington from 1908 to 1916. He remained at PLC until 1931.

ENDOWMENT DRIVE

By 1920 most Lutheran colleges were not very academically distinguished. Faculty members were not highly trained, even though natural aptitudes and dedication turned many into excellent teachers. Facilities were inadequate and the curricula were little changed from previous decades. The colleges typically did not deal with the intellectual revolutions of the recent past, especially in the areas of natural science and social science. A basic problem for the Lutheran church synods in the twenties, therefore, was to develop more intellectually respectable church-related colleges.[29]

Money for annual operations, endowment, buildings, upgraded curricula, and planning was badly needed. Accreditation concerns pushed all of this along, first in the Midwest, and then elsewhere. In 1921, for example, the North Central Association, the largest of the regional accreditation agencies, announced that as a minimum requirement for accreditation by 1927 all colleges must have an endowment of at least half a million dollars.

That was shocking. No Lutheran college, not even those that were already accredited, could meet this requirement. A wave of fundraising activities began. Professional fundraisers were sought for the first time.[30]

The best known of these Lutheran fundraisers was a Missouri Lutheran pastor named O. H. Pankoke. His standing in the Missouri Synod was not high, however, because of his cooperative work with other Lutheran synods during the war and his work for Lutheran unity in the twenties. He had developed and polished his organizational and publicity skills in the 1917 Reformation celebration, through wartime pan-Lutheran ventures, and as director of the Lutheran Bureau (a postwar publicity and information agency). He directed twenty-two fundraising campaigns for Lutheran colleges in the twenties and early thirties.[31]

In fall 1925 PLC launched the school's first endowment fund drive. The goal was $250,000. The Reverend J.A.E. Naess, the Pacific District president, chaired the drive. It was not very effectively organized, however, and got underway quite slowly. In September 1926 speed picked up a bit when the Reverend George Henricksen from Silverton, Oregon, was appointed field secretary to supervise the drive. He was thus the first development officer in the institution's history. A scheme known as the Luther-St. Olaf plan was adopted to provide direction for the months ahead. This was the Pankoke-directed campaign that had raised more than one million dollars for those schools in 1926. Oscar Tingelstad had served as "fieldman" in the large and complex organization that had functioned so well in that Midwest campaign, so by the time he would come to PLC as president in 1928 he had acquired a very sophisticated knowledge of collegiate development, planning, and fundraising procedures.

Pankoke was asked by "top officials" of the NLCA to survey the situation in the Northwest and help decide whether an adequate endowment drive could be mounted. He replied that the answer was "yes" if forty competent workers from the Midwest could help at the crucial moment.[32] One of those who came to help was a pastor named S. C. Eastvold. Pankoke was in Parkland by December 1926; once there he directed most of the planning and organization that would finally adequately launch the campaign. His plan included a blitz of dramatic and attractive publications in April, May, and June 1927 describing the needs and purposes of PLC, followed by a visit to every congregation (and every member) of the Pacific District by one of a host of thoroughly trained and carefully orchestrated representatives. Oscar Tingelstad led the fifty-thousand-dollar alumni drive, the faculty pledged five thousand dollars, and the students promised ten thousand. The campaign, under Pankoke's leadership, went very smoothly. The August 1927 *PLC Bulletin* announced with exultation: "The Goal Is Reached, Grand Total, August 5th: $290,000." It continued:

That which at the beginning of the Endowment campaign seemed well-nigh impossible, has been accomplished.... A new day has dawned for our college, a brighter future for its activities. Through the many pledges made, God has declared it to be His will that this Christian school shall continue. May it always do so to the glory of His name.[33]

The *Bulletin* listed all the gifts from individuals, congregations, and societies in Washington, Oregon, Idaho, and California, including several gifts of five thousand dollars. Pankoke considered the drive a great success, particularly since the goal had been proportionately larger in relation to church membership in the area covered than any other Lutheran drive.[34]

With this successful endowment drive, collegiate status, and normal department accreditation behind him, O. J. Ordal resigned in January 1928, pushed along by the board, which found a call for him at Our Savior's Lutheran Church in Bellingham. For the next few months the college was governed by a faculty council, chaired by Ole Stuen.

Other accomplishments mark the late 1920s. The college was securely established academically, its buildings were still adequate, and enrollment continued to mount (from 68 in 1920–21 to 178 in 1927–28). Third and fourth years of college programs did not seem out of the question for the near future. Service was still the norm for guiding educational activity. The successful fund drive seemed to put a stamp of approval on that much-repeated theme and to vindicate all the years of suffering and dedication that had led to 1927. Celebration, thanks, and gratitude were the orders of the day.

A call was extended to PLA graduate and Luther College administrator and professor Oscar Tingelstad to be the next PLC president. After seven weeks of carefully and prayerfully studying the call, he accepted it. He was always careful and precise. The Luther College paper described him as a Christian gentleman, a scholar of preeminent ability, and "part of the heart and soul of Luther College, one of her guiding lights at all times."[35] He was exceptionally well trained to be a college president and dedicated to both Lutheran higher education and PLC. The future seemed very promising. Slightly more than a year after he came to Parkland, however, the Great Depression hit.

6

Depression and War

O SCAR TINGELSTAD was the only presi-
dential candidate seriously considered by the board of trustees and its
energetic chair, the Reverend O. L. Haavik, pastor of Ballard First Lutheran Church. Despite some successes in the past few years, PLC's
existence was still precarious. One board member even thought the school
should close with Ordal's resignation, but Haavik disagreed strongly. He
knew Oscar Tingelstad was capable, exceptionally well prepared for a
leadership position, and dedicated to Lutheran education and PLC.
Haavik extended the call on 21 January 1928 and urged Tingelstad to
accept: "We need you out here . . . come and lead us and we will follow
holding up your hand as well as we can."[1]

Other faculty members urged Tingelstad to accept. Spokane College
president Carl Foss told Tingelstad he was the right person for the job,
although PLC was in a critical position and the job would mean much
worry and work. "But where on earth can a mortal get away from worries
if he desires to do some constructive and worthwhile work?"[2] After seven
weeks of consideration, Tingelstad accepted the call.

OSCAR TINGELSTAD

Oscar Tingelstad was born in North Dakota, but he grew up in Silverton,
Oregon. He attended Pacific Lutheran Academy, completing the commercial course in 1900 and the Luther College preparatory course with its
classical emphasis in 1902. He was an excellent student who remained a
lifelong advocate of classical education. Tingelstad graduated from Luther
College in 1905 and from Luther Seminary in 1907, served briefly in a
parish, and then joined the Luther College faculty in 1909.[3] He quickly
developed a reputation as a good teacher and was soon appointed the
school's first professor of education and psychology. In 1914 he became
the first registrar of the college and served with "distinction" in that
office.[4] He was quite disappointed in not being selected Luther College
president in 1922, lamenting that he thought he "had a right to be
considered for the position." That disappointment might have encouraged
his move to PLC in 1928.[5]

Tingelstad pursued graduate study in psychology and education at the
University of Chicago, receiving an M.A. degree in 1913 and a Ph.D.

degree in 1925. (He would be one of the few Lutheran college presidents with an earned doctorate.) An avid statistician, Tingelstad focused his research projects for both degrees on the decline of the "religious element" in American school readers, a deterioration he thought unfortunate. Tingelstad disliked many of the intellectual and theological tendencies that were appearing in the 1920s, especially evolutionary thought, which he believed undercut the authority of the Bible and Lutheran doctrine:

> Evolution is now descending into the common schools and spreading among the people. Irresponsibility, disrespect for authority, blasphemy, irreligion, crime, jazz, animalism, recklessness will follow in its train, because it represents a departure from that Word which is the "power of God unto salvation."[6]

Deeply rooted in the Norwegian Synod, Tingelstad was a conservative Lutheran dedicated to the Lutheran Confessions and the authority of the Bible. He centered his philosophy of education around the Bible as the Word of God, salvation by faith in Christ, and a profound respect for the value of the individual.[7] He was kind, quite formal, and deeply pious, but not a "pietist" or a "legalist." He was a scholar and a lover of words; words poured from him and a dry wit and a quick pun were never too far behind. He selflessly served others and they, in turn, responded with affection and loyalty, especially when the times became trying.

By August 1928 Oscar Tingelstad was in Parkland, ready to move carefully but resolutely into the future. He knew his tasks would not be easy, as he explained to his graduate school advisor: "It is make or break. There is a real opportunity for an institution of this type out here; but there are mountains of inertia to move, sloughs of despondency to drain, and fogs of misconception to dissipate."[8]

Tingelstad was installed as president of PLC on 14 December 1928. The *Mooring Mast* applauded Tingelstad's appointment and described his inaugural speech as "excellent." Built around six connected themes, it described the "apperceptive mass," by which Tingelstad meant one must understand the emotional and intellectual context of a situation before being able to act effectively. Noting that "the world's work is done by partisans," he invited partisanship of the right sort. Tingelstad also discussed what Christ's statement "I am the Truth" meant for education. He passionately described the United States as a "sweet land of liberty," but then added that American life was shifting west: "Westward the course of empire takes its way." Everyone, but especially those concerned with the church and its educational ventures, needs to understand the significance of that movement, he urged. Finally, he described the educational adventures in the Northwest as "pioneering on the last frontier."[9] Lars Boe, by then president of St. Olaf College, wrote after returning home from the ceremony: "I think you are going to succeed in solving the problem out there."[10] The problem, in Boe's mind, was lack of leadership. He and other midwestern church and college officials typically referred to PLC as being "out there," as though it were nearly lost in the vastness of space or perhaps located in a somewhat different world.

DEVELOPMENT AND PLANNING

Tingelstad—influenced by his study at Chicago, his administrative work at Luther, the widespread effect of accreditation in the 1920s, and his fund-raising experience with O. H. Pankoke—was determined to prepare a very careful script before he set to work. In August 1928 he thanked supporters for the recently completed and successful endowment drive and laid out the general policies that would follow.

PLC would be conservatively Lutheran with a forward-looking program, he explained. It would combine what the church needed with what the people in the Northwest wanted. It would march in step with the accreditation agencies, but also keep in touch with NLCA colleges and seminaries. There would be economical and audited management, but not retrenchment or curtailment. Tingelstad stuck to those resolutions all through the depression, even against the protests of church officials and sometimes of trustees. The problem of financial support would be particularly addressed; income had to be increased. That would be done mostly through organizing friends and supporters into a Pacific Lutheran College Development Association. Field work—public relations, student recruitment, and systematic fundraising—had to be carefully developed and organized as well. Victor Elvestrom was hired as a development field agent in 1928, as were Carl Foss in 1929, George Lane in 1930, and Paul Preus in 1931. Mikkel Lono and Carl Solling-Fynboe were hired a few years later. Nils Hong returned as principal of the high school, and the high school and college were administratively separated for greater efficiency and to satisfy accreditation officials.[11] By November 1928 the search was on for ten thousand development association members who would give "at least a dollar at least once a year." Increasing a budget by almost forty thousand dollars, such contributions, along with the church subsidy, could create financial health. The fifty-eight-thousand-dollar debt had to be reduced, but Tingelstad and the field agents were working on that as well.[12]

Although PLC was in debt, Tingelstad approved a plan to expand its grounds and facilities. The plan, presented in April 1929 by the architect Charles Altfillisch, well known for his work at Luther College, proposed that land should be purchased around the edges of the campus and up to the golf course. That would permit building homes for the faculty. "A high-grade faculty is an important asset to the school. In order to obtain it, it must be taken care of."[13] Altfillisch also proposed that a president's home be built and that the inadequate swimming pool space in the gymnasium be converted to science laboratories. In addition, he advised that the Old Main building, especially its fourth and fifth floors, be improved and that all future buildings be incorporated into a unified campus plan. Altfillisch also suggested a number of landscaping changes. His report concluded with a warning that if PLC adopted this plan it must "religiously" stick to it. Tingelstad intended to do just that.

By the end of spring 1929 the 1,526 members of the development association had given $4,326, but the debt remained untouched and a large operating deficit loomed for the year. Tingelstad was disappointed that problems had developed so quickly. He regularly invested in the stock market and followed it very closely, hoping it might pay off for the school. That year he wrote to a friend that he "had a dream once that Kansas Oil would save Pacific Lutheran College, [but] it doesn't look that way now."[14] A five-thousand-dollar emergency appropriation from the NLCA helped cope with the worst of the crisis, but the board of trustees threatened to resign if the potential deficit was not met by 1 July. The accreditation officials refused to grant accreditation until the shaky finan-cial situation was resolved, which meant additional expenditures for salaries and campus repairs. Caught in a vicious circle, Tingelstad became frustrated and exhausted.[15]

PLC's debt was quite serious. By the end of the fiscal year eleven thousand dollars had to be raised to pay back temporary loans, another six thousand was needed to meet the immediate demands of accreditation, and an income of forty thousand dollars had to be shown to satisfy accreditation officials. To raise money, PLC officials took various actions. Dean Philip Hauge and field agent Victor Elvestrom went to the Midwest in the summer of 1929 searching for funds. A special letter asking "Can we save our school on the Pacific Coast?" went out to pastors and friends of the college in a bulk mailing. PLC "has the field, the future, the mission, and is definitely on the up-grade," the letter concluded, but a combination of flu, bad weather, raised accreditation standards, and decreased church appropriations had brought a short-term pinch, it explained; "Can you help?"[16] It was a very trying summer—as it turned out, it was a dress rehearsal for the next fifteen years—but almost fifteen thousand dollars was raised and the fiscal year closed with a net gain of $211. After flurries of excitement and a sharp exchange of letters, accreditation came on 29 October 1929. The PLC faculty and staff then enjoyed a well-earned, if brief, sense of triumph and happiness.

Other Lutheran colleges were less fortunate. Spokane College closed during the summer of 1929, unable to meet the accreditation officials' requirement that nineteen thousand dollars be raised by 20 July for improvements and salaries. The academic records of Spokane College were merged with those of PLC, and a slow amalgamation of the two institutions began. The property was put in the custody of the NLCA board of trustees, where it remained until 1954 when it was sold. From the proceeds, PLC received seventy-five thousand dollars for building purposes. Spokane College's last president, Carl Foss, sent names of prospective students to PLC after the 20 July deadline and worked hard to transfer the Ohio Synod's cooperation and subsidy to PLC. That was accomplished with some exertion. The new Ohio Synod–PLC relationship was strengthened when the college hired Walter H. Hellman, an Ohio Synod member who had been teaching at Spokane College, as dean of men and professor of English and religion.[17] Calls were extended to other Spokane College people as well. Carl Foss became a field agent, and Clifford Olson was appointed coach, athletic director, and teacher of Latin and history. Olson was a 1927 graduate of Luther College, where he was a four-year letterman in football, basketball, and track. He was an outstanding football player, one of Luther's greatest, and one of seven Olsons on the 1926 team. He went to Spokane College in 1928 where, despite dismal prospects, he coached a winning football team. He was excited about being in the West and happy to come to PLC.[18] Throughout his coaching career, he helped create one of the most exciting eras of Pacific Northwest athletic history. Oscar Tingelstad had good instincts for personnel.

JESSE PFLEUGER

Walter Hellman resigned after one year at PLC to assume the presidency of Hebron College in Nebraska, but the connection between the Ohio Synod (which after 1930 became the American Lutheran Church) and PLU —the first instance of Lutheran educational cooperation in the United States—remained alive with the appointment of Jesse Philip Pflueger, one of the most beloved professors in PLC's history. His salary was paid by the American Lutheran Church as part of the agreed-upon subsidy. Pflueger's grandfather had been one of the founders of the Ohio Synod, and his father was a professor at that synod's Capital University for twenty-five years. Pflueger grew up in the Old Main building there and took every course offered by the university. He received a B.A. degree in 1907 when he was eighteen years old and B.S. and theology degrees in 1910. He studied tropical medicine at Tulane University, receiving a degree in 1914, and Indian languages and religion at Leipzig University in Germany in 1915, preparing for missionary service in India. The war made that impossible, but Pflueger worked for a year in health-related work in the Philippines. He moved to Seattle in 1916 to serve Queen Anne Lutheran Church, and in 1930 he came to PLC.

Pflueger represented the German-American Lutheran tradition in the midst of a Norwegian-American Lutheran college. It was a healthy mixture. He was a theologically conservative Lutheran, a foe of legalism, an influential teacher, a powerful speaker with an old-fashioned oratorical style, an artist, and a sports enthusiast. He was, for many years, trainer of the athletic teams. His "Roll 'em back, boys! Roll 'em back!" could be heard over the roar of thousands, and his railing at basketball officials—philosophically justified, he argued—was notoriously unrestrained. Pflueger taught PLC students ethics, philosophy, and Bible from 1930 until 1958, with only a little help from the mid-1950s onward. He was the only teacher that all students had to take during most of that time, usually for three classes. His wise and healthy advice was much sought after, and his influence was profound. He was the most highly praised PLC teacher in the 1930s and 1940s.

The Depression

The financial difficulties that PLC had faced since its founding and which had grown particularly acute in the summer of 1929 were badly exacerbated by the stock market crash and depression that burst on the scene in the fall of 1929. By 1933 the value of stocks on the New York Stock Exchange was less than one-fifth that of 1929. In 1930 between six and seven million people were unemployed; two years later the number had doubled. Conditions in the West were worse than in the rest of the country, with a lower per capita income and higher unemployment. As late as 1940 *Fortune* magazine reported that "the Pacific Coast harbored more doubts about the future of the American system than any other section of the country. The frontier had lost its magic."[19]

The depression forced PLC to try one desperate fundraising campaign after another to remain open. Tingelstad had to devote almost all his energy and time to financial matters, and the terrible pressure undermined his health. The faculty and staff had to learn how to get by with severely reduced salaries (which were cut by 38.9 percent in 1933) that often were not paid anyway. In the midst of the worst of the depression, Tingelstad wrote that "Pacific Lutheran College is the *child of sacrifice*. 'Pioneering on the last frontier,' it has been built by sacrifice, survives by sacrifice, and humbly faces the path of sacrifice also for the future."[20]

Sacrifice and difficulty were certainly commonplace. In 1929 and 1930 PLC avoided deficits by desperate June and July fundraising visitations and saturation mailings. The college again avoided deficits in 1931 and

1932 because of large special grants given by the NLCA. Deficits remained, however, in 1933, 1934, 1937, and 1941. Thus, PLC was forced to launch catch-up campaigns almost every summer, run by the field agents and supplemented by faculty and staff. Faculty wife Emma Ramstad was asked to go to the Midwest one hot summer. "I felt doomed before I began," she wrote. "We had to beg our way around. In many areas the sentiment was that we should give the West Coast back to the Indians, as it would never amount to anything churchwise."[21] Indebtedness was $64,469 in 1929; it had risen to $156,590 by 1940. The payment of 1927 endowment pledges, badly undercut by the depression, produced little income because the stock market remained sluggish and because large amounts of the endowment were transferred to "operations" or "loaned" to PLC. Virtually none of the loan was ever paid back, and the endowment was cut in half during the 1930s.

THE PREUS-ELVESTROM PLAN

In 1932, PLC advanced the largest, most comprehensive, and most daring attempt to deal with financial difficulties. It was popularly called the Preus-Elvestrom Plan. If successful, it would have brought a new pattern of institutional ownership and national financing.[22] It was put together by field agents Paul Preus and Victor Elvestrom. Preus was a midwestern businessman, banker, and brother of NLCA officials; he joined the college staff in 1931 as endowment manager, field agent, and planner. Tingelstad told him: "the position I have in mind for you would be of such outstanding importance that a different contract would be drawn than in the case of others."[23] Preus was paid as much as the president.

The Preus-Elvestrom Plan was built on the foundation of Lutheran cooperation PLC had already achieved with the American Lutheran Church. That pioneering Lutheran educational cooperation was expanded in 1932 to include the Swedish-American Augustana Synod. Both synods included PLC in their depression budgets, and both, in turn, were given the right to select trustees. The relationships established were warm and increasingly comfortable.[24] On a national scale, the Preus-Elvestrom Plan was tied to the American Lutheran Conference, an organization of theologically like-minded Lutherans formed in October 1930. "The purposes of the American Lutheran Conference were cooperation in those areas of worship, work, and witness where full unity of doctrine is a prerequisite: home missions, parochial education, higher education . . . and joint planning toward greater Lutheran unity."[25]

The Preus-Elvestrom Plan proposed joint ownership, financing, and operation of PLC by the NLCA, the American Lutheran Church, and the Augustana Synod. Money would have come from a complex pattern of gifts and loans from each American Lutheran Conference congregation, "certificates of participation and indebtedness," and a guaranty fund.[26] Preus, Elvestrom, and Tingelstad were absolutely certain the plan would solve PLC's financial problems once and for all. The PLC board of trustees approved it with some enthusiasm. Preus and Elvestrom showed NLCA officials and its advising bankers the plan in the spring of 1932, and they were satisfied as well. The only remaining hurdle was national approval by the three constituent church groups in the summer of 1932. All three had to approve before it could begin functioning. But that was not to be. The NLCA and the Augustana Synod approved the plan, but the financially conservative American Lutheran Church, while expressing sympathy and interest, did not approve it. The Preus-Elvestrom Plan remained in limbo for several years and finally died. Tingelstad lamented the decision bitterly and never quite got over the plan's rejection.

The Preus-Elvestrom Plan was complicated. Requiring national cooperation, it was probably too idealistic for its time, but it was imaginatively constructed. The plan tried to build on the Lutheran cooperation and unity already begun in the Northwest and at least suggested in the October 1930 formation of the American Lutheran Conference, which was to work for intersynodical cooperation and unity in home missions and education.

With no contingency plan, however, the financial situation quickly became desperate. Two months after the rejection of the Preus-Elvestrom Plan Tingelstad offered his resignation, but the board of trustees refused it. Frantic, Tingelstad sent a night letter to NLCA headquarters: "Situation desperate. Unless we receive the emergency appropriation or equivalent loan, we must curtail drastically or quit at the end of the first semester. Tacoma merchants cannot extend needed credit."[27] NLCA headquarters responded by sending money. PLC's credit was maintained (the faculty and staff "voluntarily" surrendered salary amounting to nine thousand dollars), but President Tingelstad's health cracked under the strain and the board relieved him of all duties except financial supervision for several months.

In addition to the timely support from the NLCA headquarters, PLC managed to weather the depression through the generosity of the Hans Dahl family. Emma Ramstad recalled that

> there was an angel of mercy in Parkland known as Dahl's grocery! I am not sure what would have happened if credit had suddenly been cut off at that wonderful store. Never were any of the faculty embarrassed or afraid to go and ask for an order "to be put on my account." Malla Dahl saved the faculty families from malnutrition and related illnesses![28]

Malla Dahl had moved to Parkland with her parents in 1893 when her father, Samuel Sindland, worked on the construction of the Old Main building. She attended the parochial school and academy from 1894 to 1908, graduating that year, but because she finished at midyear she never received a diploma. PLU officials conferred a PLA diploma on Malla Dahl at the 1977 commencement as a long overdue token of institutional gratitude. Her husband also attended PLA, and their three children attended PLC.

Even with NLCA grants and the Dahl family's generosity, PLC's financial future was precarious. A measure of the insecurity can by seen in the campus involvement in gold speculation after 1935. Daniel Flotre, a former PLC student, was involved in gold exploration in Idaho. Many PLC people purchased stock in the Gold Run Mining Company that he helped establish, hoping this would provide passage out of the depression. PLC got one free share for every ten purchased. When gold was discovered there was great elation. Nils Hong dashed off a sonnet, "On the First Milling at the Gold Run Mine," that concluded:

> Rejoicing are the owners, boss, and crew,
> And all who serve within the College walls,
> Who now as facts their airy dreams behold.

The mother lode proved elusive, however, and still another dream slowly faded away. PLU still carries 82,765 shares of Summit Silver stock (the present company) on the books at a value of one dollar.

Financial problems continued unabated in the years ahead, but Tingelstad refused to contemplate retrenchment or curtailment of programs. The faculty and students remained remarkably loyal, and the institution's strong sense of community was a shield against the unending problems. As Tingelstad wrote to the alumni and church in the middle of the 1930s: "In spite of the complaints and bitterness evident on every hand in these days, the past year has surely been a good year at Pacific Lutheran College . . . never before have we had a finer spirit at the College."[29]

CAMPUS LIFE

Although affected by the depression, academic and social life flowed along quite smoothly and pleasantly. There were some important advances as well.[30] In 1931 the third year of normal school education was added and accredited. Enrollment increased every year under Tingelstad's presidency until World War II emptied the campus of males. Most important, more than 83 percent of the 1931 normal school graduates received jobs, a record not even approximately equaled by any similar institution in the state. All 1936 graduates found jobs. In 1937 only two of forty-eight remained unplaced. All were placed in 1938.

In 1930 the students decided to publish a yearbook. The name *Saga*, suggested by Dagny Hjermstad, a "popular" high school senior, was chosen after a campus-wide contest to name the new annual. More than seventy dollars was raised by the first *Saga* Carnival held in May 1930 to help subsidize its publication.

In other campus events, Hoover defeated Roosevelt by a vote of 56–46 in a campus "straw ballot" presidential election in November 1932; Norman Thomas received seven votes. In response to a question put by the *Mooring Mast*, Nils Hong thought that the 1933 closure of the banks was a good thing: "As soon as Congress makes a law to safeguard deposits, there will be plenty of money in circulation, and our depression will be over."[31] President Tingelstad's appendix ruptured and was removed on Christmas Day 1933. Gangrene and peritonitis threatened his life for many days, but eventually he recovered. "The Lord put me to school. . . . He taught me many valuable things in the stiffest and most thorough course of instruction that I have ever taken."[32]

Music continued to flourish under Joseph Edwards's leadership. As he explained to Tingelstad after turning down the directorship of music at the "Methodist College in Tacoma" in 1928, "we have done much better work in music here."[33] The choir traveled regularly, often sang on the radio, and was critically well received. All through the 1930s the *PLC Bulletin* announced the special role of the Choir of the West:

> This organization enjoys the unique distinction of being the only college choir west of the Missouri River specializing in *a capella* music of the type that has made St. Olaf College Choir famous throughout the United States. Mr. Edwards, our Director of Music, at one time a student under F. Melius Christiansen, director of the St. Olaf Choir, is building up the Pacific Lutheran College Choir into an organization worthy of his illustrious teacher.[34]

Anna Mikelson was the first well-known student soloist. Her singing of Christiansen's arrangement of "Beautiful Savior" was much in demand and brought rave reviews. The board members were so pleased by her activities that they paid her tuition in 1931.

F. Mason Holmes, who had taught painting at PLA from 1898 to 1901, returned after three decades of traveling around the world and painting. He was a true artist, the *Mooring Mast* said, who lived only for his art. It reported that two of his paintings were in the Corcoran Art Gallery in Washington, D.C., the "finest and most exclusive art gallery in America."[35] Many of his paintings still grace campus buildings and Parkland homes. The 1930s also brought the first May Festival, in 1934, which was a "huge success." Kathryn Johnson, "beautiful in her gown of blue satin," was the first May Queen. A quartet sang and girls performed a maypole dance.[36]

There were also ongoing discipline problems, predictable in a situation where most students lived on or near the campus and where both sexes shared the same dormitory. The faculty and administration were either too strict or too lenient, depending on the source of the information. Faculty meeting minutes suggest they were very lenient. A mother complained that her son, who was expelled for drinking moonshine, was treated unfairly. Moonshine was regularly for sale on the third floor, she said: "The school is so wet it drips."[37] A pastor complained that not enough proper discipline was maintained and blamed the faculty. He told Tingelstad he did not want the students to dance, drink beer, and play cards, but wondered if even the faculty were guiltless. He had not learned any of this from his daughter, he hastened to add. "Don't hold these things against my daughter . . . for she is silent 'as a rat.'"[38]

Both father and daughter objected to the teaching of Professor Peter Jeremiah Bardon, however. He was accused of criticizing the United States and praising the Soviet Union. "I don't want any of the teachers down there to stand up for Russian communism and advocate this before any of my children. . . . Bardon should not teach at P.L.C."[39] Other letters were similarly critical. Peter J. Bardon was a tall, angular, sometimes acerbic teacher of the social sciences, which he took very seriously. He had been at PLC since 1909. He was a dedicated Christian and a lifelong Lutheran, but he believed there should be a social dimension to Christian life and thought. American Lutheran theology prior to the 1930s had little room for social ethics. As a church scholar has noted, "of the four major National Lutheran Council church bodies, the Norwegian Lutheran Church reflected the least social concern."[40] It asserted that Christian life should reform people, not programs; individuals should be changed, not the environment.

Bardon labored to instill social ethics and to educate parochial Lutheran youth about the usefulness of the social sciences, the realities of a complex and disturbing world, and the ethical constraints present in the New Testament. He would thunder at his classes, "Are we civilized?" hoping to provoke thought. In the early 1930s he predicted a Japanese invasion of the United States. One day while he detailed the possible nature of the invasion, an errant golf ball crashed through the classroom window, producing considerable consternation. Bardon was a civic-minded person as well as a social activist, visiting the sick and helping the underprivileged. His "Class Room Creed," written in 1936, was a hodge-podge of the words of classical and contemporary writers, *Christian Century* and *New Republic* quotations, and Bible verses. It championed cooperation, altruism, critical thought, freedom, democracy, the poor, and courage.[41]

The matter of Bardon's teaching was placed on the board of trustees' agenda in December 1934, and Tingelstad was apparently able to pacify the board sufficiently to keep Bardon on the faculty. Although Tingelstad consistently fought for his faculty and defended individuality very earnestly, the board continued to object to Bardon's views. "Professor Bardon has now become a liability to the school as far as financial support . . . is concerned . . . unless Professor Bardon's services are dispensed with at the end of the semester, we will pay dearly."[42]

Tingelstad defended Bardon for three more years before the board's will prevailed. A new mandatory retirement policy forced Bardon to retire in 1938 on a little more than two hundred dollars a year. He wrote to Tingelstad:

> I do not know what to do. I am stunned. The Board finally "got" me, as you warned me they would several years ago. . . . . My nature tends toward bitterness, but my soul causes me to rejoice, and be thankful—thankful that I, too, have been found worthy to suffer for the few ideas I have received grace and courage to stand up for. . . . I have found that one can get sympathetic response from so-called church leaders no more than from stone pavement.[43]

Tingelstad, deeply distressed at the turn of events, helped Bardon and his wife find housing and some supplementary income. The reasons for faculty loyalty to Tingelstad are not very hard to figure out.

Faculty diversity and academic strength were enhanced with the appointments of Michel Franck and Harold Leraas in 1935. Franck, born in Constantinople to Hungarian parents, served in the Hungarian diplomatic service and came to New York on behalf of the Budapest Chamber of Commerce. He earned a Ph.D. degree at New York University and taught languages, political science, and history at PLC. In the following years Franck, an excitable and popular teacher, became passionately interested in PLC athletic triumphs. He also developed a close friendship with Tingelstad.

Harold Leraas was a Luther College graduate with a doctorate from the University of Michigan. At Luther College he would study biology with William Strunk, who would also join the PLC faculty in 1948. Leraas was only the second Ph.D. to serve on the PLC faculty, the first in science. He soon had a bustling biology department going, and he was instrumental in establishing the strong premedical and predental programs that remain in place today. Leraas—a record-setting distance runner in his college days—also helped coach track at PLC until the outbreak of World War II.

THE LIBRARY CAMPAIGN AND GOLF COURSE

Despite the depression, Tingelstad was determined that physical development of the campus should continue alongside academic developments.

Small steps were taken in 1929 and 1930 with the construction of a new chemistry laboratory and a new biology laboratory. A president's residence was completed in 1930 at a cost of ten thousand dollars. By 1936 it was clear a library was badly needed. The space in the Old Main building was inadequate, and officials threatened to withdraw accreditation unless a safe and larger facility was provided. Classrooms were also needed. The construction of a new building would also be a satisfying blow against the depression. Consequently, an eight-year $1.5 million construction and endowment expansion program was proposed to be completed in the golden anniversary year of 1944. The first unit was to be a hundred-thousand-dollar library-classroom building. Pierce County Lutherans were asked for twenty thousand dollars and Tacoma residents and businesses for eighty thousand. O. H. Pankoke agreed to serve as the executive director of the Tacoma campaign.

The campaign to raise money for the new library was soon underway. A committee of 150 contacted the 3,500 Lutherans of Pierce County, and a 25-member advisory committee assisted in the Tacoma campaign. Problems arose at the outset, however. Pankoke and the chair of the Tacoma campaign irritated each other, and subcommittee appointments could not be filled. These minor difficulties were soon overcome, thanks in large measure to the ten-thousand-dollar corporate gift from J. Philip Weyerhaeuser, Jr., donated because "they believe in the small Christian college."[44] When the library's cornerstone was laid on 23 October 1937, Tingelstad described how Bjug Harstad's original plan for four buildings was now accomplished. "We, the people, have not perished, because our fathers had vision." Containing seventeen thousand volumes, the library was dedicated in May 1939, although it was not fully completed until the late 1940s.

Toward the end of November 1937 Tingelstad fell and broke his hip while on his way to a football game, and he was hospitalized for 110 days. Philip Hauge administered the college in his absence. Tingelstad's health had always been precarious, and there would be future hospital stays. Tingelstad talked about his health with some regularity in chapel; if it went on too long the students would grumble about "another organ recital at chapel."

In 1937 the Parkland Golf Association gave the course it owned to the college, enlarging the campus to its present dimensions. Many of the lots in the 1890 land development scheme were on the site of the present golf course, but they remained undeveloped in the aftermath of the panic of 1893. The flat expanses of vacant land worked well as a golf course, however, and it was unofficially used as such for years. Ole Stuen and J. U. Xavier stomped down grass and put down codfish cans for cups as early as 1914. It became increasingly obvious that a real golf course could be built with some effort. To that end, Mr. Alvin Lehman, the local postmaster and owner of a general store, organized the Parkland Golf Association on 6 April 1928 and was elected its president. The association authorized the sale of thirty-nine thousand dollar's worth of stock, and the funds acquired were used to buy additional lots to fill out the course and to build a small clubhouse. PLC donated some lots; in return, faculty and staff could play at half price. By the end of the spring the course was in use. It was at first a nine-hole course, but it became so popular that it was remodeled to eighteen holes in 1929. There were several avid golfers on the faculty— Ramstad, Stuen, Xavier, Edwards, and, occasionally, President Tingelstad.

The depression brought Parkland Golf Association severe difficulties. Taxes could not be paid, and even basic maintenance became a problem. At that point Cliff Olson, Paul Preus, and the college attorney, Fred Henricksen, suggested that the association assets be given to the college as a gift. The three men then had to gain the support of the creditors and convince the shareholders and college board of trustees to accept the gift. With such terrible financial problems plaguing the institution, the board was reluctant to assume possession of a liability, however useful the land might be in the long run. Olson, Preus, and Henricksen, with courage and foresight, agreed to cover any losses incurred in operating the course and also agreed that any profit would go back to the college. The offer was extremely generous. The board finally accepted this arrangement in April 1937; the original dimensions of the campus were reestablished and vital space for the future was assured. The energetic Olson saw to the management of the course. In 1940, under his direction, a football practice field, baseball diamond, and tennis courts were carved out of the course, and the eighteen holes were reduced to nine.

ATHLETIC TRIUMPHS

Clifford Olson, tapping his extensive organizational, psychological, and coaching skills and building on a long college tradition of athletic enthusiasm, began producing exciting and competitive teams in the early 1930s. Olson's first successes were in basketball, in which PLC won six junior college league championships, including three in a row in the mid-1930s. The 1935–36 team was 10–0 in league play. Gene Jack and Harold Nilsen were the outstanding players for those teams. The 1939–41 teams were equally outstanding, even though they played only four-year schools by that time. The 1938–39 team had a 20–5 record, the best in the school's history up to that point. The 1939–40 team record was 20–7, and the 1940–41 team went 19-6, winning the WINCO—Washington Intercollegiate Conference—championship. That team also defeated the University of Washington 40–30 in an early season game. Sigurd Sigurdson, a blond Icelander from Ballard and gifted all-around athlete, was the conference's leading scorer for two years, and he and the fiercely competitive Marv Harshman were regular all-conference selections. Marv Harshman later declared that "Sig Sigurdson at that time was the best basketball player I'd ever seen, including the guy from Stanford, Luisetti." Hank Luisetti was then the most famous college basketball player in the country.

Football captured the public's attention in a unique way, however, and the drama and excitement of the 1939–41 era raised PLC to a new level of visibility. People in Tacoma, the Northwest, and even New York City learned where Parkland was and that the "Marvelous Marvs" and "the aerial circus" were something special. Sportswriters descended on the campus. Tacoma businessmen and politicians wanted to be associated with the program and its coach, and Tacoma residents, including Mayor Harry Cain, jammed stadiums to watch the "Lutes" play. (They were almost never called the Gladiators, even though that was their official name.) There had never been anything quite like it in the City of Destiny. People were undoubtedly interested in pushing the grim years of the depression behind them; the razzle-dazzle of the "aerial circus" helped. Even the church officials who were so concerned about deficits and so peeved at Tingelstad for his stubbornness were excited by the athletic news that came from Parkland.

Hints of what was to come later were present in the early and mid-1930s. The 1934 team had a 5–2 record, and the 1936 team, with a 5–0–2 record, scored ninety points to the opponents' six. The teams from 1939 onward—playing only four-year schools—were the record breakers, however. John McCallum, the nationally known sportswriter, described those teams and their coach at length in *The Gladiators: A Chronicle of PLU Sports*.[45] They won three consecutive WINCO championships and produced an eighteen-game winning streak; a 23–2 record; a twenty-fourth place tie with Notre Dame, Clemson, and Rice in the Associated Press poll of major teams in 1940; the institution's only undefeated football season; and the single most exciting game in PLU football history (the 1940 last-minute 16–13 victory before fifteen thousand fans over "big-time" Gonzaga).

Why was PLC so successful in football? Much of the credit must go to Coach Olson. He had no athletic scholarships to offer, but he recruited a cluster of gifted athletes. He was single-minded, hard-working, and more imaginative as an offensive coach than his contemporaries. Moreover, against a backdrop of quite conservative, even staid football (and a dreary decade) his teams dazzled. It was not just the victories but also the "aerial circus" that attracted attention. The team passed the ball twenty or thirty times a game when most teams tried running plays almost exclusively. "I suppose I was pretty rough on my boys. But we always had a well-conditioned team; boys who loved to play. We had a type of offense that was a lot of fun, a wide-open, gambling offense, with lots of trick plays, passing, laterals."[46]

Marv "Tommygun" Tommervik produced remarkable passing statistics and records, some of which still stand fifty years later, and he was twice named a little all-American. Marv Harshman was for three years the leading scorer on the Pacific Coast, twice all-conference, and a member of the 1941 *New York Sun*'s all-American team, which was composed of players from all colleges and universities in the country. Sig Sigurdson and Earl Platt, the pass-receivers, were all-conference selections and received little all-American mention. All later played professional football. Blair Taylor was another all-conference selection. Harshman, Platt, and Taylor, as well as Tommervik, still hold records in the PLU football record book. Royal Brougham, the longtime *Seattle Post-Intelligencer* sports editor, wrote in 1940: "Martin Luther ought to be bursting with pride at the amazing feats of . . . the Lutes." David James, the *Tacoma News Tribune* sportswriter who helped make the teams famous, wrote in the 1942 *Saga*:

> We could speak of the records, the all-star honors, the pages of pictures and praise. They loomed so big at the time. But even bigger is the school you introduced to a nation, the playgrounds and athletic fields you left as a heritage to those who follow. These will be your pride when the clouds of war have passed beyond and you have come home.

The victories and national attention also brought in much-needed money for financially troubled PLC. Coach Olson—and the school—made friends with numerous Tacoma-area businessmen who were very generous in subsidizing games, paying for a new practice field, and giving other gifts to the institution, often at Christmas. Olson remembers receiving as many as ten checks as he made his seasonal rounds.[47] Athletics achieved an important fundraising and public relations breakthrough for a school that had been almost unknown to the Tacoma business community.

BALANCE SHEET

By 1940, after fifty years of institutional existence and a dozen years of Tingelstad's leadership, PLC was not a distinguished or nationally known center of learning. It was a small, regional institution, with most of its students coming from the Puget Sound area. Its ethnic ties were still strong, as the excitement caused by the visit of Crown Prince Olav and Princess Martha of Norway on 25 May 1939 illustrated, and slightly more than half the students were Lutheran. The faculty was poorly paid, badly overworked, and certainly not intellectually well known. Many were good teachers, however; they approached teaching as a vocation—in the Lutheran sense of that word—and took their duties seriously. Teaching—and teaching at PLC—was their calling. They thought education was important, and education combined with Christianity more important still. That conviction, reflected in their lives, frequently influenced and excited students, who often received a better education than experts or outsiders might have predicted. PLC teachers mediated truth and the importance of education through their personalities and lifestyles as much as through diagrams, proofs, and syllogisms, perpetuating a feature of Christian education prominent from its beginning.

Between 1928 and 1940 a number of important advances had been made. In 1939 a fourth year in education training was added and the first class graduated in 1940: PLC was finally a four-year school. There were five majors to choose from the first year: English, music, social sciences, history, and biology. The third year of liberal arts instruction was added in 1941 and the fourth in 1942. Tingelstad had worked hard to accomplish the growth of the liberal arts toward parity with the education department.

Between 1937 and 1940 the faculty was strengthened by a number of appointments. The influence of some of those individuals can still be felt. Gunnar J. Malmin was appointed choir director in 1937 after Joseph Edwards's resignation. Malmin was a pastor's son who received a classical education at Luther College ('23), where he was a cornet soloist for the band conducted by Sperati, who later recalled that "the best harmonist ever to study under me was Gunnar Malmin."[48] He conducted research in Scandinavia for the Carnegie Institute and then, giving up graduate study in history for music, spent a year at St. Olaf College, where he sang under the influential F. Melius Christiansen. Malmin taught at Drake University, then directed the choir at Dana College in Nebraska for seven years. He knew and admired Tingelstad from his student days at Luther and was happy to come to PLC when offered the position. Malmin liked the freedom in the West and found a congenial faculty, a good choir, and plenty of interest in music. He tried to get as "high a degree of perfection as possible" from the choir and to maintain a close relationship between music and the church. Malmin would significantly influence Lutheran church music and the Norwegian choral tradition on the Pacific Coast.[49] The music department was further strengthened when Elvin Akre came that same year to be dean of men and band director. He had a classical education from Concordia College in Minnesota and was also a cornet soloist. In later years he would teach generations of students American and Northwest history.

PLC also continued its strong tradition of hiring women faculty. Rhoda Hokenstad Young ('35) directed women's physical education from 1938 until illness forced her retirement in 1968. She powerfully influenced that program, especially the tradition of a folk dance performance in conjunction with the May Festival. Grace Blomquist and Anna Marn Nielsen joined the faculty in 1939. Grace Blomquist, like Akre, was a Concordia College graduate. Compared to Concordia, PLC seemed to Blomquist to be less ethnic, structured, stable, and secure. She thought PLC seemed "not very well put together," but she acknowledged it was "freer," more "democratic," and not as "pietistic," with a strong sense of community and a passion for athletics.[50] Blomquist was appointed assistant dean of women, and she taught Latin and English. She launched the children's literature curriculum and worked hard to establish a library collection to support it. Anna Marn Nielsen was an Iowa State graduate who had taught in the public schools of Iowa and taken an M.A. degree from Columbia University. She was hired as director of teacher training and directed her massive energies and powerful personality to the advancement of that program. She found Dean Philip Hauge a close ally, and she soon knew— and was respected by—school officials all over the state. Her infectious laughter regularly rolled down the halls of the Old Main. The primary reason for PLC's existence was to train teachers, according to Anna Marn Nielsen. If you challenged that, you found her a forceful adversary.

Three important faculty additions were made in 1940, two of whom had Ph.D. degrees, which was important to Tingelstad. Olaf Jordahl graduated from Luther College (where he played the tuba in Sperati's band) in 1925 and received a Ph.D. in physics from the University of Wisconsin in 1933. He taught at Luther and then at Northwestern University until 1940. Jordahl, a stern, demanding, and dedicated teacher, established the modern program in physics at PLC and helped raise standards for all the sciences. The foundations for the strong post-World War II science program were in place with Jordahl, Ramstad, and Leraas on the PLC faculty. Jordahl also taught the advanced courses in mathematics for many years, directing and upgrading that department as well. He worked at the University of California radiation laboratory during World War II as a physicist on the Manhattan Project.

The second important faculty appointment made in 1940 was Herbert Ranson, a Phi Beta Kappa graduate from the University of Kansas with a Ph.D. from the University of Washington. He was a shy man who liked golf and played the piano. He loved literature and was a quiet but effective teacher who helped move the English department more closely in line with the academic standards of the better departments around the country. He was also deeply committed to individualism: "After all I teach the English Romantics and the Concord group. And perhaps unfortunately, I also have for decades found meaningful their essential points of view—about all essential growth being individual: He who would be a man must be a non-conformist."[51] Ranson's concern about the individual and his notions about how literature should be taught brought some heated disagreements with administrative policy and academic direction, especially in the last years of the Robert Mortvedt presidency. Ranson was shy and not politically clever, but he stood up for what he believed.

The third important faculty appointment in 1940 was Theodore O. H. Karl, a pastor's son and a Gustavus Adolphus graduate who came to PLC as dean of men and professor of speech. His persuasiveness, energy, and ability to organize and delegate responsibility soon produced numerous theatrical and dramatic productions and outstanding debate successes. Students Neil Hoff and Robert Lutnes successfully competed against the finest debaters in the country over the next two years. After the war, Karl created a virtual speech-drama-debate empire, with headquarters—and trophy display cases—in the new chapel building.

These years also witnessed the professionalization of PLC's faculty and consequent fears of secularization. In 1920–21, three of the seven faculty members had bachelor's degrees. By 1940 five of the nearly thirty faculty had doctoral degrees; almost all the others had master's degrees. Tingelstad was quick to point out with pride that the institution had stuck to the policy of "accredited work only" through the past decade, despite the costs. Meanwhile, although the "aims" of the institution had not changed appreciably since 1928, Tingelstad was also concerned about the possible erosion of appropriate Christian values and the increasing secularization of faculty and students. Tingelstad believed that the larger the student body, the more likely PLC's religious character would be diluted. Size and age make for secularization, he feared. Tingelstad thought that half the students at PLC should be avowedly Christian and probably Lutheran (54 percent of the student body was Lutheran in 1941).[52]   In addition, Tingelstad wanted to achieve more balance between academic and vocational programs pursued by the students, but he also wanted the tradition of strong teacher training at PLC to continue. Between 1921 and 1937, 628 students had graduated from PLC: 267 teachers, 15 salesmen, 10 farmers, 7 clergymen, 2 attorneys, 2 physicians, 1 dentist, and many others. The issue of whether PLC would continue to be primarily a teacher-training institution would remain unresolved until the early 1960s.

Late in 1940, as a result of ongoing church concern about PLC, H. J. Glenn, pastor of First Lutheran Church in Sioux Falls, South Dakota, was appointed by NLCA president J. A. Aasgaard to investigate PLC thoroughly and report back to him. Glenn visited the campus in January 1941 and produced a generally affirmative and optimistic report. According to Glenn, the faculty was loyal and morale remained high, despite the financial problems caused by the depression. He noted that advances and improvements were taking place in the institution, and it was well regarded in the region. It was a "focal point" and a "unifying" entity for Lutherans in the West, which was gratifying and should be encouraged. Glenn also recounted the athletic successes with relish. There were problems, of course: the buildings, except for the new library, were "depressing," he wrote. "If this institution is a child of the church, it gives the appearance of a rather forgotten child." He found that insufficient money was an ongoing problem, just as it had been since 1890, certainly since 1929.[53]

President Oscar Tingelstad, Dean Philip Hauge, and the faculty and staff have to be given high marks for their work in the 1930s. PLC not only survived the worst of the depression without cutting the faculty or reducing programs, but four-year status and accreditation were achieved for both the education department and the liberal arts program during the decade. Moreover, the faculty had grown in quality and quantity, while the enrollment in 1941–42 reached 551, up from 187 in 1928–29. Athletic successes brought national recognition and new fundraising possibilities. Campus morale and community spirit remained high. Tingelstad was respected and genuinely liked by the college community, and he was deeply respected by Lutherans throughout the Northwest. The terrible pressure had taken its toll on his health, but there was still much to be done at PLC and he wanted to be a part of that work. That was what God had called him to do, he believed, and Tingelstad took his calling very seriously. But the ongoing fiscal problem would finally bring Tingelstad's forced resignation in 1943.

RESIGNATION

In 1938 Tingelstad was offered a deanship at Concordia College; he was tempted to accept the position and escape the pressures he had lived with for so long at PLC. Administration and faculty divided in opinions of what he should do. The chair of PLC's board of trustees and the secretary of the NLCA board of education encouraged him to accept the offer. He had served PLC well, they reasoned, and accepting the deanship would give him some respite from pressure and opportunities for scholarship.[54] On the other hand, the faculty and many pastors asked him to stay. Ultimately, Tingelstad stayed because he thought it was his duty to do so.

Financial problems continued, however, and pressure on Tingelstad grew after the outbreak of war. As student enrollment fell dramatically, the budget was increasingly ruined and complaints surfaced. Lars Boe, of St. Olaf College, complained about unfair PLC financial requests and arguments that he no longer trusted, especially Tingelstad's use of the phrase "the kingdom-vision" to justify decisions and requests.[55] Tingelstad snapped back an angry response: "I detest political trickery. To accuse me of it is calumny."[56] He explained that he meant by "kingdom-vision" a religious perspective to help put things in their proper order.

Meanwhile, however, the Puget Sound National Bank refused to carry an overdue short-term loan any longer. Church officials said that this situation, coming for a long time, was a reminder that Tingelstad had not always done what they wanted him to do. He accurately responded that he was constantly told to do things but not given the funds or freedom to do them. Despite Tingelstad's years of service, by November 1942 the chair of the board of trustees openly asked whether it was not time for Tingelstad to step aside: "I think you owe it to yourself and your wife to withdraw from a situation that seemingly is impossible."[57] Church officials were not going to change their position about deficits and the need for retrenchment, and resignation was the only thing that would satisfy them. NLCA president J. A. Aasgaard wrote to Tingelstad in general terms about the financial situation at PLC, contending that no matter what, "we must have a College on the Pacific Coast."[58] How to achieve that was not so clear, Aasgaard wrote. Aasgaard was a strong and capable but autocratic leader who clearly seemed weary of the problems in Parkland.

On 2 and 3 January 1943 Tingelstad wrote five long, carefully reasoned, and sometimes angry letters to Aasgaard about the situation at PLC. He wrote about the unfortunate failure of the Preus-Elvestrom Plan, which he could never quite forget. He described the successes of Lutheran cooperation in the West, the unfair charge of "alarming debt" raised by the American Lutheran Church, the impact of the war, and the differing perceptions of PLC in the West and Midwest ("Out here we are praised, back there we are censured"). Most especially, he discussed the nature of his "call" to the presidency of PLC, determined to "respect the divinity of the call."[59]

At the request of H. L. Foss, chair of the board of trustees, Tingelstad did not mail the letters until 22 January, at which time he included a letter from Foss asking for his resignation. He asked Aasgaard for a response to the points of the five letters—especially about the nature of his "call"— and advice about how he should respond to Foss's request. On two earlier occasions he had already told Foss it was "morally impossible" for him to resign. According to Tingelstad, the situation at PLC was improving and much remained to be done, but if Aasgaard thought he should resign, he would.[60]

Aasgaard never responded. He apparently had already decided a change in leadership was necessary at PLC and had a successor in mind. The board accepted the resignation that Tingelstad then reluctantly and unhappily tendered; Tingelstad was angry and hurt. He never completely recovered from either emotion, and was especially upset that he had received no response from Aasgaard. Tingelstad was a man of principle who felt he had been pushed aside like a pawn in a political struggle. In April 1943 his good friend and longtime Trinity congregation pastor T. O. Svare assured him:

> Aasgaard finally got his way. This is not a vague suspicion . . . but a vicious fact which everybody must know, if they want to know it. In what respect have Boe, Preus, Granskou, Brown been better Presidents? None at all, but they were the friends of Caesar. . . . You have made the school what it is today. I know of very few in the church who could have done what you have done, especially with so much opposition from the powers that be.[61]

Although Svare's letter was harsh and a little one-sided it was essentially correct. Tingelstad had done a remarkable job as PLC president in the midst of very trying times. The circumstances facing the church and church-related education in the West were not adequately understood in the Midwest. Though stubborn at times, Tingelstad insisted that standards and quality were essentials to a college that took education seriously. He wished to serve Lutherans in the West and to make an impact on the region. Perhaps Tingelstad had been too ambitious for PLC.

There was another side to the issue, however, that Tingelstad could not see very clearly. He was tired and ill. He desperately needed some distance from the struggles he had been intimately involved in for so long. People at PLC were ready for a shift away from Tingelstad's carefully reasoned leadership style to one of vigor and action. Such shifts are sometimes psychologically useful, even necessary, as institutions move from period to period and from one set of problems to another. The battles of the depression had been long and difficult, but now the siege mentality had to be lifted. Tingelstad was loved and respected, but many thought new leadership and a different approach were now needed. Neither Aasgaard nor the board of trustees handled a difficult situation very well, however. Nor did the next PLC president.

The hand-picked successor, Seth Clarence Eastvold, was a widely known midwestern pastor who had achieved great success in all the parishes he had served. He had a reputation as a powerful preacher and a forceful leader. Aasgaard gave him a check for forty thousand dollars and told him to keep PLC open if he could; Tingelstad had never been given such financial security. Eastvold was known to be a decisive man of energy and confidence. He unleashed his remarkable energy as soon as he arrived at PLC and seemed to be everywhere at once. Some of Eastvold's initial actions shocked and offended Tingelstad and several of the older PLC hands. Eastvold, however, totally ignored Tingelstad and never consulted with him. It was the beginning of a new era.[62]

7

Postwar Expansion

Sᴇᴛʜ Cʟᴀʀᴇɴᴄᴇ Eᴀꜱᴛᴠᴏʟᴅ was one of ten children born to the Reverend and Mrs. C. J. Eastvold. C. J. Eastvold had come to America from Norway when he was sixteen and studied for the ministry at the Hauge Synod's Red Wing Seminary. He was a pastor, president of the Hauge Synod's Jewell Lutheran College in Iowa, president of the Hauge Synod, and a member of the committee on union prior to the Norwegian Lutheran merger in 1917. He deeply influenced his son, who later told him: "When I was a little boy I hoped that I might help carry on the work you have so ably begun among us. That prayer has been gratified in my case."[1]

S. C. Eastvold also attended Hauge Synod educational institutions: Jewell Lutheran College and the Red Wing Seminary. He became an alumnus of St. Olaf College when the Red Wing Seminary amalgamated with St. Olaf after the 1917 NLCA merger. He served in the army in 1918–19, graduated from Luther Seminary in 1920, and served parishes in North and South Dakota, Minnesota, and Wisconsin from 1920 to 1943. He was a successful parish pastor who quickly developed a reputation as an energetic leader and a powerful preacher. He acquired a doctor's degree via an extension program from Augustana Theological Seminary in 1930. His thesis was a somewhat impressionistic study of Paul and Luther. Eastvold had a powerful mind, but he was not much interested in formal scholarship. He was theologically informed (within the traditions of orthodox Lutheranism), and he was widely read in areas related to his interests and enthusiasms. He wrote six quite diverse books, but in the conventional sense of the word he was not a scholar devoted to research, to the formal structure of ideas, and to logical consistency. Rather, he was an advocate who tried to rouse people to action and bring them to his views; he was a pastor, a preacher, a leader of people. He used ideas and an enormous assortment of information on all sorts of topics in his preaching and writing, but the use was pragmatic, with an eye to the task at hand. He never worried about consistency. He was an uncommonly successful leader, however, who through relentless attention to the problems of the moment found himself thrust into positions of leadership. He was eager to assume these positions. His tastes were for government and power, not scholarship, and the power he exercised was not shared in any collegial fashion. That was certainly true at PLC. College historian Walter Schnackenberg wrote that Eastvold was a "natural monarch,"[2] and while that was probably true of most Lutheran church leaders in the first half of the twentieth century, it was particularly true of Eastvold.

His parish successes, especially at First Lutheran Church in Eau Claire, Wisconsin, between 1933 and 1943 were significant. First Lutheran's benevolence giving totaled a quarter of a million dollars during those depression years, and membership rose from nineteen hundred to three thousand. Eastvold served on the executive committee of the NLCA from 1932 to 1943, and he was also on the board of trustees (and executive committee) of St. Olaf College from 1936 to 1943. He was an unsuccessful candidate for the presidency of both Augustana College in Sioux Falls and St. Olaf College. He wanted a position through which he could leave his mark. He later would be first vice president of the Evangelical Lutheran Church (as the NLCA renamed itself in 1946) from 1948 to 1960, and he was an unsuccessful candidate for the presidency of the ELC in 1954. In 1960 he considered running for the governorship of the state of Washington.

Eastvold was an orthodox Lutheran in a confessional sense, but he also carried some emphases and energies from his Hauge Synod background that were distinctive. Liturgy, music, and doctrinal systems were of no great interest to him, but preaching, evangelism, "spiritual emphasis weeks," and ethical rigorism were. Character, understood pietistically, was what counted. At educational and religious institutions, he believed, intellectual life did not march hand-in-hand with character building, but came second after it. Social life at educational institutions—student protests notwithstanding—was such a far-distant third that it could hardly be seen, and even then it was perceived very narrowly and legalistically. It was no accident that the sign presiding over the main entrance to the PLC campus during Eastvold's presidency read "Build For Character." Eastvold was an implacable foe of jazz, dancing, consumption of alcoholic beverages, and card playing. If force was needed to accomplish the goal of character building, so be it.

The theme of death—and what happened to both sinner and saint after death—also exercised Eastvold all his life and found its way into most of his preaching and much of his writing. "We are dying men in a dying world," PLC chapel-attenders heard over and over again. He once wrote: "The globe is one great necropolis. Graveyards mark the trail of humanity everywhere." The earth "is hollow with the caverns of the dead . . . and its frail shell will soon break down into eternal burnings."

Well do I remember the impressions made upon me as a child when death came and took one of my little playmates. . . . In addition, recollections are very clear of stirring times when after a hot and sultry day, big black clouds rolled up in the western sky, sending forth terrific winds, heavy thunder showers, not infrequently hail, often destroying property and lives. On such occasions . . . my childish mind was so impressed with the possibility of the final consummation of everything temporal, that nerves and fibers trembled and I shook with fear that the great judgement day might find me so far from home.

But the "ceaseless mower" who whets the scythe and dips it sometimes in blood and sometimes in a pool of disease was ready to receive sinners. The sinner had to come now, however. There could be no tarrying, Eastvold preached. Tomorrow might be too late, and the fate of unbelievers was absolutely clear. "On every chain in hell is written FOREVER."[3]

Eastvold was also a premillenialist in his theology, believing that a future thousand-year reign of blessedness will follow the Second Coming of Christ. Although millenarianism has never been formally rejected by large, mainline Christian bodies, it has generally been treated with the "greatest reserve."[4] That was true of the Lutheran synods of the time. Eastvold encountered premillenialism in the left wing of the Hauge Synod, where it was quite popular, at the Red Wing Seminary, and he learned it from his father. It struck a responsive chord. He was fascinated by all the possible configurations, mysteries, and meanings that could be drawn out of the topic, and he pursued them with loving detail, especially in his midwestern Bible studies, preaching, and radio talks. After coming to PLC, Eastvold downplayed the millenarianism he relished so dearly. He wanted to be president of the Evangelical Lutheran Church and knew that it was a potential problem. But premillenialism still energized his sermons and chapel talks in a powerful way and was never too far from the surface.

Eastvold's theology, legalism, aggressive leadership style, audacity, and determination to succeed soon occupied center stage at PLC. It was clear that he understood Christian higher education quite differently than his predecessor. Above all else, he intended to make the college into a bastion of his style of religion. For that reason, the history of the college for the next nineteen years of his presidency cannot be understood apart from him.

Eastvold visited PLC in March 1943 and expressed his appreciation for the opportunity to serve. He presented a financial analysis of the institution and described the financial request he was going to make to the NLCA as a condition for accepting the call. The board petitioned for the assistance, but it seems quite clear that President Aasgaard had already promised a special grant of forty thousand dollars to help resolve the most pressing problems. Aasgaard advised Eastvold simply to do the best he could and reassured him that if he couldn't make a go of it, it would be no disgrace.[5] The problems the new president faced were certainly substantial: declining enrollment (down to 260 in 1943–44), more than a hundred thousand dollars of debt, an unpaid faculty, and threatened credit.

Eastvold hit Parkland with his feet moving. He was ably and loyally assisted by his long-time parish secretary, Mrs. Joseph (Anna) Enge, who managed to keep track of his whereabouts while churning out enormous amounts of work at the same time. He paid the faculty their unpaid salaries. Many thought it a miracle, but there was a footnote. With the encouragement and counseling of Eastvold, most faculty members agreed to take only a part of what they were owed and apply the rest to the debt reduction program. This was in addition to the faculty pledges made to the Golden Jubilee Fund. "Hats off" to the faculty for their noble example, Eastvold wrote.

Downtown merchants were similarly approached. Would they take something on the dollar? Would they give a gift back to the school after they were paid? Some would and some would not. Debts were paid, but some residue of bitterness and suspicion was left behind with merchants that would take a long time to expunge, hampering future fundraising in Tacoma. Under this system the forty thousand dollars went a long way, however; debts were cleaned up, the faculty was paid, and credit was restored. There was growing optimism.

Eastvold had obviously come in with a rush, apparently to ensure that PLC would survive. A number of Parkland veterans—including Oscar Tingelstad—thought some of the methods used were unfortunate, even immoral. Faculty and merchants should receive all they were owed, they felt; bargaining was inappropriate. In reply, Eastvold told Tingelstad not to burden his conscience with what was no longer his responsibility.

On 18 November 1943 Eastvold was installed in office by NLCA president J. A. Aasgaard. Representatives from the American Lutheran Church and the Augustana Synod were present. Board chair H. L. Foss presided. The 2 December 1943 issue of the *Mooring Mast* described the installation as "impressive." Eastvold's speech was entitled "The Imperatives of Democracy." It was not one of his better speeches, but it introduced some of his most basic notions and was filled with wartime atmosphere: "Looted shops, ruined universities, fallen cathedrals, deserted palaces, and dead men's bones all testify to a paganized intellectualism which has left Christian education out of the plans." Spiritual neutrality has paved the way for the present-day pagan totalitarianism, he said. "The primary aim of this College is sound Biblical Christian character. We aim at Christian culture rather than commercial or vocational skills."[6] The college had to be ready for service when the war ended, Eastvold announced. That meant that financial stability and an adequate physical plant were the orders of the day; building would begin as soon as steel was available. In fact, Eastvold's greatest accomplishment as president of PLC would be the fundraising for building that dominated the next decade. It was a great accomplishment, but it was not unique and not without long-term costs.

The college continued to function through the war years, but activities were severely curtailed. Many faculty members took leaves to work in war-related employment, and others worked a double shift, teaching and then working elsewhere. Enrollment fell by more than 50 percent, and males almost disappeared from the student body. Agnes Mykland was elected student body president for the 1944–45 year, the first woman to serve in that capacity. She was succeeded by Eunice Torvend. By 1945, 372 alumni were in the armed services.

By the end of the war people wanted to reestablish their interrupted lives; for many that meant continuing or beginning an education that had been deferred. The egalitarianism of the war effort dispelled the notion of higher education as an elitist preserve. An educational and social revolution was underway in America, greatly facilitated by the 1944 congressional passage of what came to be called the GI Bill. It was designed to help veterans make an appropriate adjustment to civilian life with a tuition credit of up to five hundred dollars and a living allowance that ranged from sixty-five to ninety dollars a month. With such assistance, a million veterans went to college. Most were mature adults, which rearranged the traditional rules and regulations of collegiate life. Some of the confrontations between in loco parentis rules and the "vets" were memorable. That many of the veterans selected colleges for geographic, not theological or ethnic, reasons certainly changed the character of Lutheran colleges throughout the United States; they would not be as homogeneous as they had been before the war. By educating veterans and participating in various government programs, Lutheran colleges and universities also became "public" institutions in new and important ways. In the years after the war the Evangelical Lutheran Church would from time to time express concern about whether the traditional educational motives—preparing clergy and lay leaders and buttressing the faith of the young—were being served. But the postwar shift to include secular, "public" constituents would not be reversed.

After 1945 the crush of numbers of students at PLC became very great. There were 260 students in 1943–44; by 1945–46, over 500 were enrolled. Half of those students were veterans, and men significantly outnumbered women. In 1946–47 there were 706 students; men outnumbered women two to one, and the freshmen class was 70 percent male. The enrollment reached 1,105 by 1949–50. With the Korean War and some internal policy changes enrollment dipped a bit, then climbed slowly but steadily through the 1950s. The percentage of Lutherans at PLC remained about the same as it had been before the war, a level that was more than twenty points lower than at the midwestern ELC institutions, which were 82 percent Lutheran in 1946.

The glut of students brought shortages everywhere. It was hard to find adequately trained faculty, and classrooms and dormitories were in short supply. The federal government helped solve that crisis, at least in the short run. Both the government and the American people wanted to demobilize as quickly as possible, so large amounts of military equipment and portable housing were soon available. Army surplus bulldozers and trucks cleaned up the lower campus, and students attended classes and lived in portable, temporary units. Some of those "temporary" buildings are still in use on the campus.

Eastvold's energy, single-mindedness, and bargaining ability, aided by Aasgaard's forty thousand dollars, saved PLC in the middle of World War II, according to a popular and often-told tale that certainly has some substance and validity. (The account underestimates, however, fifty years of institutional momentum, the achievements of the 1930s, and the school's considerable experience and stubborn determination in dealing with crises). If that tale is extended to the postwar period, it gives far too little credit to the GI Bill, a rapidly expanding economy, demobilization, a population boom, and changed attitudes toward higher education. All of those factors helped create what are sometimes called the "golden years" of American higher education. Across the nation colleges flourished and grew in an unprecedented way; that was true of Lutheran colleges as well as of other private colleges in the Northwest. PLC's growth and expansion have to be placed in that context. James Hitchman's careful study of eight private Northwest colleges points out that all of them developed in curriculum, physical plant, endowment, and enrollment in the postwar period and that some made "spectacular strides," especially Lewis and Clark College, the College of Puget Sound, Whitworth College, and PLC.[7] A chief characteristic of these schools during that time was the longevity of their presidents. Eastvold was not unique in his long tour of duty. "Most of these men were builders because their institutions desperately needed facilities at the time, but they were strong leaders and men of ideas as well, absolutely dedicated to their schools."[8]

Eastvold was a remarkable man—in an era of long-serving and frequently autocratic but successful builders and leaders—who accomplished a great deal, but those accomplishments must be placed in a regional and national context and understood within the framework of the institution's history. The achievements cannot be ignored, but they cannot be transmuted into mythology either. PLC expanded and grew, as did almost all other colleges and universities in the United States. The effort needed to produce PLC's growth was very great, however; it did not happen easily.

The first item on the building agenda was to enlarge the Golden Jubilee campaign. Although the roots of that campaign stretch back to 1936, it was formally launched in 1942 with Vice President Mikkel Lono in charge and a goal of $150,000. The goal was doubled in 1944 after Eastvold came. The money came from the cooperating Lutheran synods in the Northwest and was eventually used to complete the library stacks and to build a science building. Similarly, the people of Tacoma were asked to fund the building of a new gymnasium. Businessman and philanthropist John S. Baker agreed to serve as the honorary chair of that campaign, and Cliff Olson was the active chair. It was hoped building could begin soon after the war ended. The contract for the $200,000 science building was let in May 1946; permission to build a new gymnasium was given at the same time. The need for a science facility was dramatically underscored just a few days later, on 4 June, when the old wooden gymnasium—with the science laboratories in the basement and all the sports equipment and uniforms in the locker rooms—burned to the ground. A fundraising appeal was launched the very next day and letters were quickly in the mail. A frenzy of activity followed. Some wags thought it had happened so quickly it was almost too good to be true.

Credit for the success of the Memorial Gymnasium campaign has to go to Cliff Olson and John Baker. Eastvold never functioned very well as a fundraiser with the Tacoma business community, and so that vital source of funds, which Cliff Olson had effectively opened up with the 1939–41 football successes, slowly dried up. The new president of the College of Puget Sound systematically and effectively worked into the territory. Nature abhors a fundraising vacuum. It would take a long time for PLC to reestablish friendships and beachheads in Tacoma; a major effort of fund-raising and public relations in the 1960s and 1970s was needed to accomplish that. Eastvold's strengths were in the Lutheran churches and with individuals with strong connections to churches. He managed there quite well. But in the Memorial Gymnasium campaign, it was Baker who invited several dozen businessmen to the Tacoma Club and told them he was going to support the effort generously and that they should too. Cliff Olson did the follow-up work and the funding fell into place relatively quickly.

The science building was dedicated in November 1947, followed shortly by the gymnasium's dedication in December, featuring a brief halftime address at the PLC–University of Washington basketball game by the president of the University of Washington, Dr. Raymond B. Allen.

The Huskies trounced the Lutes (as they have always been popularly called) 61–36 in the game.

A student union building was built on the foundation of the old gymnasium, which explained the somewhat awkward configuration of that building. Eastvold called the building "one of those fine touches so important to student life."[9] If it was not quite that, it was a busy place in the next few years. It was dedicated in February 1948. A sewage disposal plant was also built in 1947. Enlarged several times and soon stretched beyond its limits, it remained in use until the 1980s, when sewers finally came to Parkland. Meanwhile, the library stacks were finished by 1949, and the Old Main was refurbished with gifts from individuals and churches and with plaques that commemorated the gifts. Its top floors were finally made habitable after more than fifty years.

Much had been accomplished by the end of the 1940s. Most of the money for that had come from Lutheran churches and individuals, especially in the Pacific District of the ELC ($278,000). Eastvold had personally contacted almost every church. The ALC had also been generous, contributing $75,000. Large budget surpluses were also invested in building. Apart from one large gift from an individual—Mrs. Sophie Munson of Ellensburg, who gave $73,888.90—the gifts were relatively small. Church officials and sympathetic pastors helped in the raising of money, but it was primarily the exertions of Eastvold that paid off. Eastvold now carried three portfolios: that of president, business manager, and chief development officer or field agent. In March 1945 the *Mooring Mast* reported that Eastvold had returned from California with eleven thousand dollars for the Golden Jubilee campaign. He had visited four parishes. In the previous eighteen months he had traveled fifty thousand miles and crossed the mountains in whole or part twenty-five times.[10] His typical approach was to give a Sunday sermon in a church and then visit as many parishioners as possible. He would read a biblical text to those he was visiting, pray with them, and then make the presentation about PLC. In February 1947 Eastvold returned from a twenty-eight-day trip to Oregon and California, where he had visited "about one hundred" individuals and organizations, who had given $6,018 in gifts and pledges in amounts ranging from three to two thousand dollars. It was a very successful trip, he thought, and he was happy to come back to the college family.[11]

By 1949 national church bodies recognizing the crises facing the colleges in finances and facilities responded with "great generosity."[12] The ELC organized a United Christian Education Appeal and set out to raise two million dollars to be divided among colleges and seminaries. PLC eventually received two hundred thousand dollars toward Eastvold's dream of an imposing chapel-music conservatory in the middle of campus. The ALC launched a $3 million drive in 1950; PLC received 80 percent of the Northwest's contributions, about one hundred thousand dollars. That was earmarked for the chapel also. Augustana Lutherans paid for the organ in the chapel. These drives required much local and regional organization and visitation, but the national stamp of approval helped. The earlier Munson bequest went into the chapel fund, as did the monies that came from Mrs. Mathea Severson of Everett. "If she is able to pay the $150,000 she has pledged," the board resolved, "the chapel will be called the Severson chapel."[13] She gave about a hundred thousand dollars and her picture was hung over a doorway in the front of the chapel. For many years a picture of Christ hung over one doorway, and a picture of Mrs. Severson hung over the other.

The cultivation of Mrs. Severson was legendary. Adept at making money, she was a hard-working woman who washed clothes for others, ran a boarding house, and loaned money to fishermen and loggers at exorbitant rates of interest. She had been raised a Lutheran but attended a Baptist church. After an Everett pastor told Eastvold about her, she was visited, brought to the campus, and greeted with song on her birthday. She wanted a baptistry in the chapel, so when she toured the completed building Eastvold and Ted Karl showed her the stage, where square sections can be lifted up for stage design purposes, and told her a tank could be placed in an opening with great ease.[14] She apparently was satisfied. Ground was broken for the new chapel in 1949, and the corner-stone of the $625,000 building was laid on 7 June 1951.

Long-needed dormitories were built in the mid-1950s utilizing newly available low-interest government loans. The first three built were rather unimaginatively named North, South, and West halls. They have since been renamed Hong, Hinderlie, and Kreidler halls. By this time the campus was architecturally quite impressive.

CAMPUS LIFE

From 1945–46 onward, with the war over and the campus filled with students, activities flourished and academic life proceeded with consider-able seriousness. The *Mooring Mast* took on a buoyant air. Plays and programs flashed across the stage of the new student union building, the choir sang to large audiences, and athletic competition resumed. Marv Harshman was hired as basketball coach in October 1945 and busily prepared for what turned out to be a 6–15 season. He would coach for thirty-nine more years at PLC and elsewhere, most notably at the University of Washington. Dean Philip Hauge returned to PLC from his military service in North Africa and Italy and resumed his manifold duties on 1 January 1946. There had been many changes in his absence, he said, but returning to the college was "returning home."[15] Hauge continued his close alliance with the department of education and assisted mightily in its postwar expansion and successes. The arts and sciences were a secondary concern to him. Hauge also shouldered an enormous number of administrative tasks, leaving the president free to pursue the work that interested him most. No person ever connected with the institution devoted such steady and consistent attention to the daily routine of the college's life.

The students pushed for the expansion of social life in 1947 by asking the board to approve social dancing. A faculty committee did not support social dancing, but it did support folk dancing (or "shottishing"). But the president spoke adamantly against both and the board unanimously supported him. Eastvold wrote to Hauge that there were enough social events on campus without introducing practices that will be "hurtful." Not all the faculty will understand or agree, he realized, but they will have to "trust and obey. . . . There must be *no word, no look, no martyr silence* which may give rise to a tiny minority in the student body which may become a pressure group."[16] Meanwhile students, sometimes in large numbers, attended dances off campus. In reply to a petition favoring dancing signed by a large majority of the student body that appeared in 1953, however, Eastvold told student body president Paul Wangsmo, "If the student body president's wastebasket isn't large enough for these petitions, mine is."[17] Dancing would not be permitted for another decade.

On another front the board and, presumably, Eastvold were concerned about faculty member Michel Franck's "spiritual commitment" in 1949. When his doctrinal position was examined by Eastvold and board chair Foss, Franck said he agreed with Lutheran doctrine, especially the "real presence," and his pastor vouched for him. A board member told Franck that many people misunderstood him because of his unwise use of sarcasm and choice of friends. Franck was a volatile Hungarian with a multitude of friends. The meeting ended in a "very friendly fashion," however, and Franck was given a contract for the next year.[18]

A number of influential individuals joined the faculty in the years after the war. In 1946 Anne Knudson arrived to teach English; Ottilie (Terzieff) Little, with a Ph.D. from the University of Hamburg, came to teach foreign languages; and Leslie Eklund came as dean of men. A bumper crop arrived in 1947: Harry Adams came to teach mathematics and later physics; Paul Reigstad—who would make innumerable contributions in English, the humanities, and the fight for liberal education—came to the English department; Robert Olson, with a Ph.D. and experience at General Motors, strengthened Ramstad's chemistry program while taking a 50 percent pay cut; Burton Ostenson, a Luther College graduate with a Ph.D. from Michigan, brought sanity and thorough training in biology; another Luther College graduate, Kelmer Roe, with graduate work under S. Gresham Machen at Princeton, the brilliant intellectual leader of

American fundamentalism, came to teach religion and Greek; Magnus Nodtvedt, with a Ph.D. from the University of Chicago, brought rigor and broad training to the history department. Milton Nesvig ('35) also joined the staff in 1947. He ran the news bureau and directed publicity, organized the alumni, ran musical tours, recruited students, was a passionate fan of athletics, and in the 1960s became a vice president for university relations. He seemingly had the names and genealogies of most members of the alumni association filed in his brain ready for quick recall. He was almost never wrong. "Milt" loved the institution as much as anyone ever has and served it selflessly. He retired in 1980.

Erich Knorr, an ALC pastor with a Ph.D. in sociology and long experience on the board of trustees, came in 1949 after repeated invitations. He was a rock of stability and integrity in the troubled early 1960s. Dwight Zulauf also came in 1949 to teach accounting. He became the first dean of the School of Business Administration in 1960. Frederick Newnham brought his sonorous baritone voice, British musical training, and love of golf in 1950. He helped broaden the musical perspective on campus. Frank Haley came as librarian in 1951. With his boundless energy he soon found ways to limit administrative costs and buy books instead. The collection was significantly expanded under his leadership. His greatest contribution may well have been the design of Mortvedt Library, built in 1967; it turned out to be efficient to operate and pleasant to use. Generations of students have benefited from Haley's wisdom and foresight.

Athletic triumphs soon reappeared in Parkland with the "vets" back in school and the Marvelous Marvs coaching. Marv Tommervik's 1947 football team, for which eighty men turned out, was a physically dominating crew that ran over other teams. They defeated St. Olaf College 14–0 in what was billed as the first intersectional game between two Scandinavian colleges, and they defeated the College of Puget Sound 19–0 before thirteen thousand fans. The team won the WINCO championship and defeated Southern Oregon College 27–21 in the Pear Bowl, the only postseason bowl game the football team has ever played. Don D'Andrea, a 280-pound center was a little all-American selection, and running back Jack Guyot, a *Mooring Mast* humorist known as "Guyot the Riot," was a second-team selection. D'Andrea, Eldon Kyllo, Elmer Peterson, and Frank Spear were all-conference selections.[19] PLC also won Evergreen Conference championships in football in 1951 and 1952. Ronald Billings was a little all-American defensive back during that period, and Glen Huffman was an all-conference selection at two positions in successive years (he was also all-conference in three sports, an honor student, and a Rhodes scholar nominee). Billings and Huffman were among the last of the three-sport athletes at PLC, but scholar-athletes continued to appear with regularity.

The basketball team, led by the "court magician" Harry McLaughlin, probably the most colorful player ever to play for PLC, did well also. They won the 1948 WINCO championship, and McLaughlin was an all-conference selection for four years and regularly one of the leading scorers in the nation. After forty years he is still the third leading scorer in PLU basketball history. The 1951 team, led by Gene Lundgaard, who set a number of scoring records of his own, was the first PLC team to play in the National Association of Intercollegiate Athletics (NAIA) postseason tournament.[20]

Cliff Olson resigned as athletic director in 1948 after nineteen years of service. He left behind tennis courts, a football practice field, a baseball diamond, a running track, a golf course, and Memorial Gymnasium. He said the "two fine young coaches" could run things on their own.[21]

A variety of academic and intellectual successes and advances marked the postwar years. The dedication of the science faculty and Harold Leraas's premedical program came together with remarkable success. The first of the four-year graduates to earn a medical degree was Marc Stuen, who worked through the accelerated Navy V-12 program. In 1949 Warren Ghormley was the first student accepted directly from PLC to the new medical school at the University of Washington, and four more graduates entered that first University of Washington class. Grace Foege, in 1953, was the first PLC woman graduate to gain admittance into a medical school. William Rieke, a future PLU president, was admitted to the University of Washington School of Medicine that same year. By 1988, 438 PLU graduates had been accepted into medical and dental schools. A few students began going to graduate school also, at first in the sciences, and then a little more slowly in the humanities, social sciences, and education. Eighteen had finished doctoral degrees by 1962. Hundreds of young men went off to theological seminaries. The education department continued to maintain an excellent placement record, and in 1949 Anna Marn Nielsen reported that a third of the public school principals in Tacoma were PLC graduates.

With Ted Karl back on the faculty in 1948, theater productions appeared regularly on the stage in the student union, and forensic successes were extensive. In the early 1950s Jon Ericson and William Rieke debated Cambridge University students and represented the Pacific Coast at the West Point debate tournament. The forensics teams regularly won sweepstakes trophies in various tournaments. Karl and the cochairs of the music department, Karl Weiss and Gunnar Malmin, dreamed up the idea of a festival of the arts to be held in the spring, with performances in what was called the Chapel-Music-Speech building. The first drama-music festival was held in 1952 and featured Metropolitan Opera mezzo-soprano Irra

Petina and Shakespearean actor Clarence Derwent, who performed with a student cast in Christopher Frye's *Sleep of Prisoners.* The Seattle Symphony also played. The 1953 performance featured baritone Thomas L. Thomas and actor Walter Abel, who played the lead role in *Noah.* Two-time Academy Award winner Luise Rainer starred in Maxwell Anderson's *Joan of Lorraine* in 1954. She thought the new stage was "fantastic" but she disagreed with Karl's directing and banished him to the nether regions, recasting several parts and directing the play to her own satisfaction. Her performances both on and off the stage were memorable. The festivals continued to bring internationally known artists to the campus until Weiss's untimely death in 1957 brought an end to the cooperative venture. The student-subsidized Artist Series, however, brought music and drama to the campus from the mid-1950s on.

Politics hit PLC in the fall of 1952. The president's son Donald was a young Tacoma attorney, member of the state legislature, and a candidate for state attorney general; he was also a delegate to the Republican National Convention, where he was placed on the credentials committee. He attracted national attention with his defense of delegates from certain southern states who favored the nomination of Dwight Eisenhower. His interpretation carried the day and helped the nomination of Eisenhower. The national publicity helped his campaign in Washington. That campaign heated up when the Democratic incumbent, Smith Troy, charged Don Eastvold with accepting a Washington state veteran's benefit on the basis of residency in Parkland when he still claimed Minnesota residence.

The Young Democrats Club on campus invited Smith Troy to come and discuss these issues and his candidacy. Eastvold did not receive that news calmly. He had already excoriated and threatened to fire one faculty member for campaigning for Troy off campus. When he heard of Troy's visit he—along with Hauge—rushed over to the Old Main, shut down the meeting, and hustled Smith Troy off campus. Two students—Theodore Carlstrom and Allan Freed—who were present at the meeting were so angered by Eastvold's actions that they reported the event to Seattle and Tacoma newspapers. The event attracted much negative press attention, and an entire issue of the *Mooring Mast* was seized and destroyed. The president was deeply committed to his son's success. Political clubs were banned on campus after the Smith Troy affair, and political passivity—already strong—became even more dominant. That would not change perceptibly until well into the 1960s. Political clubs did not reappear until after Eastvold resigned in 1962, although a political science club was permitted a year or two before that. When Don Eastvold failed to get the Republican nomination for the governorship in 1956, his father was again bitterly discouraged. Pacific Lutheran University would become attached to the tail of still another Don Eastvold kite in 1960.

With the completion of a chapel facility large enough for the entire student body, the president determined that, beginning in February 1952, compulsory chapel should be the order of the day. The "vets" were gone and the student body was younger and more compliant; moreover, the president, with a number of major building projects behind him, had more time to deal with the quality of religious life on campus. No topic was more important to him. The institution needed to be a guide in religious life and a bastion against all the subversive intellectual and moral forces that threatened from without. Compulsory chapel would be an important offensive and defensive weapon. Of course there had always been chapel services at PLC, from 1894 onward, and students were always expected to attend. If they missed too many days they received friendly—and sometimes firm—counseling from the faculty and administration. PLC had been a relatively intimate family until after World War II, and such counseling was easy to accomplish. But in 1952 seats were assigned and attendance checked. Force and what H.A.L. Fisher once called the "plaster of paris of authority" would now be used to help produce virtue and character. Not all the faculty agreed with this plan, but Eastvold would not be deterred.[22] He explained the reasons for compulsion in an address to the student body on 30 January 1952:

> The undergraduate, ordinarily, is not fully competent to judge the importance of religion in his life. . . . The vogue of voluntary religion abandons the student who then becomes an easy victim of the world, the devil and the flesh . . . it is the solemn responsibility of his teachers and counselors to teach him the meaning of religion and its facts, as well as the arts and sciences.[23]

There is a compulsion in the universe we cannot escape, Eastvold said, and submission to "this coercive principle means discipline." Discipline could not be ignored in religious life. Discipline and religion would be correctly tied together, he promised, in "our kind of chapel."[24]

Enrollment growth slowed in the early 1950s. The Korean War was part of the reason, but enrollment was also influenced by compulsory chapel and Eastvold's hope that the entire student population might soon be Lutheran. The president told the board: "We will be fewer, but we will be stronger!" The percentage of Lutherans in the student body jumped eight points the next year to 66 percent. The percentage had ranged in the fifties for decades. There had been complete cooperation in the matter of compulsion, Eastvold reported. The only known exception had written "a beautiful letter of repentance and faith."[25] His unofficial poll did not record grumbling, yet much dissatisfaction continued. Students also grumbled about the lack of social life on campus. The complaint was not new. Response to the student council's question in 1952, "Are you satisfied with the social activity program on campus?" was strongly negative (118 said "yes" and 542 said "no"). There was neither enough to do nor enough places to go. That concern would continue, as would growing student apathy about politics, world affairs, and contemporary intellectual developments.

In loco parentis rules for students remained stringent. The consumption of alcoholic beverages was, of course, forbidden both on and off campus, and women could not smoke. There were no hours in the men's dormitories, but women's dormitory hours were very restrictive. In 1953–54 women had to be in by ten in the evening Monday through Thursday and Sunday; in the fall semester freshmen women had to be in by 9:15. On Friday and Saturday nights they could stay out until midnight with some leaves until one possible. Lights in freshmen rooms were to be out by eleven Monday through Thursday, and no social gatherings after evening devotions were allowed except by special permission. Dresses or skirts were to be worn to class. "Peddle pushers, jeans, and scarves on the head may be worn in the dining room Saturdays only. . . . Shorts may be worn only on the tennis courts." The published rules also stipulated that "the fudge kitchen shall be locked at all times when not in use." These rules continued well into the sixties.

By the early 1950s the board of trustees was almost completely mesmerized by Eastvold's enormous confidence, religious convictions, building successes, and nonstop activity. The board served as a sounding board for him, but he largely determined policy and carried it out. The board regularly eulogized Eastvold. In 1949 the board minutes reported, "With unusual fervency, Reverend Norgaard praised the work of the President of the College."[26] In 1953 the board issued a resolution thanking Eastvold for his ten years of service. He had guided PLC into "avenues of phenomenal growth and effectiveness among the youth of the Pacific Northwest," and the monies for development had "in greatest measure" been gathered by him. Asserting that the spiritual tone of the college had been continued and strengthened, the board, "with deep humility and thanks to God," acknowledged the gift bestowed by God in "the person and work of Dr. Eastvold."[27] The phrase "full, complete, and unlimited authority" was by then used by Eastvold to describe the presidency. By 1953 he had reached the height of his power. He looked for additional ways to extend and achieve his vision of how PLC should function. That vision became increasingly narrow, personal, and idiosyncratic.

THE EASTVOLD SHOW

S. C. Eastvold was an inordinately complex person. He favored the free enterprise system and thought capitalism was the only economic system in which liberty had flourished, but he did not like academic freedom. "Academic freedom has been used to fool young people and parents into letting communists and fellow-travelers teach a way of life that will destroy the sanctity of the home, undermine faith in God, and respect for the constitution and authority."[28] A "natural monarch," he could also be personable, warm, considerate, and full of good humor. He was determined to make a mark for himself in the church and world, but he also wanted to devote his life to service and God's kingdom. He was passionately committed to the success of PLC. He was concerned about the inadequacy of faculty salaries and frequently brought that problem to the trustees and national church leaders, yet some of the building in the late 1940s and much of the building from 1958 to 1962 was accomplished with budget surpluses produced largely by growing enrollment, heavy teaching loads, and low salaries.

Eastvold was a large man with a big voice and a compelling personality. He had extraordinary determination and a very thick skin. He could be remarkably insensitive, but at times his own feelings were easily bruised. His actions often seemed brusque and were usually unilateral, but he wanted to be appreciated and even loved for what he did, especially by the students. Most students, however, were in awe of him. Very few became personally close to him, and they certainly did not understand very well his complexities, motivations, or needs. Eastvold could not stand opposition, especially if it appeared in public. He wanted consensus. It was God's work that was being done after all; how could there be opposition? What was perhaps most characteristic about Eastvold was his ability to get remarkable quantities of work, loyalty, and obedience from almost everybody on the faculty and staff. Part of it stemmed from respect and agreement, but there was more. Eastvold knew that each individual responded to different concerns and had different needs and hopes. He succeeded in effectively addressing almost all of them. Authority, loyalty, fear, religion, past accomplishments, gratitude, the need to work for a cause, advancement, recognition, and money were all used as goals, rewards, or reminders. There is no doubt that people believed in Eastvold, but many think he also used people. He seemed to believe that the end really does justify the means.[29]

Eastvold's complexity and needs were never more apparent than in the chapel exercises over which he presided with great enthusiasm. Eastvold made chapel his own special forum. He frequently told students there had "never been anything like it anywhere." It was hard to disagree. He read and commented on the daily announcements; he referred to campus and off-campus events; he introduced visitors and speakers (often at great length and occasionally forgetting their names); he often commented on speeches or homilies after they were given, frequently extending chapel into the next class period. He regularly promised students he would "dilate" on some intriguing topic when he had more time, and he gave "shop talks" in which such concerns as tuition increases, discipline, the food service, dormitory life, and a variety of practical problems and issues were ventilated. There was no need for written campus communications; everything was done in chapel. He typically told students on Fridays that it had been "a good week" and then summarized for them why that was, sometimes with logic that was hard to follow. Students slept, knitted, daydreamed, did homework, listened, and participated. It is impossible to analyze with much precision, but students were undoubtedly affected in complex ways.

When Eastvold got warmed up, his homilies were often spellbinding. Referring to God as the "banker of the nations" over there "on the bosom of eternity," who owned "the cattle on a thousand hills," he looked forward with fascination to the awful, cataclysmic destruction of the whole world. The heavens "would be rolled up like a scroll," and the earth would go through "its last shaking fit, and would melt with fervent heat!"[30] PLC students would not quickly forget these performances.

THE STUDENT CONGREGATION

In 1954 it was decided there should be a student congregation on campus. Many students over the years had attended Trinity Lutheran Church, which had always been the college church and was just across the street from the campus. The ELC decided as early as 1949, however, that there should be a college pastor on every senior college campus. St. Olaf had such a pastor by 1951. It took a little longer to work out details at PLC, although the faculty committee governing religious activities endorsed the idea in 1949. The idea edged closer to actuality with the construction of the new chapel and seemed more necessary with the growth in enrollment. In May 1954 the faculty committee asked the administration to "secure" a college chaplain if that was now possible. The motion was sent to the board of trustees. The board approved the motion, appointed an executive committee of the board and Eastvold to call a pastor, and authorized a committee to begin plans for starting the congregation on 1 September 1955.

Two problems arose. Some members of Trinity congregation felt that Trinity was being pushed aside in the ministry to PLC students. That ministry stretched back to the beginnings of the institution, and a new church building was being planned to permit a more comprehensive ministry. A few suspected that the new Trinity pastor, the Reverend Erling Thompson, who had interned under Eastvold in Eau Claire, Wisconsin, was not acceptable to him. Some unfortunate confusion and misunderstanding followed, but plans for a campus pastor and congregation continued.

The second problem produced more heat. Students had not been consulted in any important way about the matter. The executive committee of the associated student body had inquired about the possibility of a student pastor in 1952, but no students had been included in subsequent discussions or decisions. When word of what was happening came to the student body there was considerable anger and frustration with the unilateralism and paternalism of the committee and the administration. This was compounded for some by their support for the newly formed Christian Student Association, which had been accepted a little earlier by a unanimous student vote. Student leaders wanted the student body to have a voice in this new matter that would obviously touch student life so intimately. They also wanted the student government to have purpose and integrity.

The problem was compounded by a heated disagreement between Eastvold and student leaders over the 1954 *Saga*. The Los Angeles company that was to print it burned and then went bankrupt. Milt Nesvig was able to retrieve the copy before the doors were padlocked, however, and student leaders through heroic efforts raised the necessary money to have the yearbook printed in Portland. Eastvold, who had favored the Los Angeles contract, castigated the students for the new contract and their ineptitude in the matter and claimed it was his efforts that had finally saved the day. Student leaders were furious, and student body president Erv Severtson described what had actually happened in a *Mooring Mast* editorial. Eastvold was in turn furious and had as many copies of the paper seized as possible. Tempers were very high. With all of this in the background, the first weeks of December 1954 were lively and heated with discussions, meetings, polls, and the appearance of an underground newspaper, the *Thinker*, to represent student opinion in the matter at hand and to advocate more vigorous and widespread intellectual activity on campus.

The matter of the student congregation was finally brought for a student vote on 8 December during chapel time. A fourteen-point questionnaire was distributed. The important question was "Do you at this time favor forming a Lutheran Student Congregation (Church) on the campus?" During the president's explanation four students rose (including Erv Severtson, the future PLU vice president for student life), trying to speak or make motions. Eastvold told them this was not a student body meeting and motions were not in order. Students were voting on a student congregation, however, and many wondered why student procedures were not honored. Eastvold later said that this was the only time in his life that he had cotton in his mouth.[31] There were 655 responses to the administrative questionnaire; 300 voted yes to the big question, 287 voted no, and 68 were indefinite. It was an administrative victory, perhaps, but a Pyrrhic one. The students distributed a questionnaire at the same time, on different colored paper, but with essentially the same questions, to check the accuracy of the administrative tabulation. The vote recorded was slightly less favorable: 46 percent voted for the student congregation. Resistance and anger went for naught, however; the administration went ahead with plans. Students also were not consulted or informed about the calls that were extended to prospective pastors, one of which was sent to Dr. Marcus Rieke, brother of a future PLU president.

The student congregation was launched in September 1955 with the Reverend Robert W. Lutnes, an alumnus and a gifted writer, as pastor. The Reverend Roy Olson, director of public relations and a popular chapel preacher, was deeply hurt that the position had not gone to him; he felt the job had been promised to him by the president when he began his service at PLC. Lutnes served effectively, however, and the student congregation has played an important role in campus life since 1955.[32] John Larsgaard replaced Lutnes in 1958. It seems clear in retrospect that the students' anger was not so much about the student congregation as about paternalism, unilateral administrative actions, and students' rights and procedures.

FACULTY EXPANSION

The faculty grew quite rapidly in the 1950s. Most who came were Lutheran and were attracted to the institution for that reason. They had not experienced the depression in Parkland, however, and they were not as patient as some of the older faculty with Eastvold's administrative style. They had also done their graduate study in the 1940s and 1950s and were eager to bring those perspectives into their work. They were loyal to the institution and committed to the church, but they brought new understandings of what that meant. Some made a substantial impact on the institution.

Mark Salzman came in 1951 and helped establish a more adequate physical education program for men. He coached three sports and became athletic director in 1958. Walter Schnackenberg rejoined the faculty in 1952 (he had been dean of men during the war) with a Ph.D. in history. He had been deeply influenced by Tingelstad's vision of Lutheran higher education, especially the importance of freedom and individuality. He wrote his doctoral dissertation about Norwegian Lutheran education in the Northwest. He was quite widely read in twentieth-century history and theology and was undoubtedly the first outspoken example on the PLC faculty of what Ahlstrom called the "critical tradition" of Lutheran education. He battled for the liberal arts and freedom and was an implacable foe of parochialism. Lucille Johnson and Ray Klopsch joined the English faculty in 1953. John Kuethe came to the religion department in 1954. He had done graduate work with Reinhold Niebuhr and Paul Tillich at Union Theological Seminary in New York and brought to PLC the insights and concerns he had learned there. He thus brought the first hints of neo-orthodox theology and existentialism to the campus and the religion department. His peppery, Socratic teaching style and courses that introduced Søren Kierkegaard, existentialism, the Protestant search for political realism, and the ideas of a number of modern theologians were transforming to some students. They discovered it was possible to live in the twentieth century—politically, ethically, theologically—and still be a Lutheran. Like Schnackenberg, Kuethe exemplified the "critical tradition" of Lutheranism, which recognized that dogmatism, pietism, and Eastvoldian premillenialism were not the only ways to address the Lutheran theological tradition and the complexities of the modern world. Ironically, the complex and sometimes volatile Kuethe would be a stalwart supporter of Eastvold in the difficulties that followed his 1961 resignation.

Donald Farmer joined the faculty in 1955. Some political science courses had been taught before this time, but Farmer founded the political science department on campus. Farmer's background was Presbyterian, and he found the Lutheran political passivity at PLC hard to understand and justify. He was also an intrepid battler for faculty rights and was one of the chief figures involved in the establishment of the faculty constitution in the 1960s. On other fronts, Eugene Maier brought the first Ph.D. to the mathematics department in 1955. Mathematics studies soon burgeoned. Eric Nordholm also came in 1955. He excelled in stage design and soon had a lively children's theater program going. Lars Kittleson and Arne Pederson ('49) came in 1956; Jens Knudsen ('52) came in 1957; Stewart Govig, Kenneth Christopherson, and John Schiller came in 1958; George Arbaugh and Charles Anderson came in 1959. These new faculty brought fresh energy and a rich variety of intellectual experience; they were bright, young Lutheran scholars. Anderson, a chemist with a Ph.D. from Harvard and three years of research experience at Stanford, took over the chair of the chemistry department in 1961. Arbaugh was soon chair of the philosophy department.

Student life was not as lively in the mid- and late-1950s as it had been a decade earlier, even though enrollment continued to grow. The "silent generation" had settled in. Intellectual life was spotty. Religious life was quite earnest and often deeply pious, however, reflecting the postwar religious "boom." The piety was encouraged by chapel exercises, worship services, and a number of clubs and organizations: Lutheran Students Association, Parish Worker's Club, Lutheran Daughters of the Reformation, Campus Devotions, the All-School Prayer Service, Mission Crusaders, Kappa Rho Kappa (for preseminarians studying Greek), and dormitory devotions. Sometimes pietism was thought to be a substitute for intellectual activity, and that contributed to some expressions of anti-intellectualism, or intellectual indifference, on campus. Both were encouraged by the quite widespread anti-intellectualism of the 1950s and some of the emotionalism, self-satisfaction, and mindlessness of American Protestantism. As one church historian observed, "During the Eisenhower years, Norman Vincent Peale and Billy Graham could link hands . . . and preside over an Indian Summer of revivalism and confident living." And in 1954 President Dwight Eisenhower declared: "Our government makes no sense unless it is founded on a deeply felt religious faith—and I don't care what it is."[33]

During those years, the *Mooring Mast* was understaffed and often quite tepid, despite the efforts of some editors. Bob Fleming's humor columns were a notable exception; they were often very witty. "Heigh Ho, everybody . . ." he would write and off the column would go. Debate successes continued to roll in. In 1956 the team of Thomas Swindland and Stuart Gilbreath was one of thirty-two invited to the prestigious West Point tournament. The choir continued to be well received, and musical activities abounded on campus.

The education department continued its successful placement record, and growing numbers of PLC-educated principals were found across the state. Some faculty members, especially younger ones, became increasingly concerned about the department's all-encompassing activities and the clearly ancillary role of the liberal arts in the college's academic structure. In 1945 two catalog pages described the education program and the twenty-two courses it offered; in 1955 thirteen pages were devoted to describing seventy-three courses. Concern about that growth would come to a head in the early 1960s. Meanwhile, the sciences continued to operate with dedication and success even though the staff was quite small. Forty-two students went to medical and dental schools in the fifties, and growing numbers went off to graduate schools, with those in biology and chemistry leading the way. Many of the best students in the decade chose to be science majors.

The nursing department was established in 1951 under the direction of Frieda Al Peterson and R. Eline Kraabel. Students spent their first and last years at PLC and received their clinical training at Emanuel Hospital in Portland. It was a forty-eight-month program, so summer school work was required. In 1953 Marianne Sunset was the first graduate. In 1959 the entire program was moved to Tacoma, and local hospitals provided the clinical experience. The program was expensive to operate, but it was encouraged because of the commitment to service inherent in nursing. The

Tacoma-based program proved increasingly popular and continued to grow. By 1988, some 1,883 nurses had graduated from the program.

Business administration continued to grow in popularity also. How it fit into a liberal arts curriculum and organization was not entirely clear, however. In the thirties the program was called "commerce," with "business administration" in parentheses, and it was included in the liberal arts section of the catalog. Seven courses were offered, including typing and shorthand. By 1942–43 it was called business administration, but its twenty courses were still part of the liberal arts structure and listed under the social sciences. In 1945–46 the listing was alphabetical in the catalog; it escaped from the social sciences. In 1951–52 business administration was paired with economics and consisted of thirty-five courses, including secretarial courses. By 1955 forty-one courses were offered.

SUCCESSES IN SPORTS

The most publicized successes of the decade were in athletics. The best basketball teams in the institution's history emerged after 1955, and records were compiled that have not been equaled since. From 1955 to 1964 the basketball teams won the Evergreen Conference championship nine times in ten years and went to the NAIA tournament in Kansas City seven times. There were ten all-conference players during that decade, most selected more than once; in addition, six of those players later earned advanced degrees—four earned doctorates. The greatest of the teams were those of 1956 to 1959, coached by Marv Harshman and Gene Lundgaard, that featured the famous trio of Chuck Curtis, Roger Iverson, and Jim Van Beek, as well as an able supporting cast. Those teams won 100 games and lost only 16; they were 49–3 in the Evergreen Conference (36–0 from 1957 to 1959). They won second and third place finishes at the Kansas City tournament (most experts and fans think they came within nine seconds of the national championship in 1957) and were 10–4 in four appearances there. The teams also played the most dramatic and exciting series of games any PLU basketball team has ever played against the national Amateur Athletic Union (AAU) power, the Buchan Bakers. Curtis and Iverson were named all-conference four times, Van Beek twice. Curtis and Iverson made the NAIA all-tournament team in 1957 and 1959. Curtis was PLC's first little all-American basketball player in 1959. In 1971 Iverson was named to the NAIA all-time tournament team, and in 1972 Marv Harshman and Iverson were named to the NAIA Hall of Fame. Curtis and Iverson are still the two leading scorers in PLU basketball history, Van Beek is tenth, and Philip Nordquist, captain of the 1955 and 1956 teams, is twelfth. Naturally, with such success, basketball was very popular on the PLC campus and in Tacoma during the era. Memorial Gym was regularly filled to overflowing with people and noise, much of it made by a theater organ, brought from Seattle, that used to shake the walls. The teams and PLC got a great deal of press and television coverage. It was an exciting time in the school's athletic's program.[34]

The orchestrator of those basketball successes, Marv Harshman, left PLC to coach at Washington State University in 1958. He was replaced by Gene Lundgaard. Harshman had coached thirteen years at PLC and won 236 games; he would coach thirteen more years at WSU, then complete his forty-year coaching career at the University of Washington, where he was widely recognized as one of the finest coaches in the nation. He said in 1958: "I hate to leave, but feel this is too good an opportunity in my profession to pass up. All my life I have wanted to be a coach, and I want to take a try at a big college job."[35] In vain, Eastvold urged him to defer "any decision until I have had a personal conference with you."[36] Eastvold talked about a substantial improvement in benefits if Harshman would stay at PLC, but Harshman chose to take on the challenge in Pullman.

John Fromm became the greatest PLC track and field record setter from 1956 to 1958. He won three national championships in the javelin: AAU once, NCAA twice. In 1958 he set a national NAIA record that stood for many years with a throw of 251 feet, 8 inches. Fromm also played football and held the single season rushing record until 1971.

CAMPUS CONSTRUCTION

Building activity continued in the late 1950s. A college union building was completed by September 1955, and in the fall of 1957 the board approved a million-dollar construction plan. An administration-classroom building, an addition to the science building, and a conversion of the first two floors of the Old Main to dormitory use were planned. The American City Bureau of Chicago was brought in to help with the planning and organization of the financial campaign. Clayton Peterson, who was appointed vice president in charge of development in 1960, was the agent in charge. The city of Tacoma and Pierce County were asked to contribute a substantial amount of the money necessary to build the administration building. It was to be called the Tacoma-Pierce Administration Building. The campaign proceeded sluggishly and was not very successful. By the late 1950s, PLC contacts in Tacoma had attenuated badly, and it was difficult to get business and civic leaders to help. Finally, Gerrit Vander Ende, president of Pacific First Federal Savings and a member of the College of Puget Sound board of trustees, agreed to serve as general chairman. He was a good choice, and the campaign got off the ground. At one point various individuals were brought to the campus for a general introduction to the campaign. Eastvold agreed that the meeting would be informational and that there would be no "hard sell," but when he saw the assembly he could not resist delivering an aggressive and full-scale appeal for funds, embarrassing Peterson and Vander Ende. Faculty and alumni, however, were familiar with Eastvold's single-mindedness about money and his frequent lack of sensitivity and appropriateness. The drive was badly undersubscribed, despite the seventy-five thousand dollars pledged by the faculty.[37] Large annual budget surpluses covered most of the building costs.

Two more additions to the campus of a different sort were made in the fifties. Class gifts from 1951, 1952, and 1953 helped to pay for a centrally located bulletin board in 1957—the infamous fifteen-thousand-dollar kiosk. It was to be "radical" in design but "functional" in use, Eastvold said. Located on the central quadrangle on upper campus, it had eight large panels that were attached to four thirty-foot prestressed concrete beams that angled up from the ground and met at the top. A star-shaped concrete roof covered the area, which was lighted and featured eight covered benches.[38] The kiosk, called "the launching pad" by many, became the subject of many jokes. (Students lifted a horse on to its roof one night.) The kiosk soon fell into disuse and disrepair, and it was demolished in 1966. Shortly after the kiosk was built, President and Mrs. Eastvold gave an outdoor swimming pool to the college in 1958 to celebrate their fortieth wedding anniversary and their fifteenth year at PLC. It was purchased through their son Donald and placed behind the chapel. It could be heated and covered with a plastic roof so it could be used much of the year. It was quite popular for a few years and was quickly dubbed "Seth's pool."

UNIVERSITY STATUS

In 1954 Eastvold was a candidate for the presidency of the Evangelical Lutheran Church. The Reverend Johan Arnd Aasgaard retired in 1954 as president after serving for twenty-nine years. Eastvold had for a long time dreamed of being synod president; for six years he had been the first vice president of the ELC. After all, had not his father been the last president of the Hauge Synod? Merger talk was also in the air, talk that would lead eventually to the formation of the American Lutheran Church in 1960. Eastvold knew that the president of the ELC would be in a strong position to lead any new body. With all that in mind he went to the church convention in Minneapolis with high hopes. His theological views had some support, perhaps especially in the Midwest. There was, however, church-wide concern over his administrative style, and Eastvold's hopes were quickly dashed. Dr. Frederick Schiotz was elected president on the second ballot with 968 votes to Eastvold's 413. Eastvold was unanimously elected first vice president; his explanation of the defeat, once back in

Parkland, suggested the depths of his disappointment.

Other things went sour for Eastvold at this time as well. The rather carelessly designed 1955 College Union building—his own special creation—had not been received with much faculty or student enthusiasm, which disappointed him. His son's political loss in 1956 also hurt deeply. By 1958 he was expressing concern over the theological direction the Lutheran church seemed to be taking. He wondered if early twentieth-century conservatism should not be reaffirmed more clearly. Many of the old "synod" leaders and the Haugeans agreed.

Faced with these discouragements, Eastvold began talking about retirement—he was sixty-three—and the board "in love and thankfulness for service rendered" established a substantial pension plan.[39] The board decided a better solution might be a six-month leave of absence to travel and visit educational institutions around the world; that might be just the tonic Eastvold needed. The trip was soon scheduled for June to December 1958. An honorary doctorate for Dr. Albert Schweitzer, the internationally famous theologian-organist-medical missionary, was approved by the faculty and board to go along with the Eastvolds to be conferred when they were in Africa.

The Eastvolds sped across the world: Norway, Germany, Belgium and the World's Fair, half a dozen African countries, Israel, India, Hong Kong, Taiwan, and Japan. Accounts of the journey were sent home to be published in the local press and eventually in book form, *Around the World in 180 Days*. The high point was undoubtedly the conferral of the honorary doctorate on Schweitzer. Eastvold recalled his excitement when Schweitzer discussed with him the theology of his faith, since "there are those who are suspicious about his belief in the Divinity or Deity of Jesus Christ." Schweitzer had been one of the most controversial theologians in the first half of the twentieth century.

> When I asked him if he could accept Luther's *Little Catechism* as a doctrine of faith, he witnessed that he treasured Luther's Catechism very highly. Fearing that I might have misunderstood him, I asked him about this again . . . "Do you really accept Luther's *Little Catechism* as a confession of faith?" Again he answered in the affirmative.

That was enough for Eastvold. The degree was conferred on 10 August 1958. "I shall never forget the face of Dr. Schweitzer as he humbly and lovingly listened to the fine words of the citation in the language of his heart."[40]

The Eastvolds also visited Ethiopia and there had an audience with His Imperial Majesty Haile Selassie I, Emperor of Emperors, King of Kings, Elect of God, and Conquering Lion of Judah. The emperor accepted the greeting from Pacific Lutheran College and permitted the Eastvolds to take photographs, but the flash mechanism failed twice. "How could we impose further on the patience of His Majesty! But we were determined. We would risk anything for the picture."[41] The third time the flash mechanism worked. The Eastvolds also had an audience with Bishop Theopholis of Addis Ababa. Eastvold fell asleep when Bishop Theopholis was talking and slept fully ten minutes, but when he awoke he took everything in stride as though he had not missed a word. When Bishop Theopholis reminded him that when he had visited PLC Eastvold had given the task of showing him the campus to a subordinate, Eastvold did not miss a beat either. "Ours is a democratic country," he explained, "and all participate in important activities."[42] That was not the way he administered PLC, of course. The Eastvolds returned home early in the morning to the PLC band, a large welcoming crowd, and a joyous breakfast on campus. That welcome was the "highlight" of the world tour, Eastvold said.

One of the outcomes of the trip was the decision to seek university status and return to the institution's original name. Eastvold had seen institutions all over the world, many no larger than PLC, called universities. In fact, many people he encountered did not know what a college was. The number of junior colleges in the state was growing, and the state colleges were becoming universities. The College of Puget Sound soon made the same decision. The change would bring a new system of organization, with a college of liberal arts and several professional schools organized under the university umbrella. Deans would be appointed to head these new units. A faculty senate would follow. There was talk of additional graduate work being offered, but only up to the master's degree level. The faculty, trustees, and PLC Association supported the change, and it was quite quickly set in motion. The various motives in faculty support for the change would sometimes conflict, but that was not yet obvious in 1959.

Eastvold explained his thinking in a speech to the faculty during its annual retreat in September 1959. The speech set the administrative agenda for the movement to university status, and in some respects it turned out to be a valedictory address for Eastvold. He told the faculty that yesterday was the day of the small college, but that tomorrow would be the day of the small university. He expressed every intention that Pacific Lutheran should be a superior small university. "Even Dr. Schweitzer writes his joy and approval." As the necessary changes are institutionalized, he clarified, the authority of the board "must be unimpaired and unquestioned" and "at all times the President carries the final responsibility for everything." Clearly, in his view university status did not mean democracy. Dancing, drinking, and gambling would not be allowed in the new university, worldliness would be battled, and aggressive Christianity would be basic. "We are told that we cannot entertain our young people unless we move to the borderline of worldliness. *I do not believe this!*" The faculty would be expected to conduct themselves appropriately and to attend chapel regularly, just like the students. "The Christian College [he meant small university now] must be a rampart, a fortification, a defender, a protector as over against all dangers to our precious heritage."[43]

A flurry of activities followed the decision to assume university status. A variety of consequences—many of them unanticipated and unintended— also emerged. The years from 1960 to 1962, made more volatile by the embarrassment of the Ocean Shores investment debacle and an internal self-study, were the most heated, difficult, and divisive in the institution's history. President S. C. Eastvold would resign in November 1961, in large part because of the fallout over his decision to involve the institution in the Ocean Shores land development scheme in which his son was a major figure.

8

Coming of Age

THE COLLEGE COMMUNITY was enormously busy during the 1959–60 academic year discussing what it meant to be a small university and establishing the necessary administrative structures. Philip Hauge was appointed the university dean, and Theodore Sjoding became the dean of an expanded graduate school. Erich Knorr was appointed dean of the College of Arts and Sciences. Many hoped the new university structure would strengthen the role of the liberal arts in determining educational and university policy.

John Amend, whose experience had been entirely within the public schools, was appointed dean of the School of Education and would complete his doctoral work a short time later. Anna Marn Nielsen was the logical choice for that position, but because she did not have a doctorate it was feared that might put the new School of Education at a competitive disadvantage. She remained director of teacher education, however. Dwight Zulauf was appointed dean of the School of Business Administration, and Vernon Utzinger was named dean of the School of Fine and Applied Arts. The acting director of the School of Nursing was Eline Kraabel Morken. Kristen Solberg, chair of the psychology department, became dean of students, and Linka K. Johnson became registrar. This was a lot of administrative machinery for a small school, but it was hoped the new university would quickly grow into its new structure. When some of that structure turned out to be theoretical wishful thinking, several rearrangements would be made in the next few years.

In March 1960 the board thanked God for "magnificent and almost colossal growth," often referred to in many circles as a "miracle." It then approved a ten-year, $11 million development fund campaign for building and endowment.[1] The hiring of a full-time person to lead the campaign was approved. Clayton Peterson, a Wisconsin native, was appointed to a new vice presidency for development. He had extensive experience in business, public relations, and fundraising, most recently with the American City Bureau of Chicago. He had also helped with the 1958 drive.

One major gift to the new campaign was the Ford Foundation's seventy thousand dollars to provide a closed circuit television system and enhance salaries for several faculty members who prepared to teach their classes on television. (Many thought television would be a dominant part of the educational future; closed circuit facilities were built into the new administration-classroom building.) The Ford Foundation had already given a quarter of a million dollars in 1955 to enhance faculty salaries, part of a $210 million grant to 615 private colleges. The money was to be carefully, not speculatively, invested and only the interest was to be used. The Evangelical Lutheran Church was given the responsibility of investing the money.

The president continued to be restless. In May he announced he was being pressured to run for the governorship of the state of Washington; there had also been moves to draft him for lieutenant governor and the state senate, he said. The faculty met and advised him that he should not be a candidate for governor. Erich Knorr told him he would have to resign as president if he chose to enter the political arena. That made him "furious," Knorr reported. Nevertheless, Eastvold decided not to run for public office and announced his decision in a 23 May news release. He would not run for governor, it said, even though "a professional poll indicates that I could win the election. . . . My colleagues, and the Board of Trustees of the College, tell me that it will be more difficult to find a good College President than to find a Governor for the State of Washington."[2] Eastvold's restlessness surfaced again in July when he resigned his membership in Trinity Lutheran congregation to accept the unprecedented position of honorary pastor at Central Lutheran Church in Tacoma. The Reverend Reuben Redal, who would soon emerge as a leader of "Lutherans Alert," one of the alarmed defenders of Lutheran orthodoxy, was the senior pastor at Central.

Eastvold had been hinting at the possibility of an extraordinary fund-raising triumph all through the spring. Some dimensions of that development were unveiled in June. The executive committee of the board of trustees went to Hoquiam to look at some property ("accreted tideland") on a long spit west of Hoquiam between Grays Harbor and the ocean owned by Ocean Shores Estates, Inc. The developers—who included Eastvold's son Donald—were short of cash, so in return for a loan of $250,000 (which would be paid back with interest) a gift-pledge of one hundred acres (350 lots) of land would be given the new university. Eastvold said the land was worth a million dollars. The executive committee, with Eastvold's strong urging, accepted the offer. In addition to the hundred acres, a lot was promised for a Lutheran church and a retirement home for Lutherans; the university, in turn, promised to call attention to its contribution and encourage PLU supporters to visit Ocean Shores. The university attorney, who was not asked to comment on the wisdom of the investment, said it was legally acceptable. Eastvold was absolutely delighted. He wrote: "It may be true as somebody said to me, 'This will likely prove to be the most important business transaction you have completed at Pacific Lutheran College.' Time will tell."[3] The Ford Foundation money, which had been invested by the ELC, was now reinvested in Ocean Shores Debentures. The board tacitly approved the reinvestment of the Ford Foundation money even though the speculative nature of the Ocean Shores development was at odds with the terms of the grant. Eastvold told the trustees that the million-dollar gift "makes a great beginning" in the $11 million campaign.

The rest of the summer and the early fall were taken up with discussions, planning, and events related to the new university status. It was a busy and exciting time. The faculty fall conference in early September was, in part, devoted to a study of the relation between Christian faith and the liberal arts. The main presentation was a discussion of a book midwestern Lutheran scholars had been working on for a decade: *The Christian Faith and the Liberal Arts*, edited by H. H. Ditmanson and others. The central issue of the book was whether there was a Lutheran philosophy of education. Walter Schnackenberg presented an "informal review" of the book, one of several attempts by Schnackenberg to explain and emphasize the importance of liberal education at PLU. He—and the book—attempted to relate liberal education to Christianity and Lutheranism in a deeper and more fundamental way than was traditional. The traditional answers, strained through "piety" and "orthodoxy," seemed increasingly unsatisfactory in the midst of explosive intellectual advances and reams of disturbing questions in the second half of the twentieth century. Schnackenberg clearly espoused the "critical" tradition of Lutheran education, applying that approach to a university that both was Lutheran and claimed allegiance to the liberal arts. The real problem of the liberal arts was a human one, Schnackenberg emphasized, and "it will be self-defeating if we imagine that our educational effort is *just the same* as that carried on any place else with only these 'added' differences." The differences usually "added" were chapel, piety, religion courses, dormitory devotions, a sense of community, and safety. That was not enough to justify an institution like PLU. "On the contrary," Schnackenberg contended, "the heart of the institution *must be the educational program*, and this must be the area of our Christian emphasis...the intellectual grasp of human experience, the aim of liberating education, must be found in the central problem of man and his relationship to God."[4] Among the many concerns brewing in the new university, questions about the relationship of Christianity to education and the most authentically Lutheran way of expressing that were foremost. They would soon boil over.

The formal adoption of university status took place on 14 October 1960 with an impressive and colorful ceremony. The Tacoma-Pierce Administration Building was dedicated at the same time, and the seventieth anniversary of the university's founding was commemorated. It was also homecoming weekend. Officials from the American Lutheran Church and the American academic community were present for the festivities, and four honorary degrees were granted: to C. Clement French, president of Washington State University; to Gerrit Vander Ende, president of Pacific Federal Savings and Loan; to Frederick Schiotz, president of the American Lutheran Church; and to J. W. Ylvisaker, president of Luther College. Seven more honorary doctorates would be given on other occasions during the "University Year," including one to Robert A. L. Mortvedt, who would become the eighth president of PLU in 1962. The several addresses from the dedication weekend and other ceremonies during the year were gathered together and published in a volume entitled *Contemporary Thoughts on Christian Higher Education: The University Year, 1960–61.*[5] Most were forgettable; Mortvedt's was programmatic. The *Tacoma News Tribune* devoted a large supplement to the dedication and the institution's seventy years. With a very full weekend, the university was launched.

OCEAN SHORES

On Sunday, 16 October, some of the edge was taken off the celebration by a long article written by Don Duncan and Marshall Wilson that appeared in the *Seattle Sunday Times.* The headline read: "Big Tidelands Sale at $10 an Acre Criticized." The article spelled out in considerable detail how the "accreted tidelands" had fallen into the hands of the Ocean Shores developers. As the land commissioner, Bert Cole, characterized the deal: "It's legal, but it stinks." The acreage in question had been built by tidal action after Washington became a state in 1889. There was thus some question of legal ownership. The land was accreted from Columbia River silt after a jetty was built at the peninsula's tip in 1916. In 1956 the twelve hundred acres were sold to Ralph Minard, a rancher whose family had lived in the area since 1878, for thirty-eight cents a front foot, or $12,682 in all. He had been trying to buy the land for a decade, hoping to add it to his forty-eight hundred adjacent acres. A 1928 law had determined that if the land were to be sold, the Minard family should have the first option. The state—in the person of the land commissioner—was under no compulsion to sell the land, however, and both the game department and the parks commission wanted the land developed and used for public purposes. Nonetheless, the land was sold to Minard. A month after the sale, the attorney general's office got a judicial decision legally establishing state ownership and the right to sell the land. The land commissioner's office said the land was sold "following the recommendation of the attorney general," Donald Eastvold. The attorney general's office replied that the land commissioner had made the decision. All this was done just weeks before Eastvold's term of office ended. It was that land (the 1,200 "accreted" acres and the 4,800-acre ranch) that the Ocean Shores developers bought from Minard for a million dollars early in 1960. Donald Eastvold was one of the principal stockholders and an officer of the corporation. He said the idea of developing the area had come to him when he was salmon fishing off the coast in August 1959. Popular talk circulating in 1960 speculated that Ocean Shores would become one of the great recreational developments in the United States and earn huge profits for the developers, but in the meantime development capital was needed. That was the reason for the $250,000 loan from PLU. When Dr. Eastvold was asked by the *Seattle Times* about the loan, he said the transaction was "not the public's business." Some version of this story was soon in every major newspaper in the state.

The board members (and many Lutherans in the Northwest) suffered discomfiture at the revelation. Should PLU be involved in a speculative scheme that was "legal" but "stinks"? What about the dancing, floor shows, and sale of liquor in the existing or planned restaurants and supper clubs (including one owned by Don Eastvold's second wife, Hollywood singer Ginny Sims)? Should something be done? A special meeting of the board was called to discuss the loan and unfortunate publicity.

W. R. McPherson, a Seattle real estate broker and one of the Ocean Shores developers, was at the meeting. He said the article was "politically inspired, untruthful, and slanderous," but the loan could be paid back if the board wanted that. The charge that the article was "politically inspired" seems curious. Don Eastvold, deeply involved in the Ocean Shores development, was no longer a candidate for public office (he never ran for an elective office after his 1956 primary defeat), and his father had given up political ambitions in 1960. Neither is there evidence to suggest that the article was written to revenge some earlier political activity or to advance some unnamed political candidacy in 1960. McPherson did not specify what was "untruthful" or "slanderous" in the article. After McPherson finished speaking, President Eastvold gave a long and frequently angry statement. The article was "politically inspired," he said. Not only was the investment of the Ford Foundation money a good one for the university, but it also gave society opportunities for "good wholesome recreation." It was not a risk, he insisted. He admitted there were moral problems, however; there was a bar. "I deplore bars, or the use of liquor any place in the world. About 400 square feet on this 6,000-acre tract are devoted to that bar. In this, we absolutely want no part." Remaining steady should be the order of the day, he urged, and the board agreed that a final decision about what to do should be made at the spring meeting. The board appointed a subcommittee to study the matter and report at that meeting. The committee members were Earl Eckstrom as chair, Einer Knutzen, Gus Nieman, Pastor Arthur Anderson, and Harold Widsteen.[6]

Clayton Peterson, the new vice president, arrived on campus shortly after the *Seattle Times* article was published. He was taken aback by the article but decided that because he liked the university's prospects and the faculty he would stay. There was no development plan for the proposed $11 million campaign, however. When asked about a plan, Eastvold produced the 1959 accreditation report as a development scheme. An organized and detailed plan still had to be established. In January 1961 Peterson sent a long memorandum to the board emphasizing the need for a careful assessment of prospects and clear definitions before the institution took on the new fund drive. Only after such a "self-study" was completed could action be taken, he advised.[7] The idea of internal self-study was soon launched, amid the ongoing concerns of the Ocean Shores investigation, the movement to university status, the attempt to find an appropriately Lutheran understanding of the new institution, growing faculty concern about Eastvold's leadership, and the restiveness of some areas of the College of Arts and Sciences. Together, these concerns proved to be a volatile mixture. The importance of the self-study over the next three years cannot be underestimated.

The special subcommittee reported back to the board on 3 March 1961. After consultation with numerous investment experts, the committee concluded that granting the loan had been a mistake. It violated several basic investment principles. Moreover, the university had been "deeply hurt in its public relations." The committee was convinced the board had been "negligent." The offer to repay the loan should be accepted and an investment committee should be formed to deal with such matters in the future. The resolutions were accepted. Two weeks later the board, deeply concerned about its own negligence and responsibilities and about the statewide perception of the institution in the aftermath of the revelations about Ocean Shores, authorized a thorough study of its own structure and procedures. In June a university-wide self-study was authorized. It was to be very broad and inclusive, and it was to be guided by "qualified experts."[8] By August, Walter Darling of the Fund Fulfillment Corporation of Chicago was on campus as advisor to the first stages of institutional self-study. Five areas were to be studied: 1) the structure and organization of the university, 2) academic programs, 3) student life, 4) business affairs, and 5) university relations. Never had the institution planned such a careful scrutiny of all of its component activities and parts. The faculty began cranking up for its labors and the Fund Fulfillment Corporation brought in experts to study the board, the presidency, and institutional public relations. They interviewed faculty, administrative staff, board members, alumni, Lutheran pastors, and Tacoma business and civic leaders.

SELF-STUDY

Walter Darling presented the administration-public relations studies to the board at its November meeting. A confidential letter to board chair H. L. Foss preceded the formal presentation of conclusions. Administrative changes are "urgently needed" and Eastvold will be "deeply upset by our report," the letter said. You must reach agreement by the end of the calendar year on a date for his retirement, it advised, noting that the sooner he retires, the better for the university. Eastvold did not have a term contract, but an open-ended "call." At the end of the letter was a list of all individuals interviewed, in case a charge of bias arose. There were "unusual tensions and fears of reprisals" on campus.[9]

Eastvold had agreed to the self-study with no hesitation; he thought nothing negative could be discovered. The two reports delivered to the board in November were devastating. Eastvold was both angry and deeply hurt. Two views of board authority were profiled in the first report: one assumed that leadership and control of the institution belong to the president and that the board gets in the way if it looks too closely; the other asserted that the board properly exercises an intermediate controlling function between the church and the president. It does not serve merely to approve his decisions. The board should function in this second fashion, the report said, but the "virtually unanimous testimony" of those interviewed indicated that the board had operated under the first scheme for many years—only in the last twelve to eighteen months had it begun to operate as a policy-making body. Further, the board had been careless about formal records, failing to keep an official record of minutes. That had to be corrected. The study also found that the relationship of the board to the faculty and staff caused much resentment, since communications were handled solely through the president's office. Because the new faculty senate was made up of administrators ("entirely a creature of the president"), no solution to the problem could be found there. The senate needed to be restructured, the report concluded. The board needed to meet more often than twice a year, it added, and the services of the university attorney should be used more regularly. It further recommended that the by-laws of the corporation be amended to allow two permanent subcommittees, an executive committee and a finance commitee. A board manual should be prepared. The board, determined to bring about necessary reforms, set to work at the same meeting to institutionalize the most important of the recommendations.

The report further noted that the president had too many responsibilities. He was president, business manager (and in effect treasurer), and head of the faculty senate. The positions of president and business manager should be divided, it recommended, and the president should no longer serve as head of the faculty senate. Carrying out these recommendations would also respond to the criticism in the April 1959 accreditation report: Eastvold may be the greatest strength of the institution, it had said, but complete dependence on him is the greatest weakness as well.[10] In response, however, Eastvold simply would not accept the recommendation about separating the tasks of the presidency and business operations. Combining those two offices, he had run the institution since 1943; if pushed, he would resign.

The second report, the public opinion study, was full of land mines. It was crushing to Eastvold. The good things of the institution have not come together to create "spirit" or "morale," it found. Alumni expressed too little interest in the school. The clergy were ambivalent and the general public was largely ignorant of the school. The general public thought PLU was aloof and noncooperative and so strictly Lutheran that non-Lutherans were not welcome. There was also a feeling that expedience and opportunism ruled. Eastold was identified with building up the institution, but 75 percent of those interviewed felt his mission had been fulfilled and a retirement process needed to be set in motion. The size of the institution and the times made one-man rule inappropriate. "The singleness of identification of Dr. Eastvold with Pacific Lutheran University and the University with Dr. Eastvold has represented the greatest strength, weakness, and danger."[11]

The Ocean Shores incident had not harmed PLU with the Tacoma business community, but it had seriously damaged church relations. The "unsavory reputation of Don Eastvold" had also hurt the institution's reputation. The university had not injected itself adequately into the life of Tacoma and Pierce County; it did not enjoy enough confidence with the business and professional community to launch a major fundraising campaign—"disappointment, if not outright failure" would be the result. Clayton Peterson had been correct in his diagnosis. More adequate public relations mechanisms would have to be created, and they should not be so closely tied to one individual. The faculty is divided and wants to be treated as a "community of scholars," not as employees. The report concluded: "President Eastvold is a man recognized as having done a perfectly amazing job but, unfortunately, he has been woefully lacking in his own personal public relations. He has conveyed the impression that he operates in the belief that 'The end justifies any means.'"[12]

Eastvold, already disgusted with the board for pulling out of Ocean Shores, was furious with the Fund Fulfillment Corporation's reports. Steadfastly refusing to contemplate the separation of the presidency from business management, he resigned, effective 31 July 1962. "We have built a great school," he said. "It is our fond desire that, as we sever connections officially with the school, it may be done in such a way and manner that we will have unanimity and spiritual fellowship, approved by God and well-pleasing to man."[13] The board adopted a resolution of thanks to Eastvold and presented a retirement package that was quite handsome. The board also agreed to destroy the public opinion study that it had just received and studied, except for those portions that made specific recommendations. On 6 December the board announced the procedures that would be used in the selection of the next president. It also announced that the faculty self-study would continue, with the reports due in March.

The faculty self-study was conducted under the direction of James E. Perdue, dean of the College of Arts and Sciences at the University of Denver, with Dean Erich Knorr as the general chair. A nine-person steering committee was established, as well as eight subcommittees, to deal with virtually every aspect of university life. George Arbaugh chaired the crucial objectives subcommittee, which also included Kenneth Christopherson, Louis Christensen, Arne Pedersen, and Walter Schnackenberg. Self-study in combination with the president's resignation (and efforts to undo the resignation) produced much work, serious thought, a feeling that change was possible in a way hitherto undreamed of, considerable political maneuvering, and great divisiveness in the months ahead. Much that was done was couched in terms of religion. There was frequent talk of loyalty and forgiveness. Chapel talks were often freighted with levels of meaning. It was undoubtedly the most difficult period of transition in the institution's history.

A counterattack, aimed at undoing Eastvold's resignation, started almost immediately. A letter sent to the regents (the trustees had changed their name with university status) on 8 December 1961 referred to a petition and argued that the resignation of Eastvold was not "in the best interests of the University." It asked the board to reconsider. The letter claimed that a heavy preponderance of faculty and staff favored retaining Eastvold. The letter was signed by administrators John Amend and Kristen Solberg, house father C. K. Malmin, plant manager Kenneth Jacobs, presidential secretaries Anna Enge and Lucille Giroux, and faculty members T.O.H. Karl, John Kuethe, Kelmer Roe, and William Strunk. These individuals, especially the faculty members and administrators, would be the mainstays in the Eastvold camp in the months ahead. They were frequently referred to as "the kitchen cabinet." Eastvold said he had no role in the petition activity, but he found it gratifying. He still wanted to retire, but "I appreciate the fact that nothing is so final that the Holy Spirit may not further lead and guide us."[14]

In February the *Mooring Mast* announced that both Dr. William Strunk of the biology department and Eastvold were leaving to assume leadership positions in the new and financially troubled California Lutheran College.[15] Eastvold had bought a house at the nearby Salton Sea development his son was involved in. Nominations for the presidency were flowing in (seventy by the end of January), and Eastvold had declined nomination. Later in February, Dr. Gerhard Belgum was the featured speaker for spiritual emphasis week. He had resigned from the Luther College religion department a year earlier in a somewhat similar theological-administrative struggle. The student council urged students "to begin preparing . . . for Spiritual Emphasis Week by evaluating their own Christian life through prayer." Belgum's former Luther College colleague Knute Lee, who had also resigned and now served in the PLU religion department, said, "If this boy can't keep them awake, they might as well sleep."[16]

Students were not very well informed about many of the substantive issues in the struggle, but the student body was inevitably caught up in it. The student body leaders had been battling to keep dancing off the PLU campus; now they turned their attention to supporting Eastvold. The student body president, Charles Mays, thought it was the "witness to Jesus Christ" that was at stake and that Eastvold had been a heroic witness. Student attitudes, concerns, and polarization were pushed along by Belgum's presence and activity in February, Mays testified, and students were regularly supplied with information and encouragement by faculty members and administrative personnel. Twenty-five years later Mays admitted he had not been very well informed about many of the issues and that the theology that prevailed in student circles had been "simplistic," but he added that it was a great year for learning, "some of which took years to process."[17] Mays said he would fight just as hard on the other side today.

The *Mooring Mast* tended to be editorially sympathetic to Eastvold and the status quo. Other students had different views. "The door seems to be opening and there are faint rays indicating that we will soon be able to express ourselves without condemnation or psychoanalysis. . . . The time has come for us to loosen the bonds of these medieval principles and to think in a more modern light. We owe it to God if to no one else."[18] The *Mooring Mast* was full of letters to the editor and guest editorials, some of which expressed concern about the frequent tendency to make all issues and questions into religious referendums. A future student body president wrote: "The conservative point-of-view which has so long run student affairs, has also found need to make a little noise defending against the opposition, which they feel is basically un-Christian. Must a change of policy be against or detrimental to Christian ethics?" The author did not think so and explained why.[19]

In March the board met to elect a new president for PLU. The five leading candidates were Fred Binder, Robert Mortvedt, Allen Pfnister, Sidney Rand, and Morris Wee. Robert A. L. Mortvedt led after the first round of balloting and was elected on the second; the board made it unanimous on the third. Church president Schiotz spoke to the faculty that evening, announcing Mortvedt's election and urging an end to controversy. Mortvedt was fifty-nine years old, had received a Ph.D. in English literature from Harvard, and had more than twenty years of collegiate and university administrative experience. He would need it all as he addressed a long agenda of challenging and difficult problems. Mortvedt accepted the call.

A special board resolution thanked Eastvold, detailed his accomplishments, and stipulated that the Chapel-Music-Speech Building would now be known as Eastvold Chapel. The faculty self-study reports were also submitted at this meeting (although some were not yet complete), and the Fund Fulfillment Corporation presented the rest of its reports.[20] The board continued to express its support for the self-study and the leadership provided by Knorr.

The supporters of Eastvold now turned their guns on the self-study reports. Tension grew and the heavily politicized atmosphere on campus made regular work difficult for the rest of the year. Reasons for the attempts to undo the resignation and the opposition to the self-study (or parts of it) are complex and difficult to unravel. They included loyalty to the president, respect for authority, the memory of past accomplishments, attempts to defend privilege, fear of changes that the self-study might bring, the clash of personalities, the fear of "modernism," defense of "authentic" Lutheranism, and undoubtedly much more. Disagreements continued to take on religious coloration, and attempts to enroll students and pastors in the fray continued. Eastvold played an active role; meetings of the "kitchen cabinet" took place with his knowledge and frequently in his office.

Eastvold wrote to the faculty on 10 March that the selection of Mortvedt had been the right choice. There was success at every hand, he announced, and Mortvedt would inherit that success.[21] Eastvold further reported that because of allegations of grave unethical practices, in and out of the classroom, he was withholding seven contracts. He had permission to do that, he said, even though the board had ultimate responsibility to investigate each case very carefully. The seven people—five administrators and two faculty members—were, presumably, those perceived to be the most serious, effective, and crucially placed opponents of Eastvold's administrative style, theology, and vision of education. The seven were Frank Haley, Gunnar Malmin, Milton Nesvig, Roy Olson, Clayton Peterson, Walter Schnackenberg, and Cecil Vance. But when he informed the board of his action on 13 March, the acting chair of the board told him to get the seven contracts out immediately, and they appeared on 14 March. Eastvold wrote: "Please be assured that I have not been motivated in any way by recrimination or personal animosity."[22]

April and May were filled with last-ditch attempts to scuttle the self-study, especially the work of the objectives committee and the student life committee. The statement of objectives prepared by the former was not adequately Lutheran, some conservative faculty members charged. The student life committee was accused of being too critical of past social structure and too permissive about changes, since it suggested ways to inhibit the heavy hand of restrictive, legislated morality and to move students from "spectator-life" to participatory activities and away from "hill-billy" religion.

The objectives committee became the center of the storm in the next several months. A number of battles were fought, including a battle over the nature of Lutheranism. That battle had been going on in Europe for a number of decades and in the United States since the end of World War II. The beginnings of the struggle at PLU date from the mid-1950s. In very broad terms it was a battle between "Old Lutherans" and "Neo-Lutherans." E. Clifford Nelson, the best recent historian of Lutheranism in North America, summarized the differences in this way: "Those who sought to uphold biblical inerrancy and generally to repristinate 'orthodoxy' might be called Old Lutherans; those who sought to relate contemporary theology and the Luther Renaissance to American Lutheranism, Neo-Lutherans. All, however, were speaking *within* Lutheranism."[23] The spectrum of Lutheranism was relatively broad. Old Lutherans defended biblical infallibility; Neo-Lutherans preferred to speak of the infallibility of the message ("the Word of God") of the Scriptures, thus distinguishing between the Word of God and the Scriptures, but not separating them. This view was tied very closely to the findings of Luther scholarship during the "Luther Renaissance" after World War I.

Nitpicking criticisms came to the objectives committee, but also a charge from three religion department members that the committee report's opening paragraph represented a Luther and a "reformation spirit" unknown to eminent Luther scholars.[24] The report's statement read: "Martin Luther, with other great reformers, re-established the principle of free search for truth, thereby overthrowing the ancient appeal to tradition as primary authority." That statement, and others that followed it, clearly reflected "Neo-Lutheranism." The criticism and concern, on the other hand, reflected "Old Lutheranism." The statement was also a response to the various crises and disturbances of the recent past. It attempted to explain the university in the most appropriate historical and theological context and to forge a weapon with which to fight Eastvold and some of the worst problems and excesses associated with his administration, especially authoritarianism and the sometimes capricious approach taken toward academic freedom. The statement became the focal point of the struggle during those last months because it was the faculty's own statement.

In response to the criticism about an inauthentic understanding of Luther, the committee wrote to four of the leading Luther scholars in the United States, spelled out the nature and context of the disagreement, and asked if the statement's interpretation of Luther was correct. The responses were carefully written, varied, interesting, and affirmative.[25] The dean of American Luther scholars, Professor Roland Bainton of Yale University, wrote:

> I agree with you heartily that 'a Christian College' is committed to an absolutely free search for truth without qualifications. . . . As for Luther I agree with what you say about his total impact . . . the total impact of Luther was emancipating, although obviously one should not dress him up as a doctor of the Enlightenment. One can say that in his own day he shattered the authority which chiefly impeded free investigation.[26]

One last attempt to scuttle the self-study was made at the annual meeting of the university corporation in June. Various charges had been made that the self-study had encouraged inroads of "modernism" and attempts to weaken religious practice on campus. Erich Knorr, as general chair of the self-study, wrote to the district pastors who would be present at the meeting and told them that the rumors about the self-study were unfortunate. He assured them that the studies were important and the committee members were hard-working and thoroughly Christian.[27] A week later another letter went out to the pastors over the signatures of John Amend, T.O.H. Karl, John Kuethe, and Kristen Solberg. It found fault with Knorr's letter and the whole self-study process. The "unfortunate situation" needed to be remedied.[28] Their letter had been sent with the full knowledge of Dr. Eastvold, they wrote.

The final battle was fought at a meeting of the corporation's standing committee on higher education. Eastvold appeared before the committee one evening and told the members that the self-study must be dropped, the objectives nullified, and his resignation reversed. He said the objectives committee was "embarrassed" by the statement and that they should be let off the hook by having the corporation turn it down. Moreover, he claimed, the faculty opposed the objectives statement and disliked the self-study. Kenneth Christopherson, a member of the objectives committee, had obtained a letter from chair George Arbaugh authorizing him to speak for the entire committee. Like the other committee members, Christopherson was worried about what might go on at the meeting. Listening at the open door, he asked for permission to speak. The objectives committee members were not embarrassed, he said; they did not want to retract the document, and it had the support of a large part of the faculty. Faced with this conflicting testimony, the committee decided to take no action.[29] John Kuethe asked Christopherson if he knew what his statement implied about Eastvold's remarks. Christopherson said he did.

The self-study reports were accepted by the board on 11 June. Polishing the objectives statement took another year. The resulting declaration has been an important and normative statement guiding university life since 1963. Its presence today in the university catalog does not suggest the passion of its birth nor its importance in the spring of 1962.

The *Mooring Mast* interviewed Eastvold in June. He said he thought his greatest accomplishments at PLU were the "marked development in the spiritual life on campus," full accreditation, and the buildings constructed under his presidency. The major obstacle to success had come in the last year with the Fund Fulfillment Corporation. The goal for the future should be expansion to meet needs, Eastvold urged: "The sky is the limit in this space age."[30] Clearly, some of the old bounce was still left. He was a little more frank with board member and old friend O. K. Davidson the day before he left for California: "I reserve the right to say that I have very seriously disagreed with the Board of Regents, and it is this disagreement with the Board of Regents that has brought about my request for retirement and this, I suppose, is no secret to anybody on the Board."[31]

Eastvold left for California on 1 August 1962. With the resignation of President Orville Dahl, he became acting president of California Lutheran College in January 1963. He had served just six weeks in that position when he was stricken with a massive cerebral hemorrhage. He died on 25 February 1963 in Minneapolis.

S. C. Eastvold's energy and leadership were important in keeping PLC alive during the dark days of 1943. The next nineteen years were filled with the fundraising and building activity that he organized and orchestrated. Those accomplishments were significant. Eastvold's efforts to translate his theology into an educational bastion were less successful, at least in the long run. By 1962 a substantial portion of his thology and his educational notions were on the periphery of American Lutheran theology and education. They were badly out of touch with postwar concerns and a rapidly changing, younger, and more ecumenically minded American Lutheran Church constituency. That can be seen in the 968 to 413 margin of victory in the Schiotz-Eastvold election for the 1954 Evangelical Lutheran Church presidency, in the serious problems unearthed by the Fund Fulfillment Corporation in 1961, and in the struggle to produce a statement of objectives in 1962. The theological and educational battles that were fought at PLU in the early 1960s and that resulted in the statement of objectives were battles within Lutheranism, however. The individuals and arguments involved, almost without exception, bore that stamp.

Robert Mortvedt set to work in August 1962 with the vigor and singularity that marked his presidency. There was much to do. The new university—the institution that the largest number of alumni easily recognize—began to take shape under his leadership, but the development was not easy. The structure and ethos of the institution began to change quite rapidly with the new university structure and as more ecumenical, pluralistic, and secular emphases and undreamed-of social and political pressures appeared. Stability and change were central concerns as faculty and administration tried to hang on to the best and most authentic aspects of the past despite wrenching and unprecedented changes. In the midst of all the pressures and change the university continued to grow physically and academically.

The 1960s and the 1970s were exciting decades in higher education, but they were very trying. There were important advances and many false starts. At PLU, too, it was the best of times and the worst of times.

The first faculty, 1894, 1st row: Meyer Brandvig, Mrs. Carlo Sperati, Miss Sophie Peterson
2nd row: Rev. Ballestad, Rev. Carlo Sperati, T. C. Satra, Rev. T. Larson, Rev. N. Christiansen,
W. Shahan, Rev. B. Harstad

The PLA band, 1900

The PLA Athletic Club, early 1900s

Penmanship class in Old Main (Harstad Hall), 1903

The women's basketball team, 1907

Chapel address by Ola Ordal, mid-1920s

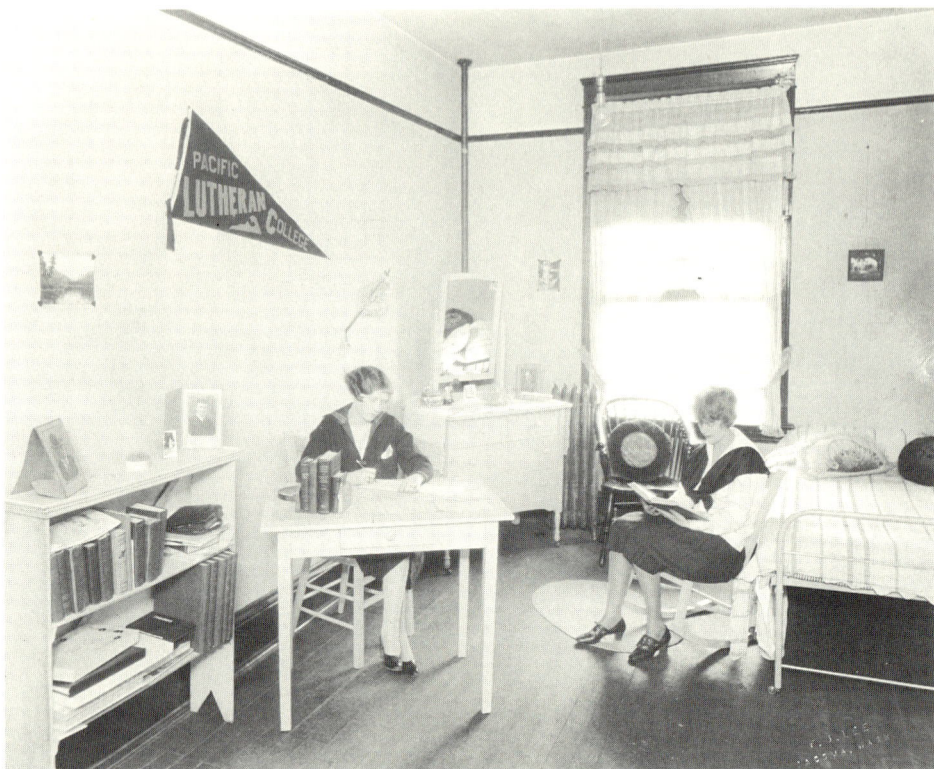
Dorm living, 1920s

Early *Mooring Mast* staff, 1920s

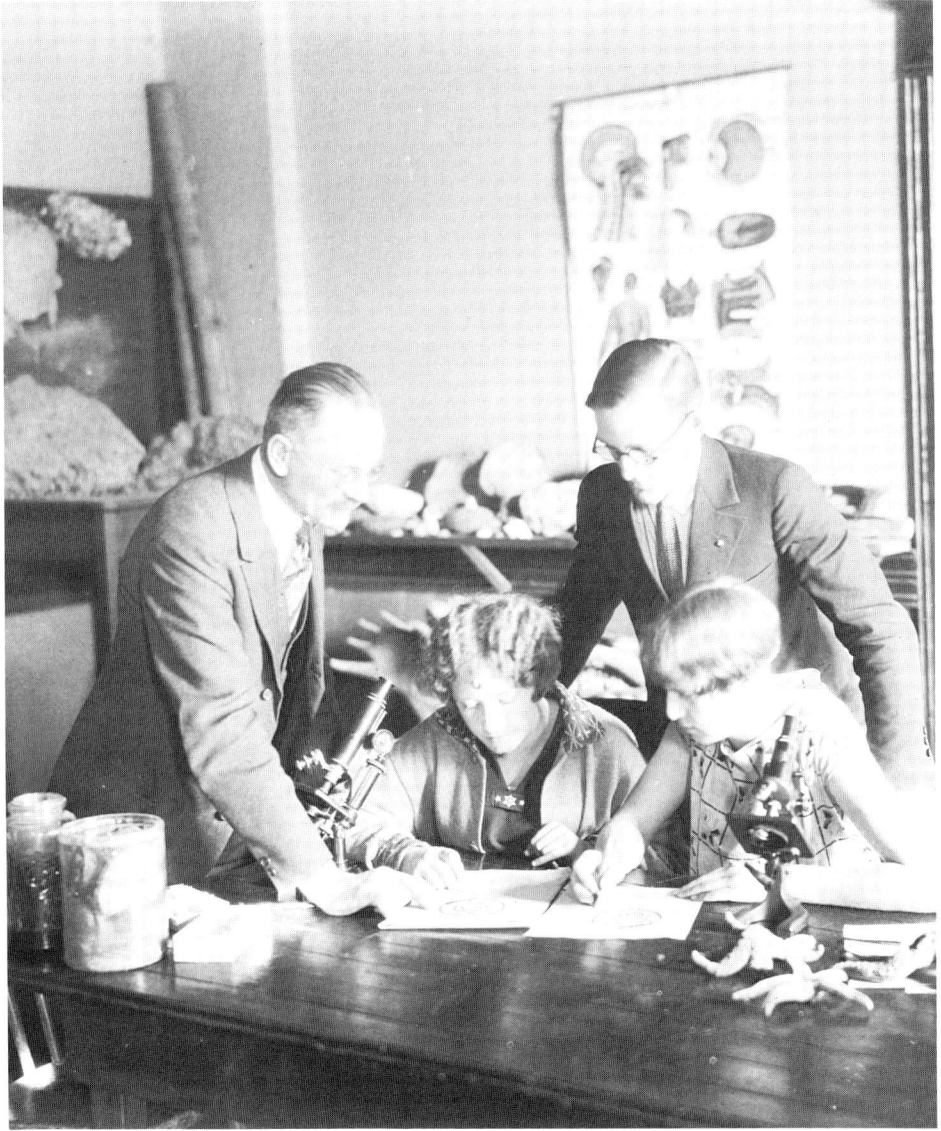

J. U. Xavier, left, instructing biology students

J. U. Xavier, Ole Stuen, and J. O. Edwards, early PLC golfers

The first Choir of the West, 1927, J. O. Edwards, center

The Philip J. Hauge family at the campus entrance, 1920s

1938 May Queen, Alice Cook, and her court

Football greats Sig Sigurdson, Earl Platt, and Marv Tommervik, late 1930s

Library reading room (now Xavier Hall), 1950

1951 debate champions Jon Ericson, left, and William Rieke, right, with T. O. H. Karl

The kiosk, late 1950s

1959 men's basketball action

Faculty Grace Blomquist (English), Anna Marn Nielsen (education), and Rhoda Young (physical education), 1960s

Gunnar Malmin, Choir of the West director, 1937-63

Robert Mortvedt, Senator Henry Jackson, and President John F. Kennedy, 1963

Lute Jerstad, 1963, after his successful climb of Mount Everest

PLU business office, early 1960s

Robert Pierson conducting an economics class, mid-1960s

Rooftop sunbathing, mid-1960s

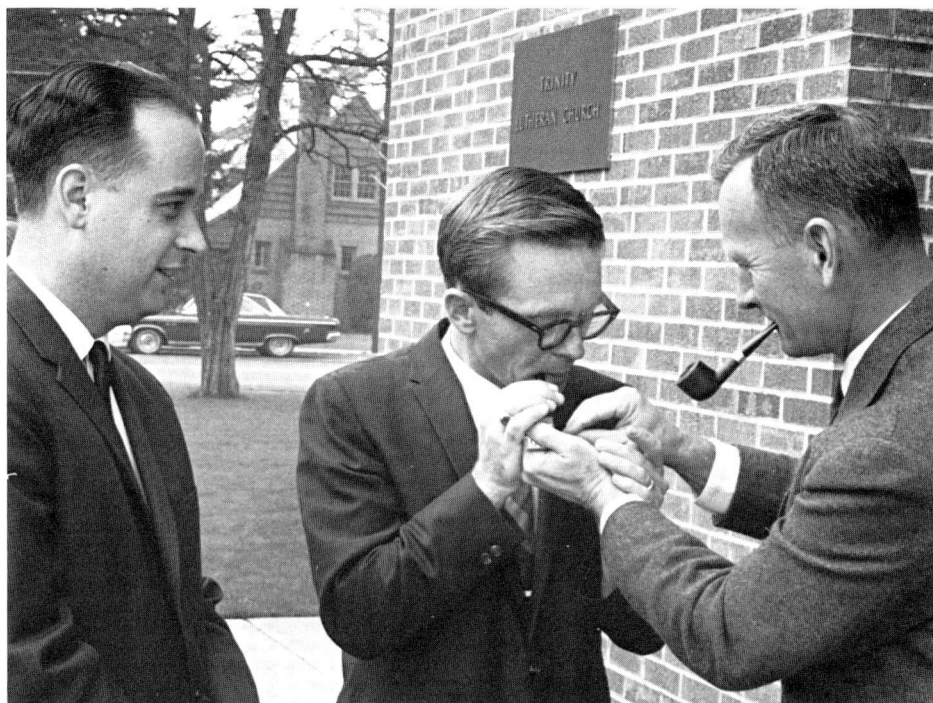

Faculty William Giddings (chemistry), Peter Ristuben (history), and Walter Schnackenberg (history)

Moving into Mortvedt Library, 1967

The archbishop of Canterbury, the Reverend Dr. Michael Ramsey, 1967

National Crisis Forum, 1970

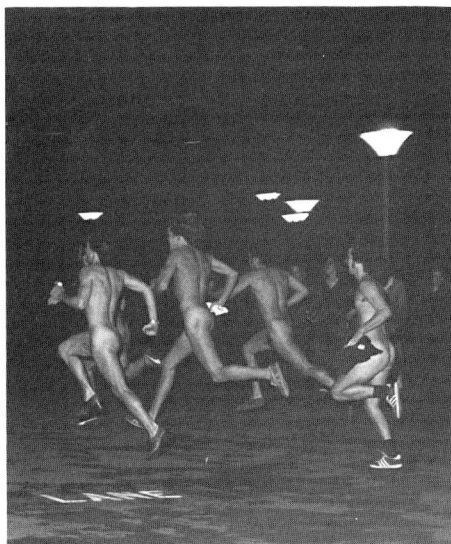
Streakers on lower campus, mid-1970s

Donald Farmer (political science),
first Regency professor, 1971

Norway's King Olaf visits PLU, 1975

Bruce Bjerke, PLU's first Rhodes scholar, 1972

Maurice Skones, Choir of the West director, 1963-83

"Frosty" Westering, head football coach since 1972

First Burlington Northern Faculty Achievement Award winners Stanley Brue (economics, left), and Stuart Bancroft (business administration, right), with President Rieke, 1987. Also honored was Paul Menzel (philosophy).

International students on campus, 1980s

The 1988 national championship women's soccer team, led by coach Colleen Hacker, far right, with Zephyr

1988-89 Fulbright scholars Grace Running, Janae Boyd, and Christian Lucky

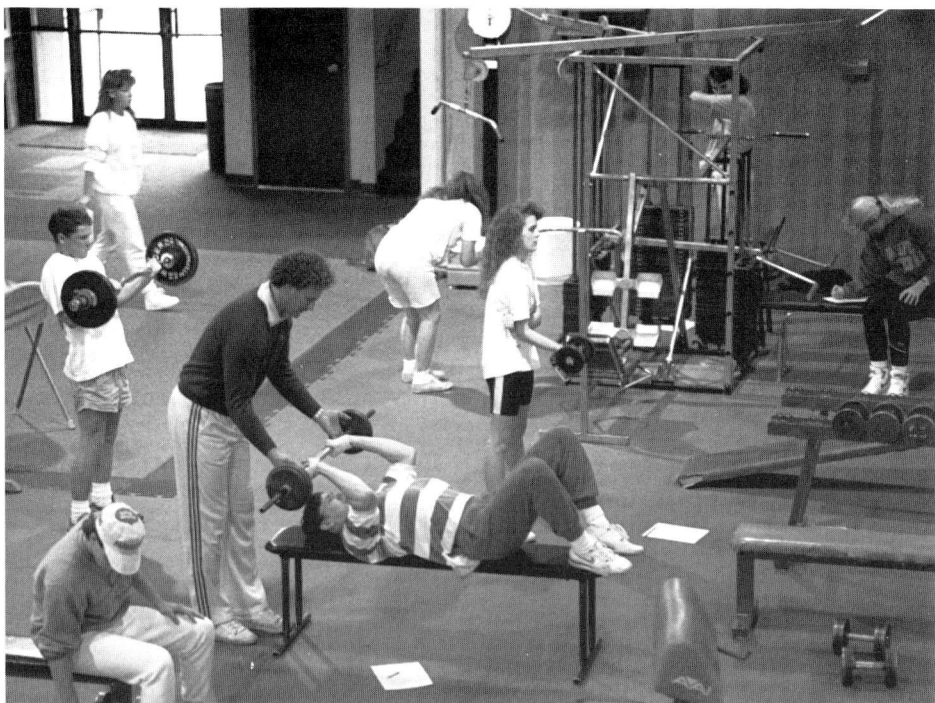

Names Fitness Center, 1988

Celebrating PLU's Scandinavian heritage, 1989

Looking to the southwest across the PLC campus (Trinity Lutheran Church in the foreground), 1938

PLC campus, looking to the west, 1954

PLU campus, looking to the southeast, 1975

9

The New University

R~OBERT~ A. M~ORTVEDT~ was born and grew up in small towns in Illinois. Both his parents were born in Norway, and his father served as a Lutheran pastor (in the Hauge Synod until 1917) for sixty years. In 1924 Mortvedt graduated *summa cum laude* from St. Olaf College, where he served as student body president and enjoyed numerous successes in debate and oratory competitions. (Another successful orator in the class of 1924 was Frederick Schiotz, future ELC and ALC president). Mortvedt undertook graduate work in English literature at Harvard University, taught at St. Olaf for several years, and ultimately received the doctorate from Harvard in 1934. His dissertation was a 472-page study of the British dramatist Thomas Morton (1764–1838). His graduate school coursework was mostly linguistic; he studied Latin, Old French, Gothic, German, Old Norse, Anglo-Saxon, and Middle English. This linguistic and oratorical training would stay with him for the rest of his life. Mortvedt taught at St. Olaf until 1937 with considerable satisfaction and success, but, troubled by graduate school debt, he grew increasingly dissatisfied with his salary. In 1937 he accepted an offer from Stephens College in Missouri and taught there until 1943. At Stephens he experimented with his teaching, wrote a book about how to study literature (*Let's Talk about Literature* [1942]), and attended a Missouri Synod congregation, where he never felt fully at home because of its antiecumenical stance.

In 1943 Mortvedt was appointed dean at the University of Kansas City. He was appointed vice president in 1948, and was acting president for a short time before he resigned in 1953 because of administrative strife. The Mortvedt family attended an Augustana Lutheran church in Kansas City and felt at home in its "ecumenical spirit."[1] Mortvedt had thus experienced much of American Lutheranism by the time he came to PLU. In 1953 he was appointed president of the Augustana Synod's Bethany College in Lindsborg, Kansas. It was in a deeply moribund condition when he arrived, but his administration helped turn the fortunes of the college around. In 1958 he became executive director of higher education for the Augustana Synod, and in 1959 he took up the same position for the United Lutheran Church in America since the two synods would soon merge together as the Lutheran Church in America (LCA). He commuted between Chicago and New York and supervised twenty-eight institutions. He decided not to continue in the position after the formation of the LCA and so was available when PLU was seeking a president in the winter of 1962.

Mortvedt was as well prepared for a Lutheran college presidency as anyone could have been, and he was ecumenical and pan-Lutheran in his understanding and sympathies. He also knew Eastvold quite well, and their relationship had been cordial over the years: Mortvedt had edited Eastvold's *Paul and Luther* in 1937, and Eastvold had tried to bring Mortvedt to PLC as chair of the English department, asking, "Why waste your time at Bethany when you can come to PLC?"[2] Mortvedt knew there were some serious problems awaiting him at the school. "I entered a situation that would demand all the tact, skill, experience and wisdom that I had accumulated over the years. . . . I was aware of the dimensions of the challenge."[3]

Mortvedt's philosophy of Christian higher education was more carefully articulated than that of any other PLU president. He had worked on it most of his adult life. The first two major addresses he gave at PLU in the fall of 1962 were distillations of that thought. The first, "Education in His Name," was given at the faculty retreat on 10 September. He talked of the long involvement of the church in education, but wondered if the church college was not now outmoded, given the growth of the large state institutions. If the church college was to be relevant, it must have a peculiar character and purpose and must make Christianity "dynamically pertinent." The state can supply education for all, but it cannot "provide an education in the name of Him whose name is above all other names!" The difference between the two kinds of education is not chiefly chapel, required religion courses, or the prohibition of social dancing, he said; rather, the Christian college must quietly demonstrate in all its relationships the fundamental commitment of its faculty, board, and administration to the "Man of the Cross." God's grace is prayed for and acknowledged at such institutions, he explained, and individual faculty would probably devote some part of each day to a period of private devotion, which would affect their teaching and the example they set. The students would know of the institution's objectives before they came. Such education would not isolate people from the world; it would instead help make the Gospel peculiarly relevant to church and nation. The Christian commitment of the faculty and staff would be basic.[4]

It was immediately clear that the new president was scholarly, strong-minded, dignified, formal, and a forceful and powerful speaker. It was equally clear that his philosophy of education was very firmly held, as the next seven years would bear out. The faculty's response to Mortvedt was enthusiastic and affirmative.

Mortvedt's inaugural address, delivered on 8 November, was entitled "In Him All Things Hold Together." Many of the same themes were reiterated. A university, he said, was a noble institution, the origins of which go back to the dawn of human desire to know, learn, and discover. He then quoted Sophocles about the wonders, as well as the complexities and limitations, of mankind:

> Wise though his plans are,
> artful beyond all dreaming,
> they carry him both to evil and to good.

The church knows that humans have minds that must be cultivated for the benefit of the church and the world; the Christian university tries to do that in a context "defined by a public avowal of faith in Jesus Christ as the only savior of the world." That is the sole important reason for the existence of this institution, he said. In conclusion, Mortvedt quoted St. Paul: "In Him all things hold together."[5]

Mortvedt was fully aware of the tension, mistrust, and difficulties that had marked the previous two years and set out to deal with the problems of the new university as quickly as possible. He set for himself and the institution a less formally stated agenda of matters that needed to be addressed. Some took longer to resolve than others. He thought the most basic problem in 1962 was that the new university clothes were too large; a clearer sense of the nature and scale of a university was needed. Further, faculty members lacked sufficient confidence, self-reliance, and academic strength. Mortvedt wanted to appoint a well-trained business manager as quickly as possible so he could be free to concentrate on educational matters. He wanted to improve the quality of chapel services to make them genuine occasions of worship, explaining that "chapel is not a forum for me or anybody else." He also decided to continue the self-study even though he was under considerable pressure to abandon it. He wanted to help improve the effectiveness of the regents' work and to streamline the rather cumbersome and ineffective academic administrative structure created in 1960. He encouraged the abandonment of the faculty senate and the creation of a more broadly based assembly-committee system of faculty governance.[6] The first years of Mortvedt's leadership were full of important changes that required considerable presidential leadership and courage—and widespread faculty effort—to accomplish. A feeling that positive steps were being taken prevailed.

Some tension and suspicion remained from the recent past, however. Some of the suspicion was related to Mortvedt's "presumed liberalism" in contrast to Eastvold's known conservatism. Mortvedt found that very curious. "In point of fact, I have always been a conservative both in theology and politics; but I was considerably more liberal than my predecessor."[7] For example, Mortvedt (and the faculty) approved social dancing within a year; Eastvold would never have done that. In another way, however, Mortvedt had developed theologically far beyond Eastvold and some faculty members long before he came to PLU. He was certainly informed about many of the latest developments in Lutheran theology. His experience at Harvard and St. Olaf, his educational work for the ULCA and the Augustana Synod, and his own growth and curiosity saw to that. He served for ten years on the Augustana Seminary board and was influenced by that small but progressive seminary faculty. He frequently crossed paths with the philosopher Paul Holmer and the theologian Joseph Sittler, two of American Lutheranism's liveliest thinkers, and they helped him crystallize his thought.[8] Mortvedt may have been "conservative" theologically, as virtually all Lutherans probably were in 1962, but he was also ecumenical and pan-Lutheran in experience and perspective and open to what was going on in Lutheran theology. With his roots in pietism, broad experience, ecumenical sensitivities, and exposure to post–World War II scholarship, he was remarkably well equipped to guide PLU in the early 1960s. PLU was not to be a bastion in the style of S. C. Eastvold, Mortvedt implied, but a dedicated Christian faculty was essential: "The unique quality of a Christian college is that it seeks to bring all knowledge within the compass of a Christian interpretation of life." Mortvedt liked to quote the Augustana Lutheran educator, Conrad Bergendoff: "A Christian college is a mission field in the continent of learning, and those who teach there are missionaries to a culture foreign to Christianity."[9]

THE 1960s

By 1962 it was clear that many of the characteristics of the 1950s "silent generation" were passing. The close identification of patriotism with piety, a by-product of the early cold war, seemed wrong-headed to many. The postwar religious revival sputtered out and revealed difficult and unanswered questions, many dating back to the early twentieth century. Intellectual life picked up momentum and the long-term impact of science, technology, naturalism, pluralism, and urban life became obvious in new and sometimes disturbing ways. Calls for change began to emerge, accompanied by a basic shift in mood. That mood shift was both intensely critical, discovering deep social and institutional dislocations, and optimistic, finding possibilities for rapid and dramatic change. The young began to mobilize, intent on achieving some of those changes and greater personal freedom. The reform-minded John XXIII was elected pope in 1958 and brought the Counter-Reformation to an end. Interfaith dialogue soon began. The key word in his pontificate seemed to be *aggiornamento* ("a bringing up to date"). The Roman Catholic John Kennedy was elected president in 1960, promising to get things going again. The civil rights movement developed momentum, culminating in the great demonstrations in Selma in March and April of 1965. The Black Power movement emerged a year later, and at about the same time the call for student power was heard. A generation gap of rather ominous proportions was opening; youth were regularly warned not to trust anyone over thirty.

All these movements and developments were exacerbated by the war in southeast Asia and the draft that accompanied it. By 1969 half a million soldiers were there, and American opinion concerning the war was badly divided. As Sydney Ahlstrom remarked: "The decade of the sixties was a time...when the old foundations of national confidence, patriotic idealism, moral traditionalism, and even the historic Judeo-Christian theism were awash."[10] For many, religion was irrelevant to the country's most serious problems, and some saw the church as an obstacle to change. By the end of the decade came a cry for a secular and demythologized interpretation of the Bible and Christianity for a world "come of age," and some were even ready to announce that "God was dead." It was a very trying, but exciting, time for a university with strong historic ties to Lutheranism that was supposed to be "a mission field in the continent of learning."

Mortvedt's first important decision was to appoint a business manager. His choice for the position was A. Dean Buchanan, a young California accountant who had just finished a four-year term as business manager for Augustana Lutheran missionary institutions in Tanzania. Mortvedt's service began on 1 August; Buchanan's began two days later. Buchanan was able and enormously hard-working; he immediately took control of all business and financial activity—finding the "most astounding practices" when he arrived—and allowed Mortvedt to turn his attention to educational issues. Buchanan proved to be especially capable in the complex activity of financing and orchestrating the nonstop building that marked the decade.

The chapel format was also changed by the end of September. It became more liturgical, a chancel choir was added, and bulletins replaced the spoken announcements. A distinction was clearly drawn between chapel and convocation. Social dancing was discussed, but it had to be approached with "great deliberation," Mortvedt said, because it was controversial and needed "sympathetic insight."[11] The choir's 1963 summer tour of Europe was approved: twenty-eight concerts would be sung in Norway, as well as others in Denmark, Germany, Switzerland, and France. It would be Gunnar Malmin's last major tour with the choir.

The *Mooring Mast* continued to be full of editorials and letters about the relationship of Christianity to learning at PLU and whether the Christian presence was growing or diminishing. That discussion would continue all through the decade. There were complaints that the student body officers were "mere puppets of the administration" and anger at the "if you don't like it here, leave" philosophy sometimes advanced by student leaders.

By February there was a reconstruction of the cumbersome 1960 administrative structure that had been plagued by too many deans and too much conflicting authority. The number of deans was reduced to two (one for the College of Arts and Sciences, and one for the professional schools), and former deans became directors. According to Mortvedt, "this arrangement greatly elevates the importance of the College of Arts and Sciences, around which the program of the university is logically constructed."[12] Nine-month contracts were also approved, to great rejoicing from the faculty. Contracts had been for ten months, requiring faculty to teach one session of summer school. That arrangement was eliminated and summer school was handled separately, but without a reduction in salaries. The change required careful financial planning, but Mortvedt and Buchanan were determined to make it work.

Lawrence J. Hauge was appointed the first full-time director of alumni affairs in 1963. He was a 1950 alumnus, a Tacoma school administrator, and the son of Philip E. Hauge. Emma Ramstad had labored in a part-time capacity for the previous nine years to organize alumni activities and had accomplished a great deal. Eastvold had never been very sympathetic, however, and had not provided an adequate budget and planning. Mortvedt thought the need to cultivate and serve the alumni was pressing; problems and some disaffection had to be addressed. For example, in 1960 only 8 percent of the alumni participated in annual giving to the school, compared to Whitworth's 14 percent, St. Olaf's 25 percent, and Reed College's 38 percent. Alumni disgruntlement had been discussed in the Fund Fulfillment Corporation's reports.

By the end of May a great deal had been accomplished. Religious life and chapel seemed healthy, Mortvedt observed, but he felt there was still too much extramural candor: "certain individuals are being indiscreet or unethical in discussing various problems with students, with each other, and with people outside the University family."[13] A ten-year development plan would soon be unveiled. The formal statement of objectives, first submitted to the board in the spring of 1962, then modified slightly by the committee after consultation with Mortvedt, was approved by the faculty on 20 April 1963, despite continued opposition from some members of the religion department. The board approved the statement in May. More than twenty-five years later, that statement continues to play an important role in university life.

Addressing another persisting issue on campus, the board followed the lead of its student life committee and the ALC, which asserted that social dancing did not cause new problems on campuses and was not a moral issue, and resolved to allow social dancing. The first approved social dance on the PLU campus was held in September 1963. It was well attended. English professor Herbert Ranson, a staunch defender of freedom and individuality, was seen whirling around the floor; he said he would not have missed the dance for anything.

President John Kennedy made a memorable visit to Tacoma on 27 September 1963. The stimulus for the visit came from Clayton Peterson, then Mortvedt contacted Senator Henry Jackson, who thought the event might be possible if a suitable site could be secured. After some planning it was decided to enlarge the event and share sponsorship with the University of Puget Sound, a relatively uncommon bit of cooperation between the two schools for that time. Cheney Stadium—the Tacoma minor league baseball stadium—was selected as the site and weeks of planning followed. The crowd was estimated at twenty-five thousand. Both faculties, wearing full academic regalia, formed two long lines from the stadium's entrance to the party platform. Kennedy arrived from Astoria, Oregon, by helicopter and was greeted by President Mortvedt and President R. Franklin Thompson of UPS, and then escorted through the faculty lines. He greeted faculty members warmly and shook many hands. His prepared speech was shelved when he saw the large number of students in the audience, and he spoke extemporaneously. It was an extraordinary day, which those present would never forget. When less than two months later on 22 November Kennedy was assassinated, the campus went into shock for days. For many, much of the attractiveness and promise of the decade seemed to disappear with that single event.

Alumnus Luther Jerstad was honored by the university in October 1963. Jerstad was one of the first three Americans to climb Mt. Everest in a historic climb the previous May. President Kennedy had hosted a reception for the climbers shortly after they returned, and they had received the Hubbard Medal from the National Geographic Society. Jerstad spoke and showed slides of the climb at a PLU convocation in his honor that was called "Bivouac at the Top of the World." The slides were spectacular and the speech gripping. In May 1964 Jerstad was the first recipient of the Distinguished Alumnus Award.

In the spring of 1964 some of the unresolved tensions and disagreements of the 1960–62 period resurfaced. Some disagreement in the faculty continued, of course, and the earlier charges, countercharges, and broken friendships were not easily forgotten or healed. A former regent, John Sather, continued to make groundless but often malicious charges about PLU and its new president. That was unpleasant, but Mortvedt took it in stride, determined not to be partisan in any way. The immediate cause of the spring 1964 explosion was requirements in the School of Education, which had dominated PLU for a long time. Dean Hauge, Anna Marn Nielsen, and, since 1960, John Amend had worked hard to maintain that dominance. Other portions of the university wanted educational policy (and policies governing teacher training) established more broadly by the entire university, however. That preference had surfaced in the self-study reports and reflected current national reforms. As part of the ongoing self-study process all sections of the university were asked to scrutinize their programs for ways to reform and reduce curriculum, if possible. Faculty in education refused. They were satisfied with their program and viewed suggestions about teacher education from other parts of the university as attacks.

By the spring of 1964 the educational policies committee brought a half-dozen proposals for reductions in the badly inflated education requirements, in particular eliminating a five-credit course in alternative student teaching. Discussions were heated, but the senate approved the recommendations. Amend was furious and Nielsen distraught. They tried a power play; both resigned (they were joined by a junior member of the education faculty, June Broeckel, a daughter of former regent John Sather) even though they had signed contracts. Mortvedt did not accept the bluff. He accepted Amend's resignation, but tried to talk the other two out of resigning because he thought they had been badly counseled and did not understand fully what they were doing. They persisted. Anna Marn Nielsen's resignation was a tragedy; she was much beloved. Her life centered around PLU students and activities and the School of Education, but she would not agree that establishing the teacher education program was the responsibility of the entire faculty.

These resignations and two earlier ones—those of Kristen Solberg and John Kuethe, for quite different reasons—along with Sather's charges, came up at the PLU Corporation meeting in June. Gossip-mongers whispered that a purge was underway and that irreligion was triumphing at PLU. Mortvedt met the irresponsible charges with a forceful and frequently angry speech. He insisted that he was not trying to destroy the School of Education, nor was he opposed to the professional schools. Nor was a power-hungry block trying to dominate the president and take over the university. "To the best of my knowledge, the resigning teachers have never attempted to correct the distorted picture that has been drawn. Their loyalty appears to have been to the School of Education rather than to the University."[14] That was the end of it. The corporation accepted Mortvedt's explanation; he could be very forceful when he needed to be. Kenneth Johnston was appointed director of the School of Education in the summer of 1964 and served until 1987. The school remained an important part of the university during these years, but it did not dominate as it had in the forties and fifties.

By 1964 most of Eastvold's strongest faculty supporters had gone. William Strunk and John Kuethe chose to go to California Lutheran College. Kristen Solberg resigned for personal reasons, and John Amend and Anna Marn Nielsen resigned in a power play. Knute Lee did not receive tenure, and his religion department colleagues Paul Vigness and Kelmer Roe retired in 1965 and 1967, respectively. Of Eastvold's allies, only Ted Karl remained. He retired in 1978.

BUILDING

The carefully prepared ten-year development program was announced in March 1964. This "Program for Long-Range University Specifics" was called the PLUS program. Its model was the kind of planning emerging out of Stanford University, and its foundation was the earlier self-study analysis. Slightly earlier a thorough investigation by Quinton Engineers of Los Angeles had resulted in a master plan for campus development and a landscape projection by Richard Haag Associates of Seattle. Both plans were incorporated into the scheme. The PLUS program cited nine achievable specifics, including a new library, and a $16.5 million goal: $14 million for capital developments and $2.5 million for endowment. The plan was followed meticulously and virtually every goal, except the endowment funding, was achieved, some ahead of schedule. At least one building project was underway every year Mortvedt was president.

A new library was essential to the PLUS program and to Mortvedt's thinking, but a rapidly expanding student population meant dormitories had to take first priority. Federal loans to build dormitories were available, and Dean Buchanan worked hard to establish good rapport with the Housing and Urban Development (HUD) officials in Seattle, which quickly paid dividends. Two-thirds of his time was soon devoted to building projects. Long-time county commissioner Harry Sprinker—a Parkland resident—played an influential role in the building successes. When Buchanan would visit him with plans that needed approval, Sprinker would put his arm around Buchanan's shoulder and walk him into the planning commission offices saying "give him whatever he wants."[15] Pflueger Hall was finished in 1963, Foss Hall in 1965, Stuen Hall in 1966, and Tingelstad and Ordal halls in 1967. The building boom provided adequate on-campus living space for the student body in the seventies and eighties. Other buildings were also constructed during the decade. Columbia Center—a dining hall and golf course professional shop—was finished in 1963. A large enclosed swimming pool was finished in 1965; student pledges, beginning in 1958, provided the funds for that facility.

In November 1964 the library drive was approved but delayed by the dormitory building. Fundraising went slowly and was frustrating. The faculty pledged $75,000 and the alumni goal was set at $250,000, but large private gifts were scarce and federal money proved elusive. Meanwhile, the old library was becoming more and more inadequate. Finally, a $250,000 gift from the Tenzler Foundation of Tacoma—the largest single gift in the history of the institution up to that time—provided the breakthrough. It was soon followed by the approval of a $571,780 grant from the Higher Education Facilities Act. The financing of what turned out to be a $1.7 million building was complete. The board unanimously decided it should be called the Robert A. L. Mortvedt Library. That was appropriate. He had seen the importance of the library from the beginning and battled to get it built. Mortvedt thanked the board for the honor "from the bottom of [my] heart." Yale theologian and historian Dr. Jaroslav Pelikan spoke at the dedication and called the library "a hospital for the soul."

Many plans were considered for moving the 140,000 volumes from the old library into the new, but they were all either too slow or too expensive. Finally it was decided that faculty and students would carry the books and periodicals across campus and deposit them on the correct shelves in the new building. Student Jim Ross was the principal architect of the plan. On Friday, 2 December, the old library closed at noon and the staff put large rubber bands around bundles of books and carefully prepared signs and directions for the move. On Monday, 5 December, classes were cancelled; people streamed into the old library, picked up bundles, and marched in a continuous line to the new library, where staff members shelved the volumes in the correct location. The scheme proved efficient, and everyone who helped felt a part of a unique moment in university life. Mortvedt Library was ready for business Tuesday morning. Two hundred forty pounds of rubber bands were used. There is no record of how much Brown and Haley candy, provided by librarian Frank Haley, was consumed.

Two more major buildings were constructed or planned late in the decade. Olson Auditorium—named for Cliff Olson—with physical education and athletic facilities and a large multipurpose auditorium was built with a federal grant, a low interest federal loan, and fund solicitation in Tacoma. Tacoma engineer, businessman, and long-time regent Tom Anderson served as general chair of the solicitation campaign. The University Center was also planned and financed in the late sixties but not completed until 1970, Mortvedt had retired. It was funded through a loan, student pledges, and an ALC educational fund appeal called LIFE (Lutheran Ingathering for Education) that was intended to bring one major building to each ALC college and seminary campus. The building activity of the sixties, which would have been substantially more difficult—and probably impossible—a decade later, made the growth and development of the seventies and eighties possible. It was a very great accomplishment.

New Faculty

Some important faculty additions and administrative changes occurred in the middle of the decade. Carrol DeBower, a determined faculty rights activist with a Missouri Synod background, joined the School of Education in 1964, the same year that church historian and former Augustana Synod member Emmet Eklund came as chair of the religion department. Eklund's presence ensured that PLU was to be broadly Lutheran in the style of the twenties and thirties, not in the narrower style of the forties and fifties. That stance was broadened even further with the hiring of Missouri Synod pastor and professor Curtis Huber as a member of the philosophy department, also in 1964. Huber had resigned from the Missouri Synod's Concordia Seminary in Springfield, Illinois, in a debate over theological issues (and a style of administration) that would soon push the Missouri Synod into fierce, internecine combat and produce many casualties and refugees. PLU became the first ALC or LCA educational institution to hire sizeable numbers of faculty members and administrators from the Missouri Synod and to welcome refugees from the savage struggle. Since 1964 PLU has hired a president, academic vice president, provost, assistant to the provost, vice president for student life, vice president for business and finance, vice president for development, chief librarian, university pastor, director of the Center for Human Organization in Changing Environments (CHOICE), and faculty members in art, religion, philosophy, education, mathematics, and music with roots in the Missouri Synod. Not all had cut ties over disputes with the Missouri Synod, but many had. The university was enriched by the infusion of talent, and its pan-Lutheran position—dating from the twenties—was strengthened. Some controversy over the nature and extent of authority and administrative style as well as occasional charges of a "Missouri Mafia" emerged as well. And contributions were not unmixed: Huber proved to be a provocative and sometimes contentious teacher and colleague but always a creative source of ideas for the institution.

Gunnar Malmin retired as choir director after the successful 1963 European tour (he continued to teach Latin and Norwegian), and Maurice Skones was appointed chair of the music department and director of the Choir of the West. Skones, a native of Montana, was a 1948 graduate of Concordia College in Minnesota, where he played football and basketball and sang in the choir under Paul Christiansen. He brought that midwestern Lutheran style of a capella music sung with control and precision to PLU, as well as stylistic changes and developments of his own. It was announced in October that the choir would present the world premiere of Hungarian composer Miklas Rosza's major vocal piece, "The Vanities of Life." Rosza, a friend of Skones, was famous as a composer of music for Hollywood movies (*Quo Vadis*, *Ben Hur*, *El Cid*, *King of Kings*), for which he had won three Academy Awards. The premiere was part of the 23 October 1965 Homecoming concert. It was a critical success. Afterward Rosza commented: "I am overwhelmed at how they sang. I had not imagined the works to be performed by memory. . . . Mr. Skones is a true choral genius. . . . This is one of the greatest choirs in the nation, with precision second to none."[16]

Philip Hauge retired from his administrative duties in 1965 and, after a sabbatical leave, taught psychology until 1968. His forty-eight years of teaching and administrative service is the longest in the history of the institution. Administratively, Hauge was replaced by two people. Thomas H. Langevin was named academic vice president. He was to coordinate all academic work on campus and direct the graduate program, evening courses, and summer school. Langevin was a member of the Missouri Synod who had spent the previous year as research project director for that body's board of higher education. In 1963–64 he studied higher education at the University of Michigan under a Carnegie Foundation grant. Langevin would find it relatively difficult to work with a strong-minded president; he resigned in 1969 to become president of Capital University in Columbus, Ohio. Richard Moe was appointed dean of the professional and graduate studies. He had taught in the public schools and been professor of education and, from 1959 to 1964, dean of instruction at Waldorf Junior College in Iowa. In the year prior to coming to PLU he had been director of secondary education at Augustana College in Illinois.

Erich Knorr retired as dean of the College of Arts and Sciences in 1966 and was replaced by Charles Anderson, the able and energetic chair of the chemistry department. Mortvedt wanted to appoint a dean from within the faculty to help give the faculty confidence in itself. Two new vice president positions were created that same year—overseeing student affairs and university relations—and there was much talk through the rest of the decade about the role of the "central administration" (the president, four vice presidents, and two deans). Many faculty members thought too much emphasis had been placed on administration and too little emphasis on faculty activity. Those concerns would surface in the struggle for the faculty constitution. Mortvedt replied that he did not feel he had developed the administration in any inappropriate way, although he was disappointed that the older faculty had failed to provide adequate leadership.[17]

Meanwhile, campus activities and concerns provided diversions. In a mock presidential election in 1964, Lyndon Johnson defeated Barry Goldwater 401–323, the first time a Democrat had defeated a Republican in a mock presidential election at PLU. After considerable discussion the athletic team's name was changed from the Gladiators to the Knights in 1960, and the 1964 football team, under coach Roy Carlson, won the Evergreen Conference championship. In 1965 PLU joined other similarly sized private schools in Washington, Oregon, and Idaho in the Northwest Conference. Its eligibility standards were higher than in any other conference in the NAIA. It was hoped cooperative academic and cultural activity would follow. Editorials and columns in the *Mooring Mast* continued to be lively. They discussed complaints about social life, intellectual timidity, "too much Lutheranism" (critics believed there was not enough thought and investigation, just passive acceptance), and compulsory chapel. Talk on the latter topic would continue for the next three years. Two students were dismissed from the university in April 1965 for maiming two Point Defiance Zoo eagles. They had broken into the cage one night and had taken tail feathers from the eagles to make an authentic Indian headdress. An arctic owl had died of fright during the eagle plucking, so PLU students raised money to bring another owl to the zoo. A year earlier, one of the students had been discovered digging up a pioneer cemetery grave looking for an authentic skull.

THE PRESSURES OF CHANGE

From the middle of the decade onward explosive and disorienting change increasingly dominated American life. Pressures of various kinds—many of them new to colleges and universities—emerged; some were present on virtually all campuses, others were unique to PLU. Together they produced a charged atmosphere. In the midst of all the calls for change, and sometimes for revolution, it was often difficult to distinguish what was enduring from what was transitory. Heated controversies and major disagreements between administration, faculty, and students (in various combinations) each year seemed to reach near-crisis proportions late each spring. Among the issues that became heated were *Mooring Mast* editorial policy; compulsory chapel; in loco parentis rules, especially as they discriminated against women; the faculty constitution; and the ongoing discussion of Christianity and education. Calendar and curricular reform were also addressed. The backdrop was filled with scenes of Vietnam, the draft, peace marches, the use of drugs, assassinations, demonstrations, and "God is dead" theology. President Mortvedt did not like some of the developments and fought them with all the verbal skill, determination, and administrative power he possessed. The faculty was divided on many issues, united on others, and did not always agree with the president. Students became more active and determined than at any other time in PLU history.

President Mortvedt was concerned about the nature of campus religious life by 1966. He told the board that it was becoming "continuously more difficult" to maintain an atmosphere conducive to vital personal and community religious life. The students and faculty represented a broad cross-section of American life—deciding to become a university had caused that, he thought—and the growing secularism in America and decline of the influence of the church were "sobering."[18] Moreover, not all students and faculty agreed with the institution's spiritual goals. In this the statement of objectives was of "critical and enduring importance. . . . Anyone who is not basically sympathetic or is overtly antagonistic ought not sojourn long or permanently abide among us." He was also concerned about student restiveness. He did not think it was their prerogative to define the objectives of the university, however much could be learned from them.[19]

The university celebrated its seventy-fifth anniversary during the 1965-66 academic year with a number of activities, including the publication of a brief but lively history, *The Lamp and the Cross*, written by Walter Schnackenberg. The *Mooring Mast* used the occasion of the anniversary to stress the need for careful institutional definition and the translation of ideals into reality. Editor Neil Waters, perhaps the most thoughtful and determined of the decade's able and reform-minded editors, asked if PLU was just a place where parents sent children for protection? He concluded that the institution had not yet resolved the issue.[20]

A heated and sharply worded exchange between President Mortvedt and the *Mooring Mast* followed the 22 April issue. It soon enrolled substantial numbers of faculty and students and simmered unpleasantly until the end of the semester. Mortvedt objected to a photograph, a column, and an editorial in the 22 April issue. A news article about off-campus drinking was accompanied by a picture of a beer mug and the caption: "My Cup Runneth Over." The beer mug had been filled with soap suds for the photograph. Mortvedt thought the caption was in very bad taste. The editorial, "On Senioritis"—trying to be provocative, as the *Mooring Mast* was wont to do, and capturing some of the anger that was present at PLU—suggested, without much research, that graduating seniors did not "give a d—n about this place and wanted out: out, where there won't be 'some idiot' telling us what to do all the time; out where we can listen to two or three consecutive sentences without hearing the name of God mentioned-one way or another...." The column was a gadfly attack on provincialism and small-town attitudes. It included some rather careless references to sex, a brief discussion about the pleasures of chablis, and a call for critical thought and discussion. The column was clumsily written, but it was passionate and antiparochial at a time when the school was still quite parochial. The conclusion was offensive to many: "Of course a few pregnancies might result during this program before it is discovered that babies don't happen from sitting in the bathtub too long, and a few waywards may end up enjoying a cold beer without feeling penitent. . . ."

The president was white with rage at the picture and articles. He called in the writers, editor, and advisor, and a heated two-hour session followed. No agreement was reached; the writers told him what they were trying to say and wrote clarifications in the next issue, but the president wanted a "genuinely thoughtful admission of error," so he wrote a long letter to the paper expressing his concerns.

I was appalled by the obvious bad taste, the harshness of the strictures against individuals and groups, and the profoundly disturbing callousness exhibited in the article concerned with sex and maturity. . . . *I object.* I do not think it is appropriate to express such views in a student newspaper at PLU. These views are against our principles and abhorrent to our taste. They put the University in a very unfair and unfavorable light. . . . If the editor continues to show the bad judgment exhibited in the articles discussed, he is definitely putting the freedom of the press in jeopardy. We have gladly given freedom, but expect responsibility and good taste.[21]

A rush of letters from both faculty and students appeared; the first week all were critical of the article and column. Opinion evened out the following week, and one faculty member lauded the off-campus drinking article's spirit of nonconformity. He was hammered by President Mortvedt the following week, but then the preponderance of letters tilted favorably toward the reporters' intentions, if not always their literal texts. The exchange of letters—arguably the most heated and interesting in the history of the *Mooring Mast*—continued until the end of the semester without resolution of the issues. The sloppy reasoning and writing probably needed to be criticized, just as student concerns needed to be supported. A stern but even-handed presidential lecture was undoubtedly in order. Whether the crimes were as serious as charged and whether it was wise, in a hot and troubled spring, to go public with the dispute is another matter. It dragged on a painfully long time and created a great deal of anger and frustration on all sides. The confrontation seemed both to summarize and to focus many of the widespread student concerns.

Editor Neil Waters later reflected on the whole matter:

It is hard to think myself back into that time, when the issues seemed both clear and critical. I thought then that we were fighting censorship and hypocrisy. On reflection I still think so. But then I saw these as manifestations of evil. Now I think they are characteristics of a recurrent phase in the life of many institutions. . . . They show up in confusing times, when the ideas and ideals that once provided common purpose to an institution's constituents seem less and less important to more and more people. Mortvedt . . . believed that at PLU the marriage between Athens and Jerusalem should be a happier union than was possible in 1966–67. I think most students at PLU in 1966–67 still supported the Vietnam war, in a lukewarm sort of way, but the possibility of being drafted on graduation and sent to Vietnam for fuzzily expressed reasons meant that for many of us, some very grown-up decisions were in order. In that atmosphere Mortvedt's Jerusalem-derived idea that the University should act *in loco parentis* was anathema, as were all its manifestations. . . . The protected world that that evoked was at odds with the world we expected to face, either in Vietnam or in an America torn by civil rights strife. Many of us wanted less protection, more inquiry, and for a few this meant more Athens, less Jerusalem.[22]

On 13 May the paper, in a "Friday Forum" supplement, presented a discussion of "God is dead" theology. A number of these forums were included during the year, and they provided thoughtful discussion about important issues. They were often very good. Whatever the merits of the 22 April issue, the *Mooring Mast* was thoughtfully edited and often very well written during these years. The 13 May issue had articles about Dietrich Bonhoeffer, Bishop James Pike, James Robinson's *Honest to God*, and much more. It was very well done. President Mortvedt picked up on it—and quoted one of the writers—in his baccalaureate speech. He railed at the "death of God" theologians and critics of religion. "I get a little impatient with the petulant critics who continuously find fault with churchgoers and their simple Christian piety and good manners and conventional morality." He concluded that there is no guarantee we can keep God alive at PLU, but the great majority of us will try.[23]

The next heated issue to arise was compulsory chapel. Well-attended and meaningful chapel exercises were central to Mortvedt's philosophy of Christian higher education. Chapel should be a pacemaker for university life. Few faculty disagreed about the importance of chapel, but many were less convinced about the necessity of compulsory chapel. The students became increasingly militant in their opposition to compulsory chapel. Part of the problem was defused by the size of the student body. Eastvold Chapel was too small to hold everyone. Various alternatives were tried, but in September 1966 it was decided chapel would be compulsory for fresh-men and sophomores in Eastvold; juniors and seniors would go across the street to Trinity, where no attendance would be taken. The issue did not die down, however. In October 1967 a voluntary chapel petition circulated and received four hundred signatures. It was carefully written and put in the context of the statement of objectives: "voluntary chapel is a frontier, an untapped frontier of Luther's spirit of free, personal search for religious truth and belief."[24] Two or three letters about chapel appeared in almost every issue of the *Mooring Mast*.

The 1968–69 ASPLU president, Steven Morrison, remembered the situation this way:

> As a pre-seminary student, calling for an end to compulsory chapel was a position not readily arrived at ... my concern arose primarily from the rather intense negative atmosphere which attended the services.... What had arisen at this point was utter indifference and apathy. Within that setting the ministry of worship is hard-pressed to survive. . . . Talking, studying, sleeping, flirting, and clowning were commonplace ... we were seeking to "kill" compulsory so "chapel" could live.[25]

Mortvedt knew the policy could not be maintained much longer, but he fought as long as he could with letters, memorandums, speeches, and administrative authority. Tensions and concerns on campus, which had surfaced in the *Mooring Mast* controversy and continued with the chapel disagreement, were heightened by increasing preoccupation with Vietnam and the draft, new attacks on campus rules, the first dismissals of students for drug use, and some expressions of student power. It was a very trying time for universities.

In January 1968 Mortvedt reported to the regents on "The Current Temper of the University." The situation was pretty good, he concluded; there was no violence and no destruction, unlike what was happening in many places. "There has, however, been a continuous state of tension, sometimes needlessly aggravated by a few students and a few members of the faculty. This is a source of concern." The prevailing mood of a small minority continues to be perpetual criticism, he remarked, despite the enormous strides taken. As for chapel, he thought the record of voluntary attendance was "deeply disappointing"; neither faculty nor students had made creative efforts to make it work. Discipline played a role in every aspect of life; could it be absent from religion? "Freedom alone is the dominant demand—freedom to do as one pleases, not freedom to obey or do what is right." Personal freedom alone cannot govern conduct, he asserted; PLU will not become that kind of institution. The stress on student power was perhaps the most disturbing element: students could participate in campus decisions, but student power was intolerable.[26] The president felt sorely beleaguered and thought his deeply held beliefs about Christian higher education were under continuous attack. The faculty respected the president and supported him in many matters, but it was honestly divided on some issues, especially that of chapel.

In October 1968 the chapel policy was changed to "positive voluntarism." Mortvedt wrote that some would feel something very important had been lost that "possibly can never again be recovered." The kind of discipline he said he found essential for his own life was no longer accepted as either necessary or desirable by a great many thoughtful and responsible people. He concluded that he had struggled and prayed ceaselessly in his six years to make chapel work, and that he would continue to do so. Chapel had been part of the PLU experience since 1894, compulsory since 1952. But this was the beginning of another era; although no one knew what would happen, the vast majority of the faculty and students thought the right decision had been made.

FACULTY GOVERNANCE

Formal discussion of the faculty constitution in April and May 1968 produced additional heat and disagreement in an already difficult and troubled time. Faculty handbooks had been published since the fifties; by the sixties they were quite extensive, describing the committee system and listing qualifications and responsibilities for faculty members and a wide range of administrators. Faculty handbooks were not constitutions, however. Given the ideas, concerns, and confidence developing from the self-study and the atmosphere of democratization and reform of the late sixties, it is not hard to understand why the faculty addressed constitutional questions. It is also understandable that it went beyond the boundaries of what a conservative and traditional president and board of regents would tolerate. The 1968 constitution was not utopian, but it was written from a faculty perspective. It was first called the University Constitution, producing a great deal of flak. The faculty committee that drew up the new constitution published the results of its labors on 25 April 1968. The committee included James Davis as chair, George Arbaugh, Larry Eggan, Donald Farmer, Lucille Johnson, Robert Pierson, and Walter Schnackenberg.

The committee members included a "Statement of Philosophy" that described their constitutional thinking. Carefully reasoned, it described legal ownership, the role of the regents, and the necessary policy-making role of the faculty:

> Since the University exists for educational purposes, the policies which govern the affairs of the University are basically educational policies. It is for this reason that the faculty must exercise its delegated role as a primary policy-making body in the University. In these circumstances, the sanction which the regents give to faculty recommendations is commonly a formal matter.

All questions with policy implications—finance, property, building, and the like—"are within the purview of the faculty and should be considered prior to the establishing of a course of action." The frequently drawn distinction between board, faculty, and administration was not drawn that tightly by the constitution; it described instead a broadly supervisory board and a faculty, with the president as its first member. The president received authority from both the board and the faculty. Administrators, appointed by the president after consultation with the faculty and approval by the board, were to provide leadership and direction and to "relieve the faculty of a myriad of essential functions." Their chief purpose should be to "cooperate with faculty policy."[27]

After observing the proper process of hearings and special meetings, the faculty enthusiastically approved the document on 17 May 1968. Dozens of hostile amendments were advanced by Mortvedt and other administrators in hopes of vitiating the document, but when Mortvedt saw the extent of faculty support he turned to the board instead. A subcommittee of the board had been working comfortably with the faculty committee, but the entire board was less supportive. Since the new constitution had to be squared with the university corporation articles and by-laws, the board held the trump cards. The board chair, Earl Eckstrom, wrote that in his opinion "this committee has gone far afield from the area in which they should appropriately involve themselves."[28] Mortvedt told the board the document needed revising. "We must be aware of the fact that throughout the country students and faculty are grasping overtly for power. What we need, therefore, is careful, thoughtful study and change."[29] Years later he recalled that he had been concerned about the faculty wasting time with the details of governance that they should devote to teaching.[30]

The faculty—and certainly the faculty committee—did not agree. Committee member and political science chair Donald Farmer saw the constitution as an attempt to create a government of laws, not men. Decisions will be made about academic questions, he said. The regents have legal power, he acknowledged, but they should not run the university or make decisions about academic matters in a day-by-day fashion. They are not educators. The choice, then, was to let either the administrators or the faculty—collectively and collegially—do it. Farmer and the committee did not like the prospect of one person running the institution; presidential power without constitutional limitations was dangerous, as numerous examples in the recent past had demonstrated. Other, more practical, questions the committee addressed included resolving who should preside at faculty meetings. The Fund Fulfillment Corporation in 1961 had recommended it not be the president; so did the committee in 1968. It was thought meetings would run more expeditiously with a faculty member as chair. This was a policy for the decades ahead, but it was also a response to Mortvedt's leadership style. His hearing loss sometimes made discussions difficult, and he was prone to give long sermonlike commentaries about topics being discussed. That was not appropriate. Mortvedt seemed to take offense at this and other proposed changes. According to Farmer, the committee did not want to offend Mortvedt, nor was the whole enterprise an overt "power grab." No matter. Dilatory administration-board tactics delayed the implementation of the document until the early seventies and its final adoption for almost ten years. Farmer estimated that only 25 to 30 percent of the original document was finally adopted, and he noted that the final version was somewhat out of balance because of the parts lopped off and the long delay.[31]

Which party was "right" in this struggle depends on one's perspective. Unfortunate misunderstandings and debates about the origin of university authority and whether it "ascends" or "descends" have been going on for centuries. The importance of the rule of law continues to be an important element in American life, however, and the centrality of collegiality at an institution like PLU cannot be gainsaid. It is at least arguable that the university would have been better off with a fully articulated faculty constitution that firmly established the rule of law and collegiality. It is never easy to give up power, however, and, for better or for worse, neither president nor regents were ready to share authority more broadly with the faculty. Descending authority prevailed.

ACCOMPLISHMENTS

Important celebrations, accomplishments, and new beginnings mark the end of the decade, as well as tensions and disagreements. Some of what happened continues to shape university life. Vice President Hubert Humphrey visited campus on 29 September 1966 and spoke to an overflow crowd in Memorial Gymnasium. The Associated Press reported that he received a "warm and noisy welcome" and the mostly student crowd "loved him." He responded in kind. Three members of the class of 1951 had by then been elected to state office: Jason Boe to the Oregon legislature, and Duane Berentson and Jack Metcalf to the Washington legislature. Boe and Berentson would later run unsuccessfully for governor in their respective states, as would Metcalf for United States senator.

The archbishop of Canterbury, the Reverend Dr. Michael Ramsey, received an honorary doctor of divinity degree on 22 September 1967. Nobody who was present would forget the archbishop's bearing, extraordinary eyebrows, or his generous remarks to the crowd:

> While I myself am not a Lutheran, I am overwhelmed with a feeling of undeserved honor and privilege and delight at becoming today one of your doctors and one of your alumni, taking my place among you who have all the privileges of this lovely campus. You have welcomed me today in the most generous and eloquent words, you have shown me a welcome of friendship which has warmed my heart. All of my days I shall cherish this honor and feel that I am one of you.

He described a university as a home of freedom, truth, personality, and religion, then ended his remarks with a benediction: "May God be with Pacific Lutheran University for many years, yes, for many centuries to come. May this university go on sending people out who will bring reality and faith home to the troubled world to which we belong."[32]

In cultural matters, too, the years were memorable. The Robert Joffrey Ballet of New York City, one of the most distinguished and innovative ballet companies in America, spent the summers of 1967 and 1968 in residence on the PLU campus. The campus community found the company's presence an exciting experience, and the shows at the end of the summer were dazzling. They brought many visitors to the campus who previously knew nothing of the institution. In 1968 the Choir of the West was chosen to present the premiere performance of William Bergsma's new choral work, "The Sun, the Soaring Eagle, the Turquoise Prince, and the God" to the American Choral Directors meeting in Seattle on 14 March. It was a musical account of an Aztec Indian sacrifice rite. The choral directors responded to the performance with a standing ovation, and the choir was described "as one of the foremost college choirs in the country."[33] The choir—and its new director—was stretching its wings.

A number of academic-intellectual developments and achievements took place in the late sixties. In 1966 the Research Corporation gave $198,567 to strengthen the science program. It eventually subsidized reduced teaching loads so that a number of faculty could undertake more research. Charles Anderson administered the program. In 1968 the Danforth Foundation announced that biologist and alumnus Jens Knudsen had received the E. Harris Harbison Award for outstanding teaching. Knudsen, a dedicated teacher, was also an artist, an occasional poet, and an enthusiastic archeologist. He had conducted research in various places around the world and had published widely, including a book, *Biological Techniques*, published by Harper and Row in 1966.

The first annual West Coast China Conference, organized and directed by students, was held during February 1968. Harvard University had been organizing such sessions on the East Coast for several years, but the supporting agency, CIRUN (Council on International Relationships and United Nations Affairs), wanted an expansion to the West Coast. Student body president Stanley Stenersen helped secure the conference for PLU. The general chair, political science student Mike McKean, spent the summer organizing the events. A number of internationally known scholars participated. The second conference was held the next year under the theme "China Today." Professors Lyman Van Slyke of Stanford, Richard Walker of the University of South Carolina, and S. T. Noumoff of McGill University participated, as did Lisa Hubbs of the *San Francisco Examiner*. History major Larry Cress was the conference chair. Most students, and certainly student leaders, were becoming more politically informed and internationally oriented. The importance of PLU's Pacific Rim location was beginning to sink in.

In 1968 students founded USSAC (University Students Social Action Committee). At first they provided tutoring services in the central district of Tacoma, then a wider range of services was attempted. Terry Oliver was one of the principal organizers. In 1969 Steven Larson, a sophomore history major, was one of two student advisors from the United States to represent the Lutheran Church in America at the fifth Lutheran World Federation assembly in Porto Alegre, Brazil. He also represented the United States the following year in Evian, France.

CORE CURRICULUM

The reform of the core curriculum became a dominant activity after 1965. The core curriculum had not been changed appreciably since the mid-thirties, although it had been enlarged somewhat with baccalaureate degree status in 1940 and 1942. The relationship of liberal education to the core curriculum had not been clearly worked out. That PLU was not a liberal arts college in the style of Luther College or St. Olaf College was evident enough; what it was or should be was not so clear. Perhaps that was something that could be decided as a last step in the self-study and the self-conscious atmosphere of the seventy-fifth anniversary celebrations. Some faculty members and students thought it was time to translate the statement of objectives into campus and curricular reality. The reform-minded *Mooring Mast* thought that might be possible.

The faculty retreat in September 1965 was devoted to an examination of some of the issues and possibilities. Three major presentations were made: Charles Anderson's "Science in Liberal Education"; Kenneth Johnston's "Liberal Education for the Professions"; and Walter Schnackenberg's "The Humanities and the Humanistic View." Johnston attempted no definitions, made no recommendations, and listed a variety of potential problems arising if changes were attempted. All education was liberating, he thought; the principal problem between professional and liberal education was "a lack of communication." More communication and common courtesy were needed in future educational discussions, he concluded. It was immediately clear that leadership to reform the core curriculum would not come from the School of Education. Anderson called for more generalists and multidisciplinary teaching and learning in the sciences. He thought curricular structure was of secondary importance to individual faculty members' imaginative guidance and instruction. He called for new introductory science courses, courses for nonscience students, and more broadly interdisciplinary advanced courses. Some of these suggestions were later institutionalized.

Schnackenberg's speech was longer than those of his colleagues and broader in scope. It continued themes he had been working with for a long time. He had just finished writing *The Lamp and the Cross* and distilled from that volume a brief summary of liberal education at PLU. He thought liberal—not professional—education had been the dominant vision of the founders, but many detours and hurdles, including depressions, wars, mergers, and constant financial constraints, had made the complete establishment of liberal education impossible. The anniversary year would be an appropriate time to set things right. Schnackenberg laid out a number of themes and elements that he thought should be part of a liberal education and PLU's core curriculum.[34] Later in September President Mortvedt appointed a ten-member core curriculum committee with Schnackenberg as its chair.

In the spring of 1966 the committee returned with a radical restructuring of the core curriculum that attempted to include noncurricular activities and vacations in its scheme, encouraged interdisciplinary seminars and independent research, and minimized the importance of grades in lower-division courses. The committee stressed that the proposal was very broad and ideal and much of the substance would have to be worked out by the faculty. It was called SCOPEXAM VI. All degree candidates would have to take a general written examination in six areas (fine arts, humanities, languages, natural sciences, social sciences, logic, and mathematics) in the spring of the junior year. The proposal addressed many additional details, including matters of residence hall living, the dining halls, and campus social life. SCOPEXAM VI did not fare well with a majority of the campus, however; it was "received"—not approved—by a faculty vote, and it provoked much discussion in the weeks following, particularly about the language and mathematics proposals, junior examinations, and interdisciplinary seminars without an agreed-upon integrative theory. The plan was thought by many to be unrealistic and unworkable, but others thought its implementation would permit thoughtfulness and creativity. New committees were appointed to address the unresolved questions of the core curriculum. Three years would elapse before all the reports would be in.

Meanwhile, the calendar and entire university curriculum came under review. Reforms, pushed hard by Mortvedt and broadly supported by the faculty, were finally agreed to at a special 25 October 1968 faculty meeting in which a 4–1–4 calendar, which had proved popular elsewhere, and a new course system were approved. Courses, rather than credits, were to be the basic units of the curriculum. Virtually the whole curriculum was evaluated, reduced (under considerable administrative pressure), and transformed into courses (which were still measured by credits, if one looked closely). Thirty-two courses were the minimum needed for graduation. In this new system the first semester would end before Christmas, and the January Interim—in which students would take just one course—would permit innovation and experimentation in teaching and learning. Off-campus courses, tours, and internships flourished. Grading for Interim courses was to be on a pass-fail basis. This 4–1–4 calendar is still in effect.

The core curriculum was finally rearranged, if not reformed, on 23 April 1969. The faculty met and agreed to stay in session until a decision was reached, despite widespread disagreement as to what should be done. They finally decided on a seven-course distribution requirement not substantially different from the old system: two religion courses and one course each from history or philosophy or literature, natural sciences or mathematics, fine arts, social sciences, and physical education. Freshmen composition would be handled on a proficiency basis, although it was soon required again. With a few revisions the 1969 core curriculum still exists also. The dreams and hopes of translating the statement of objectives into curricular and campus reality had been dashed by a variety of practical and intellectual disagreements and ongoing disagreements between the College of Arts and Sciences and the professional schools. The new core curriculum, while serviceable, was a political compromise.

By the end of the decade PLU faculty, administration, and students had assumed a much larger and more significant role in community affairs than ever before. In 1967–68 five important urban affairs conferences were held on campus, bringing experts from across the nation to discuss major urban problems. The conferences were funded by Title I of the Higher Education Act of 1965 and called "The Community Planning Project." Political science professor Lowell Culver, assisted by the department, organized the conferences, which received national attention. President Mortvedt, who provided strong leadership for the project, wrote that "it was out of concern for the need to develop better channels of communication and cooperation among governmental units and county, city, and civic leaders, as well as a strong sense of responsibility to help make the entire area a finer place in which to live and work, that Pacific Lutheran University developed the community planning project."[35]

The Tacoma Area Urban Coalition was an indirect result of the conferences, and Vice President Thomas Langevin served as university liaison to that body, as well as cochair of its education task force. Black culture programs and human relations workshops were organized on campus, and the first Teacher Corps funding in the state was granted to PLU in 1967. Arne Pederson of the School of Education drafted the Teacher Corps proposal with Tacoma school administrator Alex Sergienko and directed the quite successful program. A social action arm for the university was established in 1969. The Center for Human Organization in Changing Environments (CHOICE) was subsidized by a three-year fifty-thousand-dollar grant from the American Lutheran Church. The Reverend Robert Menzel, a Missouri Synod pastor who had directed a community agency sponsored by a number of Portland, Oregon, churches, was chosen as its director. He coordinated a large number of activities both on and off the campus before his retirement in 1986. PLU was deeply involved in community action activities by 1969, the year President Mortvedt retired.

BALANCE SHEET

In September 1968 President Robert Mortvedt announced his resignation. This was met with considerable surprise because his contract still had three years to run, but he thought it was an opportune time for transition. The PLUS program had been almost entirely accomplished, and a new, younger leader was needed to help make the crucial decisions—and organize a new development plan—for the next decade. High on the list of needs were science and music buildings; "Science and music stand on a pedestal of lonely but challenging hope . . . if we mean what we profess about a quality education *we must provide a science building soon.*"[36] In addition, Mortvedt seemed tired of the battle and the unending pressure, particularly on his health. His hearing, impaired by an attack of scarlet fever in 1928, seemed to be getting worse, which made the verbal give-and-take of university discourse troublesome, especially at faculty meetings. He suffered a relatively minor heart attack on 7 April 1969.

Mortvedt, in his last report to the PLU Corporation, said, "I have attempted from the day of my arrival to keep the institution in a close and living relationship to the Church." He called his philosophy "creative Christian conservatism." Such "creative Christian conservatism" did not always fit easily with the times, however, and the years after 1965 were filled with both agreement and disagreement. Mortvedt highlighted the building projects completed and in process; at a total cost of more than twelve million dollars, they had transformed the look of the campus during the decade. Dean Buchanan later estimated that by 1986 it would have cost more than fifty million dollars to build the same buildings. Mortvedt confessed, however, that he could not quite get over the loss of compulsory chapel: "It has been a disappointment to me personally that this central characteristic of our community has so sadly deteriorated; but there are times, even in the realm of the sacred, when one must realistically admit defeat."[37]

Among other accomplishments and developments, Mortvedt had helped the university grow into its new clothes and achieve a greater sense of confidence. The student body grew by nearly eight hundred between 1960 and 1970, and the faculty nearly doubled. The proportion of Ph.D.s grew from 23 to 27 percent during that period (with many doctoral candidates about to complete their work), and research activities and publication advanced appreciably. The decade produced books by George Arbaugh, Gundar King, Jens Knudsen, and Walter Schnackenberg. The percentage of Lutherans on the faculty fell from approximately 50 to 30 percent, however, while the portion of Lutheran students fell from 65 to 52 percent. Those figures reflect dramatic faculty and student growth, a broader ecumenical concern and approach, more aggressive recruiting, rapidly changing times, an urban location, a growing institutional reputation, increasing secularism in American life, and much more. Eighty-three graduates were admitted to medical and dental schools during the decade (compared to fifty-two the previous decade), and fifty-two PLU baccalaureate degree recipients had received Ph.D. degrees by 1966. Given regional statistics, that figure was still quite low (among private schools in Washington and Oregon only Whitworth and St. Martin's colleges had lower figures), suggesting a long preoccupation with teacher training and, probably even more important, the institution's slow movement toward baccalaureate degree status. Willamette University granted its first baccalaureate degrees in 1859, Whitman College in 1886, UPS in 1893, Gonzaga University in 1894, and PLU in 1940.

Most classes during the 1960s probably resembled the profile of the class of 1967 published for its twenty-year reunion in 1987. Slightly fewer than half of the 302 class members responded to the survey. Of the respondents, 87 percent were married and more than half of the married couples had two children. Forty-five percent of the respondents held graduate degrees, and the largest number (23 percent) worked in some branch of education. Business and health-related vocations were next with 20 percent each. Almost half of the respondents (46 percent) lived in Washington state. Many remembered a chapel speech about dippers and buckets, the *Mooring Mast* columns of Christian E. Ducation, and Joe Grande waterskiing on Clover Creek.

By 1960 a number of effective and strong departments had developed— the sciences, English, history, philosophy, education. The number had grown by 1970: the foreign languages department had weathered the coming and going of a series of bizarre characters and was quite stable; political science had grown from a single faculty member, Don Farmer, to four members; and psychology and sociology were considerably larger. The mathematics department had three faculty members with master's degrees in 1965; by 1970 there were six in the department, two with Ph.D. degrees. Business administration, under the leadership of Gundar King and Dwight Zulauf, was ready for takeoff.

President Robert Mortvedt, in the midst of a troubled and volatile decade, had helped the new university settle into its new status and then grow, both physically and academically. There were agreements and heated disagreements during his tenure, but in the spring of 1969 both faculty and students were most conscious of his strength of character, dignity, determination, and ability to focus on the central issues. The institution was much improved during his presidency. Robert A. L. Mortvedt Library stands as testimony to his leadership and vision.

It was, however, a difficult time to search for a new president. The violence and problems evident on most campuses had left many administrative candidates wary of the task. The list of presidential nominees was shorter than anticipated. After extensive screening six candidates visited the campus: Harlan Foss, chair of the humanities division at St. Olaf College; Erwin Goldenstein, chair of the history and philosophy of education department at the University of Nebraska; Kermit Hanson, dean of the School of Business Administration at the University of Washington; John Linnell, dean of Luther College; Allan Pfnister, provost of Wittenberg University; and Eugene Wiegman, dean of community education at Federal City College. Pfnister, citing professional fatigue, withdrew his name before balloting began. He was probably the leading candidate up to that time.

Of the other candidates, Eugene Wiegman, the youngest and least experienced of the group, made the most favorable impression on a broad spectrum of the PLU community. The board had established a quite democratic system of review that included faculty, alumni, students, and pastors. Wiegman had done his homework carefully. He seemed bright and fresh while some of the other candidates seemed weary and even a little jaded. He was young, 39, and seemed open to the collegiality of the faculty constitution and the democratizing concerns of the students. He appeared to know Washington, D.C., at a time when many thought that was important for the future direction of education. He was sympathetic to the institution's already established programs of social involvement. To many he was an exciting contrast to the conservative, formal, and some-times authoritarian leadership of retiring President Mortvedt. A majority in all the constituent groups favored his candidacy, but support was not unanimous. Some were concerned that he had agreed with too many about too much and that his relative lack of administrative experience would soon show up. These concerns did not carry the day, however, and Wiegman was elected quite handily. On the first ballot he received twenty-six votes with three for other candidates; the second ballot made the vote unanimous.[38] The announcement of the election brought consid-erable elation to much of the campus. Wiegman was the first member of the Lutheran Church–Missouri Synod to be elected president at an ALC college or university. He arrived with his family in the summer of 1969, thus beginning a remarkable interlude in the history of PLU.

10

The Wiegman Interlude

Eugene Wiegman was born in Fort Wayne, Indiana, and educated in the primary and secondary schools of the Lutheran Church–Missouri Synod. After serving in the Marine Corps he earned a Bachelor of Science degree (1953) in social science and teacher education at Concordia College in River Forest, Illinois. His Master of Science degree in school administration (1956) and Doctor of Education degree (1962) were from the University of Kansas. From 1954 to 1961 he was a teacher, coach, and principal in Missouri Lutheran schools, and from 1961 to 1965 he taught social science education and political science at Concordia Teachers College in Seward, Nebraska. In 1965–66 Wiegman was an administrative assistant to a Nebraska congressman, and in 1966–67 he worked with land grant colleges in extension education programs for the U.S. Department of Agriculture. In 1967 he was appointed dean of community education at Federal City College in Washington, D.C. Federal City College was the nation's first new land grant institution in fifty years and the only land grant college with a completely urban constituency. Wiegman was one of the first administrators appointed when that school was organized in the fall of 1967, and his office was charged by Congress to design new programs. Wiegman worked primarily with Headstart teachers and a teachers corps program.

The new PLU president was young, confident, energetic, and relatively inexperienced in university administration. He was politically oriented in his rhetorical style and in his approach to problems and administration, and he was quite deeply touched by the political events and personalities of the 1960s. He was also politically ambitious; he regularly implied he would not stay at PLU beyond his initial six-year contract. A product of the Missouri Synod's educational system and a member of that church body, Wiegman was the first PLU president who had not been shaped by the Norwegian Lutheran educational and ecclesiastical traditions. Wiegman, his wife Kathleen, and their six children arrived in Parkland in the summer of 1969. He set to work with great enthusiasm.[1]

The board of regents at its June 1969 meeting praised departing board chair Earl Eckstrom as a "courageous and brilliant leader." The board also thanked departing president Robert Mortvedt for his leadership, scholarship, and wise counsel, and thanked John Larsgaard for his ten years of service as campus pastor. Anacortes native Donald Taylor, who had been serving an Idaho congregation and who had two daughters at PLU, was selected to replace Larsgaard as campus pastor. At the July board meeting Wiegman's inauguration was discussed. Washington senators Warren Magnuson and Henry Jackson had been contacted, and it was announced "both want to be present." Even the possibility of President Richard Nixon as the featured speaker at the inauguration was broached.[2]

In September the faculty fall conference was held at Holden Village, the Lutheran retreat center in the North Cascades. A visible change in university policy took place when cases of beer and champagne were loaded on Lake Chelan's *Lady of the Lake* for transport to Holden Village and use at the presidential reception. Most faculty members were not teetotalers, but many noted that this was the first time alcohol was served at an official, albeit off-campus, university event. Further dimensions of the change in presidential leadership style appeared at the academic convocation in early September. President Wiegman announced to the estimated twenty-eight hundred people present that the year ahead was to be a "Year of Joy"—a year of joy in each other and joy in Christ.[3] Wiegman pledged his administration to students and to faculty rights. He had strongly endorsed both themes when he visited the campus as a candidate the previous winter. He would similarly name the next four academic years at opening convocation, dedicating them to "commitment," "reflection," "life," and "community." The announcements were soon received with some student satire and raised faculty eyebrows.[4]

INAUGURATION

Three-fourths of the way through the academic year, on 16 March 1970, the inauguration of President Eugene Wiegman was held. It was a rich, colorful, and portentous day. Dr. Frederick A. Schiotz, president of the American Lutheran Church, administered the charge of office and installed Wiegman. Washington governor Daniel Evans participated in the inauguration; senators Magnuson and Jackson and President Nixon sent wires. A luncheon for five hundred was held in Memorial Gymnasium. Two banners (the "Year of Joy" banner and a university banner) designed by art department chair Ernst Schwidder were debuted in the procession, initiating the tradition of using banners at formal university events. Music professor Lawrence J. Meyer had been commissioned to write the "Processional of Joy" that accompanied the procession of the faculty and visiting dignitaries. It continues to be used, especially at commencement, and has become a favorite of many PLU students. In his formal remarks Wiegman developed his "Year of Joy" theme. He declared that

> what the world needs is joy . . . it will be the working premise of this administration that in the decades of the seventies we shall work in new

dimensions of joy—joy in living, joy in serving, joy in ourselves, and joy in Christ. . . . Therefore, I pledge to you that I shall meet the tasks of this presidency with vigor and joy.[5]

There were four formal responses to the rite of inauguration: one from Washington governor Daniel Evans; one from the alumni association president, Roy Schwarz; one from the student body president, Bill Christiensen; and one from a faculty representative, history department chair Walter Schnackenberg.

The remarks of Schnackenberg, a veteran faculty member and the historian of PLU's first seventy-five years, were thoughtful and prophetic; many thought they were the highlight of the morning's festivities. Schnackenberg presented the new president with the university's statement of objectives and told him:

> You have read it and subscribed to it. Your profession today requires you to devote yourself . . . to its continuing realization. In this endeavor we support you with all our strength. We are mindful . . . that Faculties and Presidents have often drawn themselves up as splendid adversaries. We can assure you that we will not relax our vigilance nor faint in the lists. For the common good, we shall maintain all appropriate tensions.
>
> > If you go too fast, we shall slow things down.
> > If you go too slowly, we shall speed things up.
> > If you want answers, we shall give you more questions.
> > If you want a motion, we shall give you an amendment.
> > If you become high-handed, we shall remind you of our
> > ancient prerogatives.
> > If you want a revolution, we shall magnify the tradition.
> > If you will not change, we shall lead the revolt.[6]

A Troubled Time

The late 1960s was not an easy time to assume a university presidency. Campuses all across the United States were staggering with the tumult of sit-ins, demonstrations, and acts of violence; bitter antagonism to the war in Vietnam was widespread, and racism was attacked in aggressive ways. Dramatic changes in lifestyle continued to emerge as well: hair grew longer, hedonism and a new emphasis on self-fulfillment attracted many, a growing and guiltless use of drugs emerged, a youth culture took shape, feminism developed strong leadership and attracted a following, homosexuality came out of the closet, and perhaps most visibly of all, the sexual revolution arrived with full force, heralded by the slick pages of *Playboy* in supermarkets. During the next several exceedingly full years, nearly all of these developments, pressures, and concerns hit the PLU campus and were addressed by the students, faculty, and new president.

The first major event was the 15 October Vietnam moratorium. The faculty supported the day-long schedule of discussions and speeches, but in a closed meeting, after a heated debate, it passed a resolution stating that while continuing to endorse discussion, it would not endorse any political action groups, such as the Vietnam moratorium committees. The resolution, authored by Gundar King, Donald Farmer, and Kenneth Johnston, was aimed at clarifying the faculty's participation in the day. Farmer said: "The university as a corporate body should not take stands on political issues. The resolution would seek not to endorse political action groups."[7] Whether the resolution clarified issues for students or the general public is not clear, but hundreds of people participated in the day's events, which were capped by a fiery antiwar speech by Oregon's maverick senator, Wayne Morse. President Wiegman attended the day's activities and introduced Senator Morse in the evening. Some letters from alumni, bitterly critical of the moratorium, soon arrived. A second Vietnam moratorium was planned for 13–14 November, but it never developed much steam.

In October the ASPLU legislature adjourned indefinitely following the introduction of a bill by Nancy Lundquist and Clayton Kirking that called for adjournment of the body until it decided to attack the "relevant problems facing PLU students and the world community." The bill had been drafted in an all-night session by a cabal of student activists—John Beck, Paul Brown, Jim Hushagen, and Steve Larson—who at the same time prepared a script for a video presentation to the student legislature. The video presentation vividly contrasted some of the most potent of the world's ills with the hottest topic the legislature had been addressing— additional paper towel dispensers in women's restrooms on campus. Future Rhodes scholar Bruce Bjerke said the adjournment was the most constructive action the legislature had taken in the three semesters he had been associated with it.[8] In November President Wiegman agreed to honor student requests in support of the California grape boycott: the food service would not serve grapes.

Changes in university governance also began to emerge. The president presented the idea of an all-university commission to the board of regents in October, and by February 1970 the idea became reality. It was to be a unicameral body of students, faculty, administrators, and staff organized to study and design policy for recommendation, through the president, to the board. There were to be six students on the commission, five faculty members, four staff members, and two administrators. Some, perhaps especially the students, thought university affairs would become democratized in a new and exciting way and that students would be given more responsibilities. The president had talked of such changes as a candidate and had just reported to the ALC board of college education that "I have committed my administration to the students."[9] The body was only advisory, however, and while much talking took place in the months ahead, not very much was accomplished. The all-university commission slid into limbo after the first year. More fruitfully, the idea of a Regency professorship honoring outstanding faculty members was also discussed in the fall of 1969 and was soon established.

On 11 February 1970 a front page editorial by new *Mooring Mast* editor John Aakre asked: "Is PLU Ready for Commitment?" The paper intended to confront the campus with a number of issues, many of which would be unpopular, the editorial said, but all of which merited critical attention and commitment.[10] In March the paper discussed the appropriateness of an ROTC unit on campus, and in April it conducted a "Symposium on Population and World Hunger." The symposium featured movies, slides, speakers, and numerous activities; a special supplement featured faculty and student articles on the relevant topics. In observance of "Earth Day" later that month the paper continued its discussion of the environment. Racism and the problems of minorities on campus were discussed in a 15 April supplement, and in that same issue a recommendation of "coed" dormitories was introduced, with a survey reporting that students supported them by a 410–75 vote. A supplement on grading in the 22 April edition asked, "has it failed?" Students questioned thought grading "curbs learning" and "stifles growth."

The pace of campus life continued to quicken. In May a general strike and class boycott was called for by a joint PLU–UPS newspaper editorial protesting President Richard Nixon's extension of the war into Cambodia. The editorial urged students to find a way to express their views. Seven hundred students heard radical activist and organizer Saul Alinsky speak on campus about the importance of tactics and results. Revolutionary rhetoric was useless, he said, unless it was accompanied by realistic programs of action.

By May much of the campus and nation were in such a state of shock, anger, and outrage over Vietnam, Cambodia, Kent State, Jackson State, and much more that the faculty, pushed along by students, voted to incorporate a National Crisis Forum into the May examination week schedule. It was to serve both educational and therapeutic purposes and would tie the university's educational responsibilities to the basic issues in the national crisis—violence on campuses, conflicts in foreign policy, and generational conflict. An enormously widespread collection of activities of all kinds took place, including a solemn telephone discussion between President Wiegman and Senator George McGovern of South Dakota that was amplified so that a large room full of students could hear. Final examinations were optional in most classes for the only time in the institution's history. Many who participated felt the forum experience helped them with difficult problems and a difficult time.[11]

By commencement nearly everyone was emotionally spent, but education had not disappeared from the campus, censorship had not intruded, violence had not exploded, and administration-faculty-student relationships, while sometimes strained, were still intact. All sides should be given high marks for the 1969–70 academic year. The National Crisis Forum was one of the finest achievements of the decade. The next year brought similar activities and concerns, but the pressures did not reach the same critical proportions.

At the opening convocation in September 1970 President Wiegman announced that the academic year should be a "Year of Commitment"—commitment to build a better university and a better world, but most of all commitment to Jesus Christ. He praised and defended the students and complimented the faculty for the reforms of the recent past.[12] The "Year of Joy" theme had undoubtedly been influenced by Minnesota senator Hubert Humphrey's 1968 "Politics of Joy"; the commitment theme had been introduced by *Mooring Mast* editor John Aakre a few months earlier. An administrative reorganization was announced at the convocation. The deanships of the professional schools and the College of Arts and Sciences as well as the office of academic vice president disappeared, and a provost's office appeared.

The first PLU provost was Richard Jungkuntz, a graduate of Northwestern College in Watertown, Wisconsin, and Wisconsin Lutheran Seminary in Mequon, Wisconsin. He also had a Ph.D. in classics from the University of Wisconsin. Jungkuntz had served as a parish pastor, taught history and classics at Northwestern College, taught exegetical theology at the Missouri Lutheran Concordia Seminary in Springfield, Illinois, and served as executive secretary of the Commission on Theology and Church Relations for the Lutheran Church–Missouri Synod. He was pushed out of both the Springfield teaching position and the secretaryship for the commission by the pressures of theological reaction powerfully emerging in the Missouri Synod in the 1960s, led by that body's new president, "Jack" Preus. Preus had been president of the Springfield Seminary when both Jungkuntz and PLU philosophy professor Curt Huber taught there, and he thought both were "too liberal."[13]

Many members of the Missouri Synod were happy to see "liberals" depart; others expressed regret that Missouri moderates did not stay and fight Preus "down to the last footnote of the Canon law." James E. Adams, author of the most extensive book about Preus, suggests that Jungkuntz might have struck a significant blow against the Preus juggernaut if he had put up more resistance: a quasiheresy trial with the "articulate Jungkuntz" on the stand might have immobilized Preus for years.[14] Effective resistance, however, would have been difficult, and perhaps impossible. Jungkuntz, with his classical education and his experience with Missouri Lutheran theology and politics, began service as provost in September 1970. He served until 1988. He described his leadership style as like that of Lao-tzu: "A leader is best when he is neither seen nor heard; not so good when he is adored and glorified; worst when he is hated and despised. 'Fail to honor people, they will fail to honor you.' But of a good leader, when his work is done, his aim fulfilled, the people will say, 'We did this ourselves.'" [15]

A rich variety of issues and causes continued to attract university attention during the 1970–71 school year, although some *Mooring Mast* writers thought too little was happening. In September Glen Anderson wrote in his perceptive and witty, but often very wordy, "Parallax" column that "God is Alive, PLU is Dead," then explained that too many students were still uninformed about and not involved in activities that would lead to necessary change. There was an "abortion forum" in October, and "women's liberation" was discussed in November. On 18–19 November a "drug symposium" was held on campus with lectures, discussions, and films. An article about "Homosexuals Victimized by Society" appeared in the 11 November *Mooring Mast*. Letters critical of views expressed in the "abortion forum" also flowed in to the editor. Former president Robert Mortvedt found himself "profoundly shocked and disturbed" over views about premarital sex that appeared in the 7 October issue. Clearly, not all were happy about some of the emerging concerns, the level of passion, the use of profanity, and some of the prose styles that appeared in the paper.[16]

In his last editorial *Mooring Mast* editor John Aakre described the changes at PLU during the three-and-a-half years he had been a student: women's dormitories' restrictive hours had been replaced with a card key system; dorm visitation with members of the opposite sex, once allowed twice yearly, was allowed three times a week; two dormitories had become coed; compulsory chapel and a student congregation had been replaced by the Religious Life Council's efforts to provide greater freedom and variety in religious life; social and political involvement beyond campus had grown; and Interim had brought exciting new educational opportunities. The editorial concluded that while the changes were important and beneficial, much more still needed to be done.[17] The pace must not be allowed to slacken, Aakre urged.

Vigorous attacks on campus rules surfaced in the spring. One editorial and letter after another described how freedom and growth were inhibited by the antiquated campus rules. Glen Anderson wrote: "The University ought to quit sticking its administrative nose into a number of matters involving student life. That lame old *in loco parentis* argument has been used . . . in too many ways."[18]

The intense preoccupation with the war in Vietnam and the changes in American society did not distract PLU faculty and students from serious academic activity, however; a significant number of accomplishments emerged in the early 1970s. External events seemed to stimulate intellectual life. The accomplishments were built on a long tradition of intellectual seriousness and dedicated teaching, pushed along by a larger and more diverse faculty and the movement to university status. Some of the achievements were noteworthy. The relatively small, regional institution was beginning to attract national attention.

In spring 1971 the undergraduate program of the School of Business Administration was accredited by the American Association of Collegiate Schools of Business. Only 150 of 2,500 institutions conducting business administration programs were accredited, so the achievement was significant. The movement to accreditation was pushed along by the aggressive leadership of Gundar King and a priority allocation of funds from 1970 to 1972, when the rest of the university agreed that the business administration budgets should be enlarged to push for accreditation. The additional monies were used to enlarge the business faculty and curriculum.[19]

The 4-1-4 calendar system with the January Interim for experimental and off-campus courses received a positive reaction from both faculty and students. It was a time for "freedom" and "calculated risks," the *Mooring Mast* said. The institution was also making a concerted effort to recruit foreign and minority students, and a full-time coordinator for minority students was hired.[20] The number of minority students grew larger than at any time in institutional history, and by September 1971 seventy foreign students from fourteen countries attended PLU. Fifty-eight of those students were from Hong Kong, most recruited by physics professor K. T. Tang.

The number of alumni going on to graduate and professional schools also leaped in the late sixties and early seventies. Policies and concerns underway for more than a decade were beginning to pay off. Ninety-three graduates were admitted to medical and dental schools between 1969 and 1975, more than in the previous decade. Relatively large numbers of graduates began going to law schools as well; the numbers had been negligible in the two previous decades. The numbers of graduates going on to doctoral study became increasingly competitive with those of the better private schools in the Northwest and the better Lutheran colleges: fifty-two had received Ph.D. degrees by 1966, 151 earned doctorates between 1967 and 1976, and by 1984 the total number had grown to 313.

Individual students also began to receive recognition for their academic achievements. Mikkel Thompson, a composer, student of linguistics, and triple major, won PLU's first Woodrow Wilson scholarship in 1970. The Wilson awards went to the most intellectually promising college graduates who planned to be college teachers. Thompson said he wanted to teach comparative Indo-European grammar; he is presently a Lutheran pastor. Walla Walla resident Bruce Bjerke, a history major and 1972 graduate, was PLU's first Rhodes scholar. Bjerke was active in student government and worked in Senator Warren Magnuson's office as a summer intern; he also sang in the Choir of the West and played a lead role in the 1971 production of *Man of La Mancha*. Bjerke is now a Seattle attorney. In 1974 Carol Hidy Suess, an English major, was PLU's first Danforth Foundation scholar. The highly competitive awards (96 awards to 1700 applicants) went to intellectually accomplished students with a strong moral commitment who contemplated college teaching careers. Suess presently works for the Hewlett-Packard company. In 1975 Ann Mehlum of Florence, Oregon, an economics and Norwegian major, was PLU's first Fulbright scholar. She studied the impact of North Sea oil on the Norwegian economy in Bergen, Norway; she is presently the vice president of a bank. Between 1975 and 1989 eighteen students won Fulbright scholarships.

Alumnus and medical student Tom Gumprecht wrote to the *Mooring Mast* in October 1971 about PLU. He discussed the strengths of his education and the tendency of students in the early seventies to denigrate educational and religious institutions. PLU is a good school, he said, and students should not underrate it; it is not a "closed institution," a "monastery," or a "sunday school," he argued. At the University of Washington medical school, he observed, "PLU graduates are as well prepared academically, professionally, socially . . . as people from any other institution." He wrote that PLU graduates are "well regarded here." The reason for that, he thought, was that PLU graduates have a greater sense of direction and values and a truer sense of vocation than many others.[21] Gumprecht's reflections were helpful reminders in the midst of a difficult time, when critical analysis, change, reform, and often denigration seemed to be the dominant themes motivating the most active, outspoken, and accomplished students.

Even with educational and social reforms and widespread student achievements, the lack of money continued to be a problem at the university. By February 1972 President Wiegman had concluded that an endowment drive was necessary and that PLU must act boldly to increase the endowment from its modest level of one million dollars. He proposed a three-year (1972–75), $5 million campaign to the board and said: "I will assume chief responsibility . . . I am confident it can work. I am convinced there is no other way to put this University on the path of excellence."[22] Wiegman's concern about endowment was tied to development activity generally and to the pressing need for a new science building.

The financial and development problems were connected to legal problems as well. Wiegman later told the board that the 1971–72 academic year
should have been called "The Year of Litigation." The university was
involved in suits and countersuits with the architect and builder of Olson
Auditorium, and the county was trying to levy taxes on university
academic facilities. But the most trying legal problem was posed by a
former student who was legally restrained from entering the campus
because of severe misconduct; he had threatened harm to both university
property and individuals, including the president. He had also brought a
$200,000 lawsuit against the university. All these legal problems were
eventually resolved satisfactorily, but for the moment they took enormous
time and energy. Despite them, the president remained optimistic: "I have
not changed my mind that PLU is on the threshold of entering the realm
of the prestigious and outstanding small universities."[23]

To move PLU more effectively into the realm of "prestigious and
outstanding small universities," Wiegman appointed a fifteen-member
"commission on academic excellence" in April 1971. It was chaired by
English professor Paul Reigstad and met regularly over the next two years,
laboring with an impossibly broad mandate and a long and varied agenda
of curricular and noncurricular issues. The final report was delivered to the
faculty on 9 May 1973. It was introduced by a statement about "the
Christian University" that built on, but extended, emphases in the 1963
statement of objectives. It read, in part:

> Pacific Lutheran University identifies itself unreservedly as a Christian
> University. Moreover, it understands this identity from a distinctly Lutheran
> perspective. Only so does it maintain its integrity as a university without
> compromising its character as Christian. For a university that is Lutheran,
> faith cannot tyrannize reason nor can culture be subsumed under the faith.
> To do so only leads to legalism, which is the greatest enemy of the Gospel,
> and to a religious pretense, which is the greatest enemy of knowledge.

The statement then asserted that the university should be a place where able
people, committed to the objectives, should attempt to make freedom a
reality but at the same time welcome "the inevitable dialogue that will
follow when 'Christ' and 'Culture' share the same setting."[24]

The report emphasized the necessary centrality of liberal arts education
at PLU and listed a number of specific recommendations to advance
academic excellence. A long section detailed how the faculty should be
improved and supported. The quality, quantity, and mix of students was
discussed. Methods to improve the quality of life on campus were detailed,
including Phi Beta Kappa affiliation. The need for new facilities in science
and music was underscored. Program development and review, graduate
programs, continuing education, and fiscal policy in relationship to insti-

tutional goals were also considered. Some faculty members and administrators were disappointed because the document was not more dramatic, but given faculty diversity and disagreements, the broadly representative committee, and the flux of the early seventies, the carefully reasoned and pragmatic report was understandable and quite useful. Many of the suggestions were incorporated in the next few years, and if more of them had been seriously addressed the results would probably have been better still.

The cultural high point of the mid-seventies was undoubtedly the May 1974 West Coast premiere of Polish composer Krzysztof Penderecki's "Passion According to St. Luke." Penderecki is one of the best-known composers of the late twentieth century, and the "Passion," which premiered in Europe in 1967, is considered his masterpiece. According to *Mooring Mast* reporter Judy Carlson, it blends Gregorian chant, folk music, nonverbal choir sounds, and modified serialism in an eclectic style.[25] It was presented as part of a week-long Festival of Contemporary Music and utilized the Northwest Boys Choir, the Choir of the West, soloists, a narrator, and the PLU Orchestra under the baton of Jerry Kracht. The stage in Eastvold Auditorium was filled to overflowing with performers, and the total effect of the music was extraordinary. Junior music major Cindy McTee was invited to go back to Poland with the Pendereckis after the composer heard one of her compositions during the week. It was arranged that she would teach the family conversational English and he would tutor her in composition at the conservatory.

"No Confidence"

From the beginning of his service at PLU, President Eugene Wiegman proceeded jauntily and confidently; his leadership style certainly differed from that of Robert Mortvedt, but that was at least in part what had made him attractive to his strongest supporters. He spent relatively large amounts of time off-campus and was active in the Tacoma Area Urban Coalition and other social action agencies, which earned him praise from the *Tacoma News Tribune* and some other participants. Difficult problems had been taken in stride during the first years of his presidency, but by the beginning of the second year new problems, and considerable uncertainty, began to emerge as well. The presidential style wore thin for many, and more substantive problems appeared.

The matter of style had been satirically addressed in the *Mooring Mast* in September 1969, shortly after Wiegman assumed office. The columnist "Superlute" wrote about the coiffure of the new president ("Dr. Clairol" he was called), his attendants, and his "J.O.Y. Wagon." The columnist complained that witnesses "attempting a closer look at Dr. Clairol ... were almost trampled to death by the hoards of worried lieutenants and potential cookie pushers who follow 'Dr. C.' wherever he goes."[26] "Superlute" was amusing, but also perceptive. The more substantial problems included financial concerns (particularly about leased airplanes for presidential travel, a presidential speechwriter, entertainment expenses, Gonyea House decoration costs, and general confusion about criteria governing budget construction and spending), the president's apparent inability to work effectively with the central administrative staff, his constant need of the limelight, and the embarrassment some faculty and students increasingly felt as the president represented the university.

Concerns in some quarters had been present from the outset. The faculty presidential selection committee was divided over Wiegman's candidacy, as were some faculty members and regents. There was concern about his style, but even more concern about his lack of administrative and financial experience in higher education. His experience at Federal City College was brief and quite limited. A. Dean Buchanan, PLU's vice president for business and finance, strongly opposed Wiegman's candidacy; he was "shocked" by some of Wiegman's comments and his vote-oriented approach to problems, even budgetary and financial ones. In a 1986 interview Buchanan recalled that Wiegman "knew very little about higher education finance." Buchanan went to see ALC president Frederick Schiotz the morning of the presidential selection, hoping to stop the proceeding, but Schiotz said things had gone too far.[27] Wiegman was elected president.

Almost as soon as he arrived in the Northwest, Wiegman got off on the wrong foot with many pastors of the North Pacific District of the ALC. At the close of his keynote address to the pastors at their annual conference in Gearhart, Oregon, he told them that he was running PLU and would brook no interference from them; they should stay in their own bailiwicks. His remarks caught everyone by surprise and angered many; the address set the tone from the outset with that very important constituency.[28] Wiegman may have spoken from the perspective of his Missouri Lutheran experience, but his remarks were at odds with the relatively close and cooperative relationship that had long existed between PLU and the North Pacific District and its pastors. Former president Robert Mortvedt had worked very hard to nurture that relationship; future president William Rieke would do the same thing. Wiegman's first year also brought some sharply worded letters from district clergy and alumni over the institutional involvement in the Vietnam moratorium.[29]

By November 1970 some members of the alumni board were concerned about presidential leadership at PLU. On 11 November they met with three faculty members, the ASPLU president, and the campus pastor to discuss their concerns. That meeting led to a 27 November alumni board meeting with Wiegman, and because concerns were not allayed at that meeting, a number of alumni board members asked the board of regents to discuss the problems as soon as possible. There were three primary concerns as summarized by M. Roy Schwarz, the immediate past-president of the alumni association and the organizer of the meeting: first, some feared that the administration was moving the institution away from its Lutheran and Christian heritage; second, some worried about the way the institutional image was projected by the president; and third, some felt concern about Wiegman's administrative skills, wasteful spending, and the "handling" and "manipulation" of people. A list of examples followed each point.[30]

On 11 December the executive committee of the board took up the questions at a special meeting in Seattle and discussed them at considerable length. They talked about Wiegman's 1969 speech to the district pastors, his reputed ridicule of Norwegians and Republicans, his attempt to disband the student congregation (because "it is the last bastion of conservatism on the campus"), and his treatment of campus pastor Don Taylor (about whom Wiegman remarked, "I will not tolerate staff I cannot work with"). The choir trip deficit and the university's leasing of an airplane for presidential transportation were also discussed.[31] The executive committee, after a long discussion and after talking to Wiegman, decided to do nothing more. Wiegman pledged his full cooperation with the board; he had weathered an early and rather serious storm.

Concerns also began to emerge from the faculty. They perhaps first began as a reaction to Wiegman's treatment of the political science department. That department, led especially by Lowell Culver, had organized pioneering urban affairs programs in 1967–68 that received national attention, and the department helped organize one of the nation's first urban coalitions in Tacoma. Culver first represented the school in the urban coalition, and Vice President Thomas Langevin soon played an important role as well. All of this activity had been strongly supported by President Mortvedt. When Wiegman came he was excited by and committed to such political activism, but he was apparently determined to represent PLU himself and curtail the political science department's involvement. Culver's activity received no more administrative encouragement; Culver recalled later that Wiegman "took over the urban coalition and threw me out."[32] The political science department members initially did not receive raises in their 1970 contracts, despite various achievements (for Culver those achievements included promotion, appointment to a gubernatorial committee, nationally recognized urban affairs accomplishments, and the publication of a book). After vigorous protests, chair Donald Farmer was able to get minimal raises for his two colleagues, but virtually nothing for himself. In part as a result of these tensions Culver left PLU a year later to take an urban affairs teaching position at Governor's State University in Illinois. In January 1971 Farmer was selected by his faculty colleagues as the first Regency professor at PLU; the honor certainly reflected his long-term contributions as a teacher, scholar, and faculty leader, but it was also a plebiscite on the recent past and a signal to Wiegman. There is no evidence the message was received.

Unhappiness continued to grow. In October 1972 two letters from religion professors to the bishop's office expressed concerns over the religious direction and drift at PLU, administrative confusion, and the presence of too many "Missouri types" who did not understand the ALC tradition.[33] In December Dean Buchanan exploded to North Pacific District bishop Clarence Solberg: "How long, oh, how long is the Board going to continue to put up with this gross incompetence and total failure to lead, to act fearlessly and resolutely and support a politician who is concerned with only *his* image—not the university's."[34]

Student leaders also became disenchanted as the 1971–72 academic year proceeded. One of several items concerning students was the push for a twenty-four-hour dormitory visitation policy. Wiegman continued to announce that his adminstration was committed to students and indicated support for such a policy when talking to students, but he did not support it when the board, resolutely opposed to the policy, expressed itself. The gap between his public announcements and what actually happened produced anger and frustration. The vice president of student affairs, Dan Leasure, had to take the heat. Leasure was liked and respected by the students, but he was in an intolerable situation, caught between the board, the president, and determined student leaders.[35] Leasure resigned in the summer of 1972. The *Mooring Mast* reported that "PLU lost a great man when Dan Leasure resigned this summer. . . . His shoes will be hard to fill."[36]

Other personnel and organizational problems began to chafe badly. Campus religious life was reorganized in 1970 with the creation of a Religious Life Council that was to supervise and coordinate all religious groups and activities on campus, including the student congregation. Some thought the growing diversity of university life required these changes; others wanted the student congregation to remain basic. It had hitherto been an autonomous American Lutheran Church congregation under the authority of the president of the North Pacific District of the ALC. The new council reported to and was directed by the president, and some feared that this was an administrative "takeover" of religious life and a blow aimed at campus pastor Donald Taylor. After the changes, pastors would be called to be ministers to the university and would serve as "part-time" pastors of the student congregation. In 1971 new pastors were nominated and Gordon Lathrop—not Donald Taylor—was ultimately called. Wiegman was clearly delighted; strong disagreements between Wiegman, leaders of the student congregation, and Taylor had been obvious for at least a year. The replacement of Taylor produced considerable anger and a standing ovation for

Taylor at the PLU Corporation meeting in June.[37] The church expressed itself by electing Taylor to the board of regents.

Milt Nesvig was soon shunted aside as well. Wiegman told him he would run public relations himself; he wanted the university publication *Reflections* to be the "arm of the President to the public." Similarly, he told graphics consultant Kern Devin: "You should have been in my office … the first week I was here to explore my philosophy, but that was not done and I wait for no man, as you well know."[38] Art professor Walt Tomsic was appointed graphics consultant, subject to Wiegman's direction. Nesvig's title was changed from "vice president of university relations" to "assistant to the president for church relations and publications"; he was wounded at what appeared to be a demotion and wondered if he should resign, but friends advised him to stay and he did. Alumni director Jon Olson also resigned over a disagreement with the president about the nature of his responsibilities (and because of an attractive offer from another institution), and football coach Roy Carlson was replaced in a controversial and unexpected action.[39]

The pace of concerns quickened as the new year began. On 12 January 1973 Walter Schnackenberg, the faculty representative to the board of regents, sent to the faculty a thirteen-page questionnaire with a wide range of questions about university administration, governance, standards, and educational policy. The responses would help him carry out his responsibilities, he wrote, and the questionnaire was "not aimed at any office, any structure, any hierarchy … or system past or present." That may or may not have been true, but of the 70 percent of the faculty who responded, 84 percent found administrative leadership at the present time was "middling" or "weak"; 72 percent felt there was too much administrative expense.[40] Faculty concern was becoming sharply focused.

On 6 February 1973 Dean Buchanan resigned. That was the proverbial straw that broke the camel's back. Buchanan decided he had to dramatize the problems of presidential leadership in the most effective way possible and to let the board know the magnitude of the problems; he felt so strongly that he was willing to "resign and sacrifice" himself.[41] Buchanan had played a major role in the development and building activities of the previous eleven years and was widely respected on campus; he had a national reputation as a collegiate finance officer.

The faculty responded to the general situation and especially to Buchanan's resignation with anger and vigor. There was widespread talk that something had to be done. The members of the educational policies committee, after its 8 February meeting had been adjourned, decided faculty frustrations and concerns should be discussed at the next day's faculty meeting and that a resolution of concern should be sent to the regents. The resolution was drafted the next morning by Curtis Huber,

Philip Nordquist, and David Olson; the resolution was discussed by interested parties at a noon caucus and some strategy was planned. Word quickly filtered back to the president's office and board chair Michael Dederer was notified, but nothing more was done. Copies of the resolution were duplicated and the resolution was introduced at the faculty meeting. Nordquist moved to suspend the rules "to allow the introduction of resolutions relative to the resignation of A. Dean Buchanan." The motion carried unanimously. Then religion professor Emmet Eklund carefully and without a trace of rancor read the three resolutions.

The first resolution extended the faculty's appreciation to Buchanan for his years of distinguished service. It carried unanimously. The second resolution asked for faculty representation on the search committee that would look for Buchanan's successor. It carried. The third resolution summarized faculty "dismay and profound concern" and asked the board to "speedily address itself to the issues described above." Five clauses expressed faculty concerns:

> Whereas, we the Faculty of Pacific Lutheran University have become greatly concerned about the loss of able qualified administrative personnel; and
>
> Whereas, we have grave disappointment at the absence of sound policies which provide assurance of achieving our stated educational objectives; and
>
> Whereas, we do not find a climate of confidence and trust within which able persons may serve the interests of the University with integrity; and
>
> Whereas, we have not been convinced that the established economic priorities adequately reflect our commitment to excellence in education; and
>
> Whereas, the evidence provided by recent surveys of campus opinion concerning executive leadership raise serious questions about our success in stimulating confidence in and giving direction to the University Community . . .[42]

The third resolution was discussed, there was a brief recess, and a move to defer action was defeated. After voting by secret ballot, the faculty passed the resolution ninety-seven to thirty-two, with four abstentions. Walter Schnackenberg, the faculty representative to the board of regents, was charged with the responsibility of presenting the resolution and faculty concerns to the board at its 26 February meeting.

Despite efforts by the drafters of the resolution to keep the matter within the borders of the campus, the *Tacoma News Tribune* was alerted by an anonymous source and ran front-page articles the next two days. The Saturday headline read "PLU President Wiegman Criticized by Faculty," and the article summarized the previous day's events, reporting that the faculty had passed a resolution "amounting to a vote of no confidence in University President Eugene Wiegman."[43] That was the first time the phrase "no confidence" was used, although it would be repeated in the future. The 11 February headline read, "Dr. Wiegman Still Smiles After Faculty Criticism." Wiegman said his love and concern for the faculty and the entire university had not been diminished by the criticism directed against him by the faculty.[44]

Those who supported the resolution chose not to discuss the matter with reporters until the board had acted, but some opponents of the resolution did speak. One spoke about procedural questions, the absence of fairness, and the abuse of the faculty's own rule of faculty meeting privacy (a reporter had apparently entered the room as the meeting was coming to an end). Another suggested that the conflict was between two varieties of Lutheran piety, about a presidential style that some found offensive, and about liberal politics and social activism. That reasoning did not square with the carefully written faculty resolution. A third, in a portmanteau charge, described the supporters of the resolution as "a strange coalition" made up of "tweedy associates," "young turks," "Norwegians who feel their piety has been subverted," and "faculty members who . . . feel vulnerable and threatened by the general outlook in education."[45]

The *Mooring Mast* carefully reported the events the next week. The cover drawing by artist Dennis Andersen depicted a badly tilting, baroque-appearing ship with recognizable PLU features. The caption read: "Behold the sinking ship of state." A long article by editor Duane Larson detailed the previous week's events. It reported that officials of the North Pacific District of the ALC had also drafted a resolution to the regents about the loss of "qualified and able" personnel. Students' concerns were detailed in the article. In an editorial, Larson criticized the person who tipped off the *Tacoma News Tribune* about the faculty resolution and allowed the event to go public. He was also sharply critical of the "shoddy journalism" of the Tacoma paper, citing its failures to obtain proper objectivity and to contact students. The editorial continued:

> As to varied comments from "members" of the faculty and administration, such comments have bordered on the ridiculous, smacked of anti-intellectualism and have most often been uttered from a context of absolute puerility. Such theorization as "German-Norwegian Lutheran cultural splits" is indicative only of exasperated smoke-screening and has most likely damaged rather than helped the intended defendant.[46]

The *Mooring Mast* supported the faculty in its resolution and expressed its belief that the faculty had acted reasonably. Campus clerical and library staff also supported the faculty action and sent notice of that support to the regents.

The 26 February board meeting was long and heated, stretching from 1:00 to 11:00 P.M. Hundreds of students held vigil in the hallway outside the Regency Room and remained until after the meeting was adjourned. Testimony was heard in both open (from Walter Schnackenberg, who was savaged by some regents, and ASPLU president Don Yoder) and closed sessions (from Dean Buchanan, Richard Jungkuntz, and dean of students Philip Beal). Yoder had consulted with approximately twenty student leaders before the meeting and prepared a statement that concluded: "As a result of our concern for the future of Pacific Lutheran University we have become convinced that it is necessary that PLU seek to obtain a new University President."[47]

After the testimony and much discussion the board finally voted to retain Wiegman; the motion passed by a margin of fourteen to eleven (half a dozen members had already left because of the lateness of the hour). The board announced "that a lack of communication has existed. President Wiegman has assured the Board of his determination to re-establish open lines of communication with the faculty, and the Board in turn pledges itself to the same task."[48] A four-member board committee was established to evaluate the presidential performance and report back to the board. The members were Thomas Anderson, Melvin Knudson, Gerald Schimke, and David Wold.

The board announcement was received with shock and disbelief by many. Much more than communication problems had been presented in the day's testimony. A 1 March *Mooring Mast* editorial criticized the board for not listening to students in any serious way.[49] The editorial thanked Buchanan, Jungkuntz, Schnackenberg, Beal, and Yoder, noting that they had sacrificed a great deal and deserved great respect. In the week following the board meeting students circulated a petition and collected 843 signatures. It expressed disagreement with the board decision and asked the board to reconvene, reconsider the decision, and involve students in the reconsideration.

The board committee met with the faculty on 2 March. Board members Thomas Anderson and Melvin Knudson read statements; Walter Schnackenberg reported on his presentation to the board, and Donald Farmer, the alternate faculty representative to the board, commented on the limitations of the methods used by the board to elicit information, concluding that he did not think the board had really listened to the faculty.[50] The faculty voted unanimously to support the ASPLU and the students who had signed the petition asking the board to reconsider. Philosophy professor Curtis Huber summarized the feelings of many faculty members when, in a brief statement, he said: "The achievements of the President are neither minimal nor unappreciated." He listed some of the achievements, which included democratizing processes, introducing the idea of the Regency professorship, and opening doors to wider community involvement. Huber then explained:

What creates intensity in my unease, and doubts about our future, is that in the midst of these contributions the President has managed, whether by inattention and error or lack of wisdom I do not know, to alienate a vast number of the very staff he has ostensibly sought to serve, and which has been recipient of these benefits. By relying so heavily on the raw political process instead of scholarly persuasion and sensitive judgment to accomplish his aims, he has often given the general impression that he valued successful manipulation of persons more highly than principled direction of the University's development, and that clever strategy and personal victory were more to be prized than the achievement of University goals. However small and seemingly insignificant the individual offenses and exploitations may have been, their vast number has created, in my opinion, a dangerously pervasive dissatisfaction and lack of trust in the President's dedication and ability to pursue the highest welfare of the institution. I do not deny his dedication. I cannot rely on it.[51]

The rest of the spring was filled with much activity, including meetings between President Wiegman and student and faculty groups to address the "communication" problem. Summaries of these meetings were recorded and sent to Wiegman and the board committee. A pervasive theme continued to be lack of confidence; it was sometimes quite strongly stated.[52] In February and March letters also poured in from alumni, pastors, and friends of the university. They almost all supported the faculty resolution: of the thirty-seven letters representing forty-seven people received by board chair Michael Dederer, thirty-four supported the faculty resolution and three opposed it—all written by people Wiegman had served with outside the university. One of those letters made some interesting points:

> I wish to offer Eugene Wiegman my support against the ill-conceived resolution of his faculty at Pacific Lutheran University. Ever since his arrival in Tacoma a new spirit and *service to the community* has been most apparent. . . . This service to the community and the *palpable spirit of happiness* and youth at the university since Dr. Wiegman's arrival are in marked contrast to the stiff, proper and provincial "image" reflected by P.L.U. in previous years. . . . I would be sorry to see P.L.U. slip back to its parochial ways.[53]

Almost all the letters that supported the faculty position were also strongly stated and spoke more directly to matters that were included in the 9 February resolution. One, written by an alumnus and son of a pioneer faculty member, was particularly perceptive.

> Dr. Wiegman does not project the image that I feel is compatible with the role of an administrator of a Christian institution of higher learning. If he has humility, the publicity given him has not reflected it. I recall great astonishment on finding his picture some thirteen times in an early issue of the

"Reflections" shortly after his arrival. This seemed to set the tone.... The role of a college president in any institution is a difficult one and it must be especially so in a small school affiliated with the Church. Students and faculty should be able to identify with characteristics which include humility, consistency, the ability to foster trust relationships and genuine feelings of concern. In the news media Dr. Wiegman does not come across strongly in these areas.... This faculty cannot be forever effective working in the shadow of an administrator whose objective seems aimed at self-fulfillment.[54]

What the final outcome of the resolutions, letters, memoranda, delibera-tions, and discussions might be remained unclear through the rest of the spring. The board had acted ambiguously, and the expressed concern about communication had not resolved the problems. Board chair Michael Dederer and several board members remained firm defenders of Wiegman, and it was not at all clear what might be presented to the PLU Corporation at its June meeting or what that body might do. Confusion and frustration were widespread. Wiegman kept in close touch with Dederer all through the spring. On 1 May he wrote:

I am of a mind that there are some deep-rooted problems at this University to which I am willing at this time to address my administration.... In addition to the fickleness of the faculty, I am heartsick at the lack of leadership and expression of Christian virtues by many clergy and lay people of our A.L.C. The members of the L.C.A. and non-Lutherans have expressed greater Christian character lately, in my opinion. . . .[55]

On 15 May it was announced that President Eugene Wiegman and the board of regents, by joint action, agreed that the president would identify future goals and objectives of the university in the ensuing year and that he would take a presidential leave with full pay and benefits for the year commencing 1 August 1974. This announcement resolved some issues, but was still quite vague. Would President Wiegman retain full authority in 1973–74? Would he return after the leave was over? Who would administer the university during that year? The faculty continued to feel frustrated and concerned; many board members also expressed considerable confusion about what exactly had been done on 15 May.

Concern mounted all through May, and criticism continued unabated. The faculty liaison committee sent the board's communication committee a summary of the faculty opinion that had come out of the spring meetings with the president. It concluded that the communication gap "has not been remedied," that the president "has not increased his support from the faculty," and that of all the documents received, "not a single one supported the President."[56] The alumni board also issued a statement of concerns. President Emeritus Robert Mortvedt and his wife, Gladys, refused a

Wiegman invitation to come to campus because "to do so would be to give the erroneous impression to you and others that we are supportive of your current administrative practices and leadership, which would be hypocritical on our part. We very much regret that we cannot support you." Mortvedt lamented the "irreparable" loss of Dean Buchanan and then discussed a tasteless photograph of Wiegman, accompanied by a mawkish poem about resurrection, that had appeared in the Easter edition of the *Mooring Mast*:

> I realize that there are some harmful stories and representations which are erroneous, or which are beyond your control. But an incident over which you did have control was the recent *Mooring Mast* picture of you lying prone with a bouquet in your hands, flanked by students in an attitude of prayer, and accompanied by its offensive subtitle. In my opinion, you showed incredibly bad judgment in posing for such a picture. It hurt you and it hurt the University. No president has the right deliberately to hurt the University. The welfare of the University should tower above all individuals, regardless of station.

The letter, especially the last two sentences, spoke volumes about Mortvedt. He advised resignation.[57]

One voice of university support was finally heard. Richard Moe, who directed the School of Fine Arts as well as the summer school and graduate programs, wrote to the faculty liasion committee after it had sent its memorandum to the board. He said he knew no one who had worked as diligently and unselfishly as Wiegman to fulfill the expectations placed on him. "I have absolutely no reason to do anything but trust him, and, further, I have no reason to question his motives . . . I believe he has been a devoted servant of PLU in everything he has done. Thus, I conclude he has been maligned and viciously attacked for no good reason."[58]

After much concern and jockeying, the confusion about Wiegman's status was finally resolved at the annual PLU Corporation meeting in June. On 7 June the North Pacific District convention of the ALC passed a resolution asking the PLU Corporation to begin searching for an acting president as soon as possible and for a new president to replace Dr. Wiegman at the expiration of his term. On 8 June, at the corporation meeting, Wiegman announced that after the 1974–75 leave he would not be a candidate for the PLU presidency. Wiegman had released an advance text of his statement that had not included that phrase, but apparently he changed his mind before he read the statement. Seattle businessman and board chair Michael Dederer, who retired from the board after the corporation meeting, was still convinced Wiegman was the right person for the PLU presidency and that the disagreement was entirely "politics." The faculty and student "attempt" was something regents must stand up to, he insisted; such resistance "would have been much easier in our case had it not been for the Corporation that we also had to fight with. Had it not been for the Corporation being involved I would have been prepared to personally fight this to the last ditch, but a fight with the Church would have been a losing battle."[59] In June 1974 Dederer suggested to the presidential selection committee that the members should consider the "possibility of re-employing Gene Wiegman if he would be interested."[60]

THE LAME-DUCK YEAR

In the midst of the barrage of criticism and concern, President Wiegman did admit that he had, perhaps, spent too much time off campus and had lost touch with the faculty. He said he was limited by the board in what he could do as president, however, and he neither publicly admitted that there were any significant problems with his administration nor proposed any structural or procedural remedies.[61] He did suggest that cooperation was the answer. He called the 1973–74 academic year the "Year of Community." He told the fall academic convocation:

Where there has been discord, let us together listen anew with all our senses.

. . .

Where there has been restlessness, let us together accommodate new ideas with all sincerity.

Where there has been a hinderance of progress, let us together facilitate cooperation at every level.

I make this pledge to you with all earnestness: I SHALL DO MY LEVEL BEST.[62]

Perry B. Hendricks, Jr. was appointed vice president for finance and operations to replace Dean Buchanan. He was an Iowan with a B.S. degree from Iowa State University and an M.B.A. degree from the University of Denver. He was the cofounder, treasurer, and business manager of a private school in Colorado, and he had served twelve years at the University of Denver, most recently as director of grants and contracts. Hendricks's position was part of a new administrative reorganization scheme designed by Harry Prior and Associates that was accepted by the board in October. The plan established three vice presidential positions and a provost's office, centered more activity in the development offices, and reduced the number of people who reported to the president.

Leadership problems, tensions, and disagreements did not disappear with Wiegman's June 1973 announcement or with his call for a "Year of Community." In February 1974 Clayton Peterson resigned from his position as vice president for development under considerable and persistent pressure from Wiegman and a few board members and accepted a position at Children's Orthopedic Hospital in Seattle. On 27 December 1973 Wiegman had written to the executive committee of the board of regents: "It is never easy to recommend that a high ranking officer of the university not be reappointed to a position, but I am now ready to make this recommendation to you."[63] Given Wiegman's anomalous situation, there was considerable irony in this turn of events. Peterson had many strong points, Wiegman wrote, but he had lost his ability to lead and manage. The relationship between Wiegman and Peterson was undoubtedly complicated; they represented two quite different personalities and visions of how a small university should operate, as well as conflicting understandings of fundraising and development. The president and some board members wanted immediate fundraising results to meet the short-term financial pressures of the early seventies; Peterson took a longer view of development, one that required careful homework, a clear sense of what was to be accomplished, detailed plans, and ultimate results that would benefit the institution beyond the immediate campaign or quest for funds. The PLUS campaign was his model. Development required assiduous labor, a long vision, and patience, he thought. In his memorandum Wiegman proposed two alternatives for Peterson: a different but less important job on campus, or a position with the ALC and its $25 million United Mission Appeal.[64] Peterson rejected both options and resigned.[65] With that action all of Mortvedt's vice presidents, with whom Wiegman had indicated he was eager to work, had either resigned or been demoted.

Peterson had made significant contributions to PLU during his fourteen years of service. He had established an up-to-date development office, helped organize the PLUS campaign, reestablished friendships with the Seattle-Tacoma business community, conceived of the Q Club, and made the first contacts that resulted in President John Kennedy and Archbishop Michael Ramsey coming to Tacoma. He—like Dean Buchanan—would be missed. Peterson's position proved hard to fill, and the university lost several years of carefully organized development activity with his resignation; the science building was not built for another decade, and the earlier announced presidential search for endowment monies proved ineffectual. The church elected Peterson to the board of regents in 1975, where he served for nine years. He was decorated by the kings of Norway and Sweden, and in 1985 he received PLU's Distinguished Service Award.

On 12 March the outspoken atheist Madalyn Murray O'Hair spoke on campus about the separation of church and state. The reaction to her presence and speech was large and almost entirely negative; the *Mooring Mast* reported more than one thousand responses to the president's office.[66] An embattled Wiegman attempted to explain the university position to various constituencies and individuals, supported by a faculty resolution that reaffirmed commitment to the concept of a Christian university as a proper forum for the examination of all sorts of ideas and viewpoints, especially controversial ones, including viewpoints that "many of us find personally repulsive."[67]

A number of ideas for university expansion emerged in the spring. In an April memorandum to the faculty President Wiegman suggested the possibility of establishing a PLU branch in Hong Kong that would offer two years of general education. Wiegman had just spent eight days in Hong Kong with physics professor K. T. Tang; he was convinced a branch campus would benefit PLU and encourage even more able Hong Kong students to come to PLU (210 highly motivated Hong Kong students had atended PLU in the previous five years). The notion was discussed by committees and individuals for the rest of the year, but it was pushed aside by both faculty and regents after Wiegman left. Land was very scarce in Hong Kong, and building would be prohibitively expensive. Slightly later in the spring the president asked the educational policies committee to address the possibility of adding health sciences options—possibly including a medical school—to the university's academic structure. He had been approached by some Pierce County physicians who were unhappy with services provided by the University of Washington. That possibility never reemerged after scrutiny by the natural sciences faculty. Plans for a badly needed science facility had not yet been developed; discussion of a medical school seemed premature.[68]

On 17 May at the athletic department's PLUTO (PLU Traumatic Occurrences) awards banquet, awards were given to the athletes and coaches who had produced the year's biggest gaffes. President Wiegman received the first award. The university's irrepressible sports information director, Jim Kittilsby, presented the president with the "Paddlin' Madalyn Home" award. Kittilsby had dreamed up the PLUTO awards; he also discovered or remembered the gaffes, invented the award titles, and wrote the lyrics that were sung with the presentations. These banquets were typically hilarious, sometimes outrageous, and one of the high points of the spring semester for PLU athletes. Wiegman, as his final year at PLU was drawing to a close, received his award with good humor.

SHORT-TERM PRESIDENCIES

Short-term and frequently controversial presidencies were quite widespread in American colleges and universities in the early seventies; PLU's situation was not unique. In those overheated years criteria used in presidential selection often proved to be inappropriate, and radical (or reactionary) presidential agendas frequently produced serious controversy. Many of the presidents selected proved to be too administratively inexperienced to handle the manifold reponsibilities of the office. Seven of the eight Washington and Oregon private colleges James Hitchman included in his 1981 study changed presidents in the early seventies. "The tenure of several replacements was short, coinciding almost with the strange interlude of the Nixon-Ford presidencies. Willamette got rid of Roger Fritz when he proved that he was the wrong man for the job. Linfield replaced Gordon Bjork, whose attitude antagonized town and gown. PLU brought in Wiegman to get along with dissidents, let him go because he did not satisfy faculty and church."[69] The list of angry and aggrieved constituencies was much longer than Hitchman suggested, however. Wiegman has the unique distinction among PLU presidents of angering or alienating all the institutional constituencies simultaneously.

In his relatively short tenure as president, Eugene Wiegman brought some changes to PLU that were beneficial; forces leading to greater pluralism continued to emerge as well. Wiegman was exuberant and confident, but tight budgets soon posed problems, and the development program lost ground as well. He was a relatively inexperienced and sometimes careless administrator who paid too little attention to what was happening on campus and far too little attention to the painstaking, step-by-step solutions needed to address academic, financial, and development problems. Too frequently charm, a politicized leadership approach, and a rhetorical style that quickly lost its punch were substituted. Wiegman soon lost the confidence of most of his administrative cohorts and a large percentage of the faculty; church leaders and students were not too far behind.

The university weathered the crises of the early seventies and the breakdown in presidential leadership quite effectively, however. The financial and personnel costs were damaging, but institutional momentum continued. The institution had grown in confidence and stature since the difficult transition to university status fifteen years earlier, and it acted with determination at this critical juncture. The university would not be deterred from pursuing long-term goals that were important and within reach. The achievements of the next few years indicate the proximity of the goals and testify to the importance of the faculty and student action. Walter Schnackenberg's remarks at the 1970 inauguration of Wiegman echoed in many heads throughout 1973 and 1974: "If you become high-handed, we shall remind you of our ancient prerogative. . . . If you will not change, we shall lead the revolt."

Eugene Wiegman has held a variety of positions since leaving PLU, but he continues to live in Tacoma. He ran unsuccessfully for Congress in 1976. From 1977 to 1981 he served as commissioner of Employment Security while Dixie Lee Ray was governor. In 1983 he talked of filing for the late Henry Jackson's Senate seat, and in 1984 he was an "unofficial" candidate for governor of Washington. He ran unsuccessfully for state land commissioner in 1984. From 1983 to 1985 he served as interim lay pastor at Luther Memorial Church in Tacoma, and on 13 December 1987 he was ordained into the ministry of the American Lutheran Church and called as associate pastor at Luther Memorial Church.[70] Given Wiegman's combative announcement to the ALC pastors at Gearhart in 1969 and his "heartfelt" concern over the lack of ALC pastoral leadership and Christian virtue in 1973, his ordination seems a little ironic. Wiegman is presently the executive director of the Family Counseling Service of Tacoma and Pierce County.

At the May 1974 board of regents meeting it was announced that Provost Richard Jungkuntz would serve as acting president for the ensuing year. Jungkuntz announced, "I am not the president's 'successor'; one thing I would not do is criticize my predecessor. The record speaks for itself. He faced certain problems and dealt with them in his own way."[71]

The 1974–75 academic year went quite smoothly. The "Processional of Joy" was not heard at the opening convocation in September, however, and the year was not named and no new banner was unfurled. After students complained about the absence of the "Processional of Joy," Jungkuntz promised that the music and the use of special banners would resume in the future.

The year brought other changes in leadership as well. At the end of February Gene Lundgaard resigned as basketball coach after a 14–12 season. Responding to recent criticism that PLU athletic teams had too few black athletes, Lundgaard had recruited four black players out of the junior college ranks the previous year—the first black basketball players at PLU. Two of them, Jeff Byrd and Tony Hicks, were the leading scorers both years they played. In 1974 Hicks was the top scorer of the decade, averaging 22.4 points per game. In his seventeen-year career, Lundgaard led his teams to a 280–174 record, ten conference titles, eleven playoff appearances, and four national tournament appearances. He remained on the faculty and was replaced as basketball coach by Ed Anderson, who had just guided the junior varsity team to a 20–2 record.

In March, after four years of estimable service as campus pastor, Gordon Lathrop resigned to accept an appointment as professor of pastoral ministry and seminary pastor at Wartburg Theological Seminary in Dubuque, Iowa. In April a sixty-thousand dollar grant from the National Endowment for the Humanities was announced. It was the first such NEH grant in Washington state. It was to be used to develop introductory studies leading to an integrated core curriculum in the humanities. PLU's alternative core curriculum, the Integrated Studies program, ultimately emerged out of the studies and experimentation. Curtis Huber was the project director.

In February 1975 the board and the presidential search committee launched a long, careful, and nationwide presidential search. They sent more than three thousand letters soliciting nominations and received 205 nominations. After a lengthy process, three candidates were brought to the campus: Darrell R. Lewis, associate dean of the University of Minnesota's College of Education; Edward A. Lindell, dean of the University of Denver's College of Arts and Sciences; and William O. Rieke, a 1953 PLU alumnus who was the chancellor for health affairs at the University of Kansas. Provost Richard Jungkuntz had been nominated by several faculty members and was interviewed by the search committee, but it concluded "that the records show that at the present moment in time Dr. Jungkuntz does not have the experience to match maximally the needs of the University."[72]

Rieke, the leading candidate, was quickly named the eleventh president of Pacific Lutheran University. Rieke came highly recommended with a great deal of medical school administrative experience. He quickly unleashed his energy, charm, and persuasive abilities on the various constituencies that had been disaffected in the recent past. Sunnier dispositions and changed attitudes were soon apparent.

11

Stability and Change

WILLIAM O. RIEKE was the second alumnus and the first native Washingtonian to be named PLU president. He was born in Odessa, near Spokane, and grew up in Cashmere on the eastern slopes of the Cascade Mountains, where his father had established a bank during the depression years. His grandfather, the Reverend Henry Rieke, was a pioneer Lutheran missionary in the Pacific Northwest. Rieke was a 1953 *summa cum laude* graduate of PLU, where he was active in student life and an accomplished debater. In 1958 he took his M.D. degree with honors from the University of Washington School of Medicine and joined the faculty of the Department of Biological Structure, where he taught until 1966. He won several outstanding teacher awards and was soon among the international elite in the field of transplant biology; some of his original research made heart transplantation possible. Between 1957 and 1973 he published more than fifty papers and abstracts dealing primarily with cellular immunology.

In 1966 Rieke went to the University of Iowa medical school as professor and chair of the anatomy department. A colleague there reported that Rieke inherited a run-down and academically impoverished department and quickly breathed life into it, making it the most popular teaching program among the basic science departments.[1] He served briefly as acting medical school dean at Iowa. In 1971 Rieke was appointed vice-chancellor for health affairs and professor of anatomy at the University of Kansas Medical Center; he also directed the medical school. His achievements there were outstanding. A former colleague wrote: "Almost singlehandedly he has mobilized the interest of the citizens of the state and of the state legislators in the affairs of the medical center.... What was a mediocre institution has become first-rate."[2] A former University of Washington colleague described Rieke as a born administrator who was thorough, fair, and objective; he thought PLU would be very fortunate if it could persuade him to come as president. He concluded with some wonderment: "I must say, frankly, that I do not understand why he would be willing to move from the kind of position he holds at the University of Kansas ... why he would wish to become President of a much smaller University."[3]

Rieke admitted he was not interested in the presidency of PLU to enhance his personal status. "I currently have all the prestige, power *and* problems I desire. I would consider being President . . . because [PLU] gave *me* a great deal in terms of a quality education and a sense of direction for life. Only if I could help develop similar experiences for the youth of today would I wish to be the President."[4]

Rieke was the first choice of the presidential search committee and the board of regents. After some negotiation, he accepted the offer tendered and was named the eleventh president of PLU in February 1975. He told Ray Ruppert of the *Seattle Times* that the time was right. He had "attained" in his own field and shown he could administer a major state medical institution, but he felt restricted by certain limitations in that kind of setting.

> There was a side of my life you can't practice at a state institution . . . the blend between what we believe and what we learn and think. So I was looking for an opportunity to find a setting in which that could happen. This is a place where it could. . . . We are not a church. We're an educational institution. Our first goal has to be first-rate education. But we want to do that in a setting that is Christian with people who are professional and Christian scholars.[5]

PLU was also his alma mater, he added, and the Rieke family missed the mountains and the ocean.

On 12 September 1975, in conjunction with opening convocation, the inauguration of President William Rieke was held. The "Processional of Joy" was played by the combined orchestra and band, and the Choir of the West sang. The rite of inauguration was administered by the Reverend David Preus, president of the American Lutheran Church, and the presentation of the President's Seal was made by board chair Thomas Anderson and Provost Richard Jungkuntz. Rieke's speech, entitled "Education with Edification for Enablement," was tightly constructed, a little wordy, and reiterated themes he had already presented. It was delivered at a rate of speed that astounded many hearers and remained typical of presidential speeches in the future. The new president said:

> Pacific Lutheran is first and foremost an institution of higher learning. It is not something else. Education in its highest quality and best academic rigor is . . . the mission. . . . But edification . . . is also an important part of mission of PLU. This integrated, comprehensive search for God's truth, whether in nature or in faith, leads to a synergistic effect between education and edification such that the two together impact the student in a manner that is greater, more productive, and more relevant to the whole individual than each can do separately.[6]

The president told the regents at their first meeting in September that all indicators for the forthcoming year were positive and that a busy, productive, and gratifying year was anticipated. Rieke would remain affirmative in his public presentations and administrative style. A new and "continually

updated" master plan for program and physical development was necessary, however; in the next few years five-year plans, questionnaires, and the
search for and use of relevant data would become hallmarks of the medical
scientist turned president. A serious and constant public relations effort
aimed at disaffected constituents was also undertaken. "It is most important
that vigorous efforts be made in establishing and renewing good, external
relations with the Church, the community, and all of PLU's constituencies.
The President pledges much of his energy to meet this need."[7] The president
and his wife (Joanne Schief, '54), who worked with great effectiveness as a
team, were on the road almost every weekend for the next several years. The
new president was received with enthusiasm and gratitude by all of PLU's
constituent groups, which was quickly manifested in all aspects of university life.

The institution survived the traumas and embarrassments of 1969–74
with no special difficulty. There were costs, particularly in fundraising,
development, and personnel, but institutional strength and momentum
proved to be substantial and were evident in the achievements and developments of the next several years. Music and athletics were soon in the
headlines, and academic advances, innovations, and successes brought
national attention to the university.

ACHIEVEMENTS IN MUSIC

Music was the first extracurricular activity at PLU, dating from Carlo
Sperati's organization of bands and choirs in 1894. Continuing to occupy
a central and honored place in the university's life, it has enjoyed remarkable successes and growth in the last fifteen years. Many of these successes
were achieved by the Choir of the West and its dynamic conductor,
Maurice Skones, but the relatively young and energetic music faculty
present in the department by the seventies helped bring about achievements, developments, new beginnings, and considerable ferment that can
be seen at almost every turn.

In the summer of 1977 the choir toured Europe for the third time since
1964. It made a powerful impression on audiences and critics; Oslo critic
Torstein Glythe thought it "unbelievable" that full-time students could
achieve results that would be envied by many professional choirs. "The
choir had good voices in all sections, but with an evenness, a breath
technique and precision that I find it difficult to remember having heard
before. . . . In the motet by Reger I was really taken aback. It was a really
inspired performance."[8] The choir was described as "one of the finest
University choirs in America."[9]

In February 1979 the choir sang in New York City's Lincoln Center to
excellent reviews:

There are many superior college choral groups around the country, but not many of them would probably care to tackle the demanding and musically rich program offered by the Choir of the West.... these young students from Pacific Lutheran University ... not only surmounted almost every challenge splendidly, but also did so while singing the entire concert from memory .... The Haydn mass was in some respects a mere warmup for the major tour de force of the concert, Richard Strauss' German Motet, Op. 62. This a capella score is rarely performed, and for good reason: it is twenty minutes long, the 16-part texture is cast in Strauss's knottiest chromatic style, the vocal range spans more than five octaves and, in the words of one choral director, the piece is quite simply 'the hardest choral work, of a tonal nature, ever written.' The music is extremely lovely.... No chorus will ever sing it flawlessly, but the Choir of the West brought a remarkable degree of confidence, secure intonation, and concentrated intensity to the task. Again, the consistency of tonal beauty was astonishing, especially so in music of such complexity.[10]

In February 1980 the contemporary music program and the Contemporary Director's Ensemble celebrated their tenth anniversaries. They were the brainchildren of energetic and personable twentieth-century music enthusiast David Robbins, who joined the faculty in 1969. He was determined that PLU students and audiences should be appropriately introduced to contemporary music and new performance techniques. Twenty-five concerts and twenty composers' forums had been held during the decade, which featured 119 major works, 109 student compositions, and quite a lot of Robbins's showmanship. Many of the composers had attended the presentation of their works. The entire music department had cooperated in the enterprise, but Robbins felt two people were worthy of special mention for their support—department chair Maurice Skones and orchestra director Jerry Kracht.[11]

In 1983, after nineteen years of service, Skones resigned to head choral activities and graduate programs in conducting at the University of Arizona. In his years at PLU Skones had achieved a national reputation for the choir, seen a fivefold increase in music majors, helped bring national accreditation, and encouraged the emphasis on contemporary musical forms. He was succeeded as department chair by Robbins and as Choir of the West director by Richard Sparks, a faculty member at Mt. Holyoke College who had been educated at the University of Washington. Sparks was the founding director of Seattle Pro Musica and had conducted the Northwest Bach Festival in Spokane for three years. He quickly shaped the vocal and stylistic range of the choir in a distinctive way. Robbins commented: "Outstanding choirs often develop a glorious sound that sets them apart from other choirs. Sparks strives for a variety of glorious sounds true to the music being performed." In a fifteenth-century work the sopranos should sound like boy sopranos, Robbins said; a Germanic work should sound Germanic and a French choral work should have its identifiable sound.[12]

Sparks soon directed a triumph of his own. Benjamin Britten's profoundly moving "War Requiem" was presented in Seattle and Tacoma on the twenty-fifth anniversary of its premiere. Included in the performance were PLU chorale ensembles, the orchestra, the Northwest Boys Choir, a chamber orchestra, and soloists—250 people in all. Louise Kincaid of the *Seattle Post-Intelligencer* called it an "inspired event":

> The credit for such polish and taste must go to Sparks. Never a showman or one to grandstand, he is a musician's conductor. Rarely has a choir sounded so well-rehearsed. Under the masterfully detailed baton of Sparks, the sections were astutely balanced, the shape of the work was clearly defined and the phrases and dynamic levels were performed with intelligence and direction.[13]

ACHIEVEMENTS IN SPORTS

Athletics was the second organized extracurricular activity to develop at PLU; basketball was the first team sport for both men and women, baseball was next, and a variety of other sports soon followed. Sports competition generated passion from the outset, and large numbers of students participated. There had been many accomplishments as the decades unfolded, but after the mid-1970s the extent of participation and levels of team and individual accomplishment reached new heights. By the eighties PLU was more successful at balancing academic activity and athletics and at competing at local and national levels than any other institution in the 500-member National Association of Intercollegiate Athletics. Athletic excellence and the concept of the student-athlete were taken seriously at PLU.

Although he had a long and healthy tradition to build on, much of the credit for recent success must go to athletic director and physical education dean David Olson. He graduated from Concordia College in Minnesota, took his doctorate at the University of Iowa, and served eight years as athletic director at Wartburg College in Iowa before coming to PLU in 1968. Olson was determined to maintain the institution's emphasis on academic excellence, but thought that excellence in athletics and fitness should be striven for as well. He was also committed to extensive participation and to women's athletics. In 1973 expansion and financing of the women's program was given an enormous boost by an anonymous gift of $420,000 in the form of two trusts. Soon PLU could boast of twenty-two men's and women's varsity sports—more than at any other NAIA school

in the Northwest—thirty activity courses, a professional physical education program, and intramural and fitness activities. Olson also held several
local, regional, and national offices, culminating in his presidency of the
NAIA in 1985–86 and appointment to the United States Collegiate Sports
Council, which is responsible for arranging and managing the World
University Games. In 1988 he was elected to the NAIA Hall of Fame for
"meritorious service."

The most successful athletic teams of the past two decades have probably
been alumnus ('69) Mike Benson's men's tennis teams. Since he began
coaching in 1970 the teams have compiled a 259–121 dual match record,
won fourteen conference and eleven district titles, and advanced to "nation-
als" thirteen times. Benson has been named district coach of the year twelve
times. The men's and women's swimming teams have not been very far
behind, dominating conference competition and regularly placing at national meets. Since 1966 twenty-six men have been named all-American
swimmers, as have twenty-one women since 1977.

If the tennis and swimming teams have produced the glossiest records,
the football teams have produced the most headlines, with conference and
national championships, Tacoma Dome games, and overseas tours. The
orchestrator of these accomplishments has been Forrest "Frosty" Westering, a large, amiable, affirmative figure who came to PLU in 1972 after
coaching stints at Parsons College in Iowa and Lea College in Minnesota
and the acquisition of a doctorate from Northern Colorado University in
1966. His coaching methods encompass motivational psychology, slogans,
techniques that encourage team cooperation and closeness, affection and
concern for his players, Christian values (Westering has been an enthusiastic member and national leader of the Fellowship of Christian Athletes),
and a sophisticated and relatively complicated "big play" offense. He has
also been ably assisted and complemented by long-time defensive coach
Paul Hoseth. Westering has insisted over and over again that his teams do
not play to win—they try to play to their best ability. He told *Mooring Mast*
reporters in 1976:

> I don't really think you play to beat the other guy, even though that's what
> the scoreboard shows. You play to play at the highest level you can, and then
> the score is gonna take care of itself because if you play at a high level, you're
> gonna win many games and you don't get uptight then. I've watched a lot of
> teams crumble.[14]

In a 1986 article by *Tacoma News Tribune* sports editor Bart Wright that
appeared before the annual UPS game, Westering was described as a
"balding, bulging, Christian, all-American, Yogi Bear Buddha figure with
a headset and a clipboard."[15] He certainly attracted attention, as did his
array of such slogans as "other teams come to beat us, we come to be us."

Westering's record on the field speaks for itself, however. Under his leadership football accomplishments from 1972 to 1987 have been remarkable. Westering is the winningest PLU football coach ever with 127 victories. His teams have won seven conference championships and have been ranked in the top ten of the NAIA final rankings nine times. They have made seven national playoff appearances since 1979, winning twelve games and losing five; they have won two national championships (1980, 1987) and have twice been "runners-up" (1983, 1985). Westering was NAIA national coach of the year in 1983, and he has more victories (160) than any other active NAIA Division II football coach. Seventeen players have been named NAIA all-Americans since 1975, including John Zamberlin, a fifth-round draft choice of the New England Patriots who played five years in the NFL. Since the early 1940s ten Lutes have had tryouts with professional football teams.

The most extraordinary individual athletic achievements were those of three women, Diane Johnson ('82), Valerie Hilden ('88), and Sonya Brandt ('89). Johnson won four all-American honors in three sports—cross-country, Nordic skiing, and track. Sportswriters could not find another three-sport all-American. She also graduated with a 3.7 grade point average in mathematics, won the George Fisher Scholar-Athlete Award, and was selected to Who's Who in American Colleges and Universities. Hilden, a nursing major, won all-American ranking eight times—four times in both cross-country and track—an achievement unprecedented at PLU. She was also a two-time national cross-country champion, and her 1988 victory led coach Brad Moore's women's team to the national championship. Brandt, a business administration major, was the first four-time all-American performer in NAIA women's soccer. She led coach Colleen Hacker's team to the 1988 national championship.

The fusion of academic and athletic excellence, broad participation, and national competition has reached remarkable levels since 1985–86. That year twenty-five PLU athletes were academic all-Americans; of 510 awards given by the NAIA, one in twenty went to PLU. There were 119 participants on eleven teams in national competition in 1985–86, 115 on thirteen teams in 1986–87, and 118 on ten teams in 1987–88. In 1988 the 118 national competition participants represented 21 percent of the institution's 566 intercollegiate athletes. In 1987–88 PLU won the Northwest Conference's Jane McIlroy–John Lewis All Sports Trophy (which measures the overall strength of an institution's athletic program) for the third straight year; that year it also won ten conference championships and was runner-up for five. The football team won a national championship, as did the women's softball team. The softball victory, along with a third place finish at the national cross-country meet, a fourth place finish at the national swimming meet, and postseason competition in soccer and track, propelled the PLU women to their first-ever title in the NAIA Sports Information Directors' Association All-Sports competition. The men's teams equaled their best-ever finish with a ninth place ranking. When combining points from both the women's and men's divisions, PLU's overall 1987–88 athletic program ranked first in the NAIA.

ACADEMIC AND INSTITUTIONAL ADVANCES

A number of important administrative appointments were made in 1975–76, soon after Rieke arrived. In November 1975 Donald Jerke was installed as university minister. He was a graduate of Concordia Seminary in St. Louis and had served as campus pastor at the University of Oregon for eight years. He teamed up with James Beckman, who had served in a similar capacity with Gordon Lathrop before his resignation. Tragically, Beckman would die of cancer the next August, shortly before his twenty-ninth birthday. Jerke was appointed vice president for student life in October 1978 and served three years in that position before he died of a heart attack in October 1981. He was thirty-nine. In 1976 the Reverend Luther Bekemeier, a Missouri Lutheran pastor from Chicago with fourteen years' experience in fundraising and public relations, was appointed vice president for development. His first responsibility was to organize and launch a fund drive that would permit the building of a new science building. Also in 1976, John Heussman succeeded Frank Haley as director of the library. He had worked in both private and public institutions in Illinois and Nebraska. Haley had served for twenty-six creative years with his unique administrative style, and similarly Heussman brought twenty-six years of experience.

Department, school, and program accreditation dramatized the next several years. In April 1976 the School of Business Administration's M.B.A. program was accredited by the American Association of Collegiate Schools of Business. Only six private schools in the West were similarly accredited: PLU's was the only accredited night school program in the Northwest. In 1960 three faculty members taught business administration; by 1976 there were seventeen faculty, and both the B.B.A. and M.B.A. programs were accredited. At that time, more than seven hundred baccalaureate degrees had been granted in business since 1960, and more than two hundred M.B.A. degrees had been awarded since that program began in 1965. In 1982 the PLU accounting program was one of the first eighteen programs to be nationally accredited. PLU was one of the smallest institutions in the nation to be so honored. The aggressive and single-minded leadership of Gundar King and the irenic abilities of former dean Dwight Zulauf were producing substantial results.

Elsewhere in the university, the School of Music was accredited by the National Association of Schools of Music in 1979, and in 1982 the chemistry department was ranked among the top 3 percent of departments in the country at universities that do not grant doctorates. Only fourteen of those top departments were in the West, and only eleven of the elite schools had produced more National Science Foundation fellows between 1974 and 1979 than PLU.

In 1977 the National Endowment for the Humanities gave PLU two hundred thousand dollars to continue the experimental, team-taught, interdisciplinary Integrated Studies program. More than thirty faculty members were working on the project, which would eventually result in an alternative core curriculum–"Core II." Project director and philosophy professor Curtis Huber said: "It's the most marvelous redeeming experience I've ever had with faculty in my entire life. It's making liars of the people who claim that professors are a stubborn, ingrained bunch that just want to do their own things in their own little world."[16] The program soon received national attention, and Huber was regularly on the road describing it to other institutions.

Student academic achievements continued as well. Acceptances at medical and dental schools continued at twice the national average. Six students won Fulbright fellowships in the seventies, and five won National Science Foundation and Rotary International fellowships. In 1978 Carol Staswick, a *summa cum laude* history major who played the violin in the university symphony, won PLU's second Danforth fellowship.

In 1977 both an intensive self-study and a consultant's survey concluded that a natural sciences hall and a center for the performing arts were essential to PLU's future, and a feasibility study was launched. Those needs had been widely recognized since the late sixties, of course, and had been explicitly announced by President Mortvedt before he retired in 1969. The adventures of the early seventies, however, lost nearly a decade in development momentum. The feasibility study led to the organization and November 1978 launching of the $16.5 million capital fund campaign called "Sharing in Strength." The honorary chairs for the drive were North Pacific District Bishop Clarence Solberg, alumnus and University of Washington basketball coach Marv Harshman, and alumnus and business leader Gus Anderson. A $5 million science building, a $3 million fine arts building, refurbished facilities, and endowment growth were to be the primary goals. Rieke reported to the board that the recruitment of campaign leaders had gone very well. He asserted that "there is a vast reservoir of concerned, committed individuals throughout the Northwest . . . ready and willing to share their time, talents and resources on behalf of PLU."[17] The campaign received a big boost in the spring of 1981 with a $1.5 million gift from the M. J. Murdock Charitable Trust of Vancouver, Washington; it was the largest single gift in PLU's history. The regents authorized the science building plans in October 1982, and ground breaking took place the following May. The price tag had jumped to $6.9 million. When the science building was dedicated on 27 January 1985, the regents chose to honor the current PLU president by naming it the William O. Rieke Science Center. The final cost was $8.9 million. In May 1985 the "Sharing in Strength" campaign ended; more than $17.4 million had been raised, but spiraling costs made it impossible to build the planned fine arts facility. Private funding was pursued for that building.

The new, attractive, and much more spacious science center, badly needed for a decade and a half, was received with enthusiasm by the science faculty and students; they soon wondered how they had managed as well as they had in Ramstad Hall. Science had not been the only area of intellectual activity and accomplishment at PLU since the late 1930s, but it had been the major one. By almost any measure used—the success of the premedical and predental programs, the number of doctorates earned by graduates, funding for facilities and research, faculty publications, proportion of "distinguished alumnus" awards received by graduates (nearly half), national reputations of faculty—the achievements of the natural sciences division were noteworthy. It was assumed that the new facility would permit even more creative and effective teaching and scholarship.

After World War II, many PLU science graduates brought together service, scholarship, and often administrative skills in productive ways that sharply underscored the educational values of their alma mater. The careers of many alumni illustrate this rare combination. For example, William Foege ('57) played a dominant role in the eradication of smallpox in the world with his "surveillance-containment" strategy, and he later served as a top administrator at the Center for Disease Control, the World Health Organization, and the Carter Center. He is currently director of the Task Force for Child Survival, whose central mission is the eradication of polio in the world. Four alumni who became medical school teachers and researchers have been especially prominent: the University of Washington's Anita Hendrickson ('57), specializing in neuroanatomy and glaucoma research; the University of Kansas's Grace Foege Holmes ('53), specializing in child development; the chair of the surgery department at the University of Illinois, Lloyd Nyhus ('45), a heart transplantation specialist; and the University of Washington's Eugene Strandness ('50), specializing in vascular diagnosis and therapy. Chris Tarimo ('64) headed the Tropical Pesticides Center in Arusha, Tanzania, and developed the science curriculum for all Tanzanian schools. William Rieke ('53) made fundamental contributions in cell immunology research and directed the University of Kansas medical school before coming to PLU. M. Roy Schwarz ('58) provided important administrative leadership for regional and cooperative medical training while at the University of Washington, headed the medical school at the University of Colorado, and is presently vice president for medical education and science of the American Medical Association. Fred Wikner ('52) is a former director of the SALT task force for the Department of Defense and one of the nation's foremost authorities on national security technology and policy. Ronald Heyer ('63) is an internationally known herpetologist and a curator at the Smithsonian Institution, and David Wake ('58) is a well-known vertebrate zoologist and a museum director at the University of California at Berkeley.

Several other development gifts, expansions, and accomplishments highlighted the mid-eighties. In 1982 PLU leased the vacant Parkland grade school to relieve space problems and address community needs. A number of academic and service programs were soon located there, and the building became popularly known as "East Campus." In September 1984 the Names Fitness Center, the gift of Scott and Sis Names of Tacoma—a 5,500-square-foot facility attached to the north end of Memorial Gymnasium—was dedicated. It featured state-of-the-art weight training facilities and other conditioning equipment with full-time staff assistance.

Also in 1984, the university petitioned the state Higher Education Facilities Authority for the issuance of $10.75 million in tax-exempt bonds to purchase science building equipment, renovate Ramstad Hall, and add a third floor to Mortvedt Library. The bonds were issued, and all the projects were completed. The $2.1 million Carlisle Dietrich Library Addition was dedicated on 8 September 1987; Dietrich, a physician who lived in Parkland, had given half a million dollars to complete funding for the project. President Emeritus Robert Mortvedt delivered the dedication: books, he said, are "the really great teachers, for they preserve the finest products of the imaginations and intellects of their authors. Moreover, they are infinitely patient, always waiting to be used."[18]

KPLU, the university's National Public Radio affiliate, came of age during the eighties. It began as a ten-watt station in 1965 under the direction of Paul Steen and the electronic wizardry of chief engineer David Christian. In 1969–70 power was increased to forty thousand watts and in 1980 to one hundred thousand. With the help of "translator stations," its news, public radio features, and all-jazz format can be heard from Vancouver, British Columbia, to Vancouver, Washington. The combination of offerings—but especially NPR news and the all-jazz format begun in 1983—have been well received, and the number of listeners and amount of gift revenue have dramatically increased since that time. The station has projected an audience of one hundred thousand listeners and ten thousand "members" by the beginning of the university's centennial celebration. With listeners across western Washington, KPLU is a powerful force in local broadcasting and an important public relations tool for the university.

The energies of the period after 1975, sometimes channeled by the availability of federal grants and the access to new facilities, brought several new majors and academic concentrations to the university curriculum. The social sciences division proved especially fecund with majors in anthropology, marriage and family therapy, and social work emerging out of the sociology curriculum. Multidisciplinary and cooperative Global Studies and Legal Studies programs also emerged. In the humanities division, Norwegian and Scandinavian Studies majors helped keep the institution's ethnic heritage alive. The Integrated Studies program was an independent entity, but it had strong ties to the humanities. In 1979 the revolution in computer usage transformed the mathematics department into the mathematics and computer science department, and in 1981 a computer science major was established. Dramatic growth in numbers of faculty and majors accompanied the changes. In September 1986 a new computer engineering major was established; it was the first such blending of computer science and electrical engineering in the state. An artificial intelligence program for undergraduates was also launched, one of a handful of such undergraduate programs in the country.

INTERNATIONAL EMPHASIS

The curriculum was also increasingly internationalized. Foreign study grew dramatically, the number of international students increased, and faculty from all disciplines became involved in a variety of international exchange and advisory activities. In 1978 a Foreign Area Studies program was organized under the leadership of history professor Mordechai Rozanski. It brought multidisciplinary resources to bear on the study of the world's regions. In 1980 Rozanski was appointed director of the new Office of International Education, which worked to develop an international focus across the curriculum. A wide range of activities soon emerged. The establishment of the Foreign Area Studies program made PLU a "showcase institution" in the handling of global studies, according to the U.S. Office of Education.[19] Rozanski also spearheaded the development of regional programs and consortia aimed at increased knowledge of the dimensions of global interdependence. Between 1978 and 1982 more than half a million dollars in federal grants poured into the institution to subsidize these developments. By 1982 a Global Studies major was approved. It was interdisciplinary and "complementary"—that is, it had to be a second major complementing a regular disciplinary major. The new program had an introductory "global perspectives" course, a concluding seminar, and focuses on various clusters of world regions. In addition, "global issues" concentrations enabled students to develop additional skills and perspectives. The program was complicated and required careful coordination, but it allowed a relatively small institution to address the complexity of global issues in ways that single departments could not manage.

In 1982 business professor Thad Barnowe taught management and organizational practice at China's Zhongshan University on a Fulbright grant. He was the first Fulbright lecturer in business to teach in China since 1949, and the first foreign professor to teach a subject other than languages at Zhongshan since the Cultural Revolution. Exchange programs for both students and faculty were soon arranged with Zhongshan and Chengdu University of Science and Technology. In 1986 sixteen students went to Chengdu, along with chemistry professors William Giddings and Charles Anderson. Faculty and students continue to go to Chengdu, and the relationship with that institution remains cordial. In exchange, several Chinese professors have made their way to PLU for study, teaching, and stays of various lengths.

Larger and larger numbers of international students also came to PLU in the eighties. In 1984, 218 students came from thirty foreign countries, a number that had doubled in the previous two years. By 1988 more than 6 percent of the students at PLU were international students—the largest numbers came from Hong Kong, Malaysia, and Norway.[20]

The university's ethnic and historic ties to Scandinavia were kept alive and strengthened in the midst of these global concerns and developments. The emergence of Norwegian and Scandinavian Studies majors in the seventies suggests this, as do the development of a special collection in the library devoted to the Scandinavian immigrant experience and the construction of a Scandinavian Cultural Center. These developments have been strengthened by visits of Scandinavian royalty. In October 1975 thirty-five hundred people filled Olson Auditorium to see Olav V, the seventy-two-year-old king of Norway. (He had visited PLU as crown prince in 1939.) President Rieke presented him with a special silver medal designed by sculptor Tom Torrens, and ASPLU president Martha Miller conferred the title "honorary student" on him and presented him with a "12th man" t-shirt.[21] A rune stone sculptural grouping near Eastvold Chapel was dedicated on 8 September 1976. The shape and positioning of the stones recreated the rendering on the special medal given to the king. The sculpture—designed by Torrens—was given by the Norwegian-American Sesquicentennial Commission as a lasting commemoration of the king's visit and the beginning of Norwegian emigration to the United States. Clayton Peterson, a member of the commission, was credited with encouraging and coordinating the sculpture's sponsorship.

In September 1982 Swedish film and stage stars Max von Sydow and Bibi Andersson paid a three-hour visit to PLU to help launch the year-long Scandinavia Today celebration. They were followed by King Carl XVI Gustav and Queen Silvia of Sweden, who visited campus on 17

November. The king was given the President's Medal and the queen received a glass sculpture created from Mount St. Helens's ash.

The achievements and developments at PLU by the beginning of the eighties were often striking. Enormous amounts of work and dedication to teaching were paying dividends. Much had certainly happened since university status was established in 1960—greater community visibility, physical growth, dramatic enrollment increases, increased faculty size and competence, widespread student achievements—and virtually all aspects of university life seemed to gather speed after 1975.

In the fall of 1980 President Rieke reported to the university that "we are as a University now at that point where we are ready for the next incremental step that will take us from an excellent to a superior institution."[22] A few months later, in a ninetieth anniversary special supplement to the *Tacoma News Tribune*, Rieke warned that the source of our greatest problems and our greatest challenge will be "the stupendous pace of change itself." He then outlined how the institution through its liberal arts emphasis and the development of new programs was trying to cope with the challenges and change. He also continued his search for data by which to measure PLU's educational successes, failures, and direction. In 1981 he undertook a survey of alumni who had graduated since the transition to university status in 1960–61. The results were remarkably positive. Human services vocations still predominated among alumni, and 96.1 percent of the respondents either agreed or strongly agreed that they had received a good education. Why had they come to PLU? Over 97 percent said the institution's academic reputation was the primary consideration, size and parental influence were tied for second at 82 percent, 76 percent stressed the liberal arts emphasis, and 61 percent emphasized the Christian environment. Nearly 88 percent of the respondents said they would go to PLU again barring financial constraints. A 1986 survey produced similar results.[23] An earlier survey in 1976 had reported that 71 percent of responding students indicated they chose PLU because of academic quality, while a similar survey in 1964 determined that just 58 percent had selected the school on that basis.

In the eighties academic achievements continued, but growing numbers of students preferred job-oriented majors, and the numbers going into service occupations and to graduate school diminished. Many faculty members thought intellectual passion had declined as well. Business administration and computer science attracted many students, law school applications boomed, and the premedical and predental programs continued to attract able students from around the Northwest. Applications to theological seminaries fell off rather badly, however. In the decade, five students won Rotary International fellowships, nine won Fulbright fellowships, and a number of science students won handsome awards. Most notably, Mau Lun Yip, a native of Hong Kong and 1988 graduate, was one of nine undergraduates nationwide to win a Howard Hughes Medical Institute doctoral fellowship in biological sciences. He chose to study at the California Institute of Technology.

The quality of the faculty advanced in a number of important ways after 1975, including acquisition of terminal degrees, participation at conferences, scholarly publications, successful competition for grant funds, and appointments to visiting professorships. Teaching remained the primary activity and responsibility of the faculty, but many recognized that if a university is to make an impact on its region and provide leadership for church and state, teaching and scholarship must be integrated and both must flourish. That was beginning to happen in exciting ways at PLU.

By 1986, 70 percent of the 280 faculty members had doctoral degrees, compared to 58 percent in 1975. Publication, performance, and other professional achievements were quite widespread throughout the university. For example, between 1985 and 1987 the faculty of the School of Business Administration published sixty articles, cases, and reviews as well as several textbooks. In the 1960s four books were published by faculty authors; between 1970 and 1975 three faculty members published books. From 1975 to 1988 more than twenty-five books were published. These included a number of textbooks (including Stanley Brue's four coauthored economics texts, one of which is the best-selling introductory text in the field), monographs, edited works, volumes of poetry, and novels.

Several faculty members had acquired international reputations by 1988. K. T. Tang, who fled China in 1949 and received a doctorate from Columbia University in 1965, is known for his research on quantum theory of reactive, dissociative, and inelastic molecular scatterings. His research has been supported by numerous grants, and he has published more than seventy articles and lectured in China, Hong Kong, Taiwan, Germany, Norway, Canada, and throughout the United States. He has been a visiting professor of physics at the University of Wisconsin and a visiting scientist at the Max Planck Institute in Göttingen, Germany.

Fred Tobiason, a PLU alumnus (1958) with a Ph.D. degree from Michigan State University, is a physical chemist with interests in wood and polymer chemistry. He has published more than twenty articles and contributions to books, delivered an equal number of papers, worked extensively with industry, and lectured in Finland, Yugoslavia, Japan, and the United States. He is currently working on research projects with university professors in Germany, India, and the United States. He also has a great interest in environmental issues; he has lectured and published extensively on a variety of subjects, including water quality, dragonflies, woodpeckers, chipmunks, and sapsuckers.

Christopher Browning, an Oberlin graduate with a 1975 Ph.D. degree from the University of Wisconsin, is an expert on modern German history, particularly the Holocaust. Author of two important books and nearly twenty articles, he has lectured, given papers, and served as an expert witness at international conferences, symposia, and trials in the United States, Canada, Great Britain, France, Germany, and Israel. He has been a visiting fellow at the Institute for Advanced Study of the Hebrew University of Jerusalem and a visiting professor at the University of Wisconsin. He is the primary author of the forthcoming "Final Solution," which will be the definitive book on Nazi Jewish policy and its implementation in Europe during the second World War, published as part of the Yad Vashem Society's projected twenty-four-volume comprehensive history of the Holocaust.

Other kinds of recognition have also come to the university and its president. In November 1986 the Exxon Education Foundation ranked William Rieke among the top 5 percent of the nation's college presidents. In October 1987 *U.S. News & World Report* gave PLU the highest ranking of any Northwest comprehensive university in its biennial survey of American higher education. PLU ranked eighth in the Midwest and West comprehensive university category; fellow Lutheran-affiliated Valparaiso University was ranked first. Data came from a survey of college and university presidents; President Rieke found it "especially gratifying to be praised by your peers."[24] By 1988 PLU was not only nationally ranked as a comprehensive university, but it also had become the largest private college or university in the Northwest with 3,950 students and the largest Lutheran college or university in the United States.

In 1987 three vice presidential appointments were made, and in 1988 a nationwide search was launched to replace retiring Provost Richard Jungkuntz. It was hoped these appointments would help maintain institutional momentum and carry PLU past its centennial into the last decade of the twentieth century. Donald Sturgill, a graduate of Portland State University with an M.P.A. degree from the University of Washington, was appointed vice president for finance and operations. He had been controller at Western Washington University since 1976. S. Erving Severtson, a faculty member since 1966 and a 1955 PLU alumnus, was appointed vice president and dean for student life. And on 30 November 1988 President Rieke reported that J. Robert Wills had accepted appointment as provost. A 1962 graduate of the College of Wooster with a Ph.D. degree in theatre from Case-Western Reserve University in 1971, Wills taught at Wittenberg

University from 1963 to 1972 and served as dean and director of graduate studies in theatre art at the University of Kentucky from 1972 to 1981. Since 1981 he had been dean of the College of Fine Arts, professor of drama, and holder of the Effie Marie Cain Regents Chair in fine arts at the University of Texas at Austin. He has published widely, written several plays, and directed or produced more than four hundred plays. In accepting the appointment at PLU, Wills said: "To my mind the church-related, Christian institution makes possible the richest kind of educational adventure because it adds the dimension of faith to the context of learning."

In 1987 Harvey Neufeld, a 1954 alumnus who had served the institution in a variety of capacities since 1965, was appointed vice president for church relations, a newly created liaison position to work with the vastly larger church constituency that resulted from the organizational structure of the newly merged Evangelical Lutheran Church in America (1988). Region One of the ELCA includes six synods stretched across the enormous expanse of five states—Alaska, Washington, Oregon, Idaho, and Montana. It comprises 628 congregations, compared to 314 congregations in the former North Pacific District of the American Lutheran Church, and 262,698 members. Ownership of PLU is vested in those congregations. That constituency is a far cry from the five congregations, two ordained pastors, and 250 adult members of the Norwegian Synod that founded PLU in 1890. The coming together of the structures and possibilities of the ELCA and the successes and recognitions of PLU's recent past suggest that the second century of PLU's history might be rich and productive in ways as yet undreamed of.

THE CHRISTIAN CONTEXT

PLU has always taken its Christian moorings seriously, and it has taken learning seriously as well; it has resolutely searched for the correct relationship of those parts of its identity. This is, of course, the almost two-millennia-old question of Athens and Jerusalem raised by Tertullian. At least through the mid-1960s such institutional efforts were primarily concerned with working out differing perceptions of what it meant to be Lutheran and how that applied to higher education. The 1963 statement of objectives was written within that context. At that juncture, just as earlier in PLU's history, Lutheran identity was preserved, but with some parochial narrowing side effects. Was it possible to remedy that problem? How could PLU be authentically and ecumenically Lutheran and academically serious, yet avoid what many from the late 1950s onward thought were debilitating side effects? More diversity, more scholarship, more tolerance of dissent, and fewer restrictive rules were among the solutions advanced.

Many critics of those efforts, however, feared that the integrity of PLU would be jeopardized by pluralism, secularization, and the lack of discipline. The long-term development of secularization and pluralism, while not terminal problems for the Christian perspective, certainly pose a number of serious and intriguing challenges. It is important to remember, though, that Luther understood "secular" to mean nonredemptive but not God-forsaken, and that Western civilization has become increasingly secular at least since the Renaissance and perhaps since Plato's fourth century B.C. Greece.

The explosive social, political, and intellectual developments of the 1960s brought pressures for change and seemed to underscore secularization and pluralism in new and powerful ways. Maintaining authentic identity and responsible action became severe challenges as relentless change occurred. Some of the educational theory that had undergirded Lutheran institutions, as well as the consensus of values that had dominated American life, began to break down. By the early seventies that consensus seemed to be gone, and America found itself awash in a sea of individual preference. As individual preference took hold of private morality and public life, religious and educational communities suffered, consensus was often denigrated, and private benefit outdistanced institutional loyalty.[25] Church-related educational institutions seemed to be poised on the cusp between secularity, pluralism, rampant individualism, relativism, and innovation on the one hand, and value-oriented education, community, tradition, heritage, and continuity on the other.[26] It was a remarkably confusing and trying time.

In the years after 1975, in the midst of this tumult, the administration, faculty, and regents of PLU addressed questions of identity and mission with considerable regularity. No new institutional consensus was achieved, and old values were stretched. Pluralism—and, some thought, secularity—continued to emerge, but the theological understanding of what a Lutheran university should be was carefully addressed; the relationship between faith and learning continued to be a matter of concern and discussion.

From his first appearance on campus after being selected as president, William Rieke has been quite clear about his position: "The justification for PLU's existence . . . is to provide the extra dimension of relating Christ to all of life . . . and to the highest possible quality of academics."[27] Details about what that meant were harder to explicate, but they were the stuff of future discussions, and the concept of education within a Christian context soon appeared. It had been implicit in some of Rieke's earliest speeches. A year earlier, in 1974, the centennial historian of St. Olaf College described how that institution was taking the same tack: "St Olaf has not tried to be an all-purpose college, but has declared its intention to pursue liberal learning within a Christian context."[28]

In October and November 1977 the notion of "quality education in a

Christian context" was discussed in three public forums. The discussions were organized by campus minister Ron Tellefson. At the president's directive that phrase soon made its way onto university stationery. Not all thought it was appropriate or descriptive. At the same time "mission statements" were discussed with the regents and with various church representatives on campus, at regional retreats, and at national workshops.

In March 1979 the *Mooring Mast* devoted a long issue to the church-relatedness of PLU. Student interviews and articles and statements from university ministers Ron Tellefson and Don Jerke were included. PLU, they said, was a church-related university, but it did not claim to be a Christian university. That was a new distinction, but one that would be quite regularly drawn from that time forward. "Christian" could apply to a church, but not to a university that was concerned with a multitude of activities, most of which were undeniably "secular," Jerke observed. "PLU is a place where we can keep asking what it is to be a Christian and a place where it is okay to ask that question." Tellefson quoted the phrase in the statement of objectives about the institution being a community of professing Christian scholars, but then added that not all in the community were Christian scholars. The university community, like the apostles, he said, was made up of believers and unbelievers; it was a mixture of faith, unbelief, and skepticism. "The mixture of unbelief and skepticism exists side by side not only in the community, but inside each individual."[29] That "Christian scholars" phrase, previously understood more literally than Tellefson suggested was now the case, had been important in formulating the statement of objectives and achieving the approval of the regents and church. It had been strongly supported and understood quite explicitly by Robert Mortvedt during his presidency.

Discussions of identity and mission also took place in a larger context. In the seventies the American Lutheran Church developed an understanding of its colleges as extensions of the church. It defined them as "the church in mission in higher education" and affirmed a redemptive and reconciling role for education, in addition to its investigative and creative activities. The LCA worked on the partnership between church and college during those years as well.

The division of college and university service of the ALC supported a number of national conferences and workshops on the context and mission of Lutheran higher education during the seventies: at Concordia College in Minnesota (1974), at Luther College in Decorah, Iowa (1975), and at Luther-Northwestern Seminary in St. Paul, Minnesota (1978). A regional conference was held at California Lutheran College in 1979. The presentations at these conferences were often thoughtfully done, and the discussions were frequently freewheeling. In February 1981 the division subsidized a conference and intensive dialogue on "Community and Pluralism at PLU." It was held at the Lake Wilderness Retreat Center, and twenty-four faculty and staff members participated. The president wrote to the participants: "At a Lutheran church-related university a continuous dialogue must focus on the nature of the academic community in its search for a healthy pluralism within the Lutheran-Christian context. At PLU the creative tension between faith and culture, between Christian affirmation and pluralistic probabilities, can be especially fruitful."[30] Yale University historian Sydney Ahlstrom, Provost Richard Jungkuntz, and a number of faculty members spoke at the retreat. The retreat spilled over into the next academic year and produced a speech about pluralism and PLU's history at the faculty fall conference and the appointment of an ad hoc committee on Christian context with Ron Tellefson as chair. Forums were held in September and October and other activities followed. In 1982 the *Mooring Mast* featured a series of articles exploring the "L" in PLU.[31]

In 1985 Provost Jungkuntz discussed "Can a Context Be Christian?" in the university publication *Scene*. Strictly speaking, he said, a context and a university cannot be Christian, but PLU understands itself as characterized by wholeness, a unified wholeness greater than the parts, and what makes PLU's context Christian is its "intentionality," out of which its essential nature and existence come. He thought that had been true from the beginning in 1890 to the latest affirmations found in the 1985 five-year plan.[32] In that document, the first priority stated: "The University will continue as a small Liberal Arts University of the Lutheran Church." It spelled out in considerable detail what that meant.

The resignations of campus pastors Ron Tellefson (who joined the university's development office) and Ron Vignec (who organized a mission in Tacoma's economically depressed and racially diverse Salishan district) brought a team of three new university ministers in 1986: Susan Briehl, Daniel Erlander, and Martin Wells. That Briehl and Wells were spouses added a rare distinction to the campus ministry. Together the three new pastors brought rich, diverse, but complementary abilities, worked together comfortably, and inevitably addressed the question of university identity. Erlander said that "campus ministry is a space for grace." They labored to provide worship opportunities for an increasingly diverse student body and faculty and to serve the campus community. The confluence of personalities gave the university an unusual but special team to bear witness to its various commitments.

By 1988 the PLU faculty was more academically and religiously diverse than it had ever been, but members were still concerned about religious matters personally and professionally. A May 1988 questionnaire sent to the faculty, to which more than 60 percent responded, elicited a number of interesting responses. Sixty-eight percent of faculty respondents indicated that religious questions were either very important or somewhat important in the educational processes of the university, and 81 percent said religious issues were very important or somewhat important in their lives. Only 56 percent reported that they belonged to a church or synagogue, however. This last figure undoubtedly suggests something of the widespread privatization and individual preference that emerged so powerfully in religion and morality since the sixties. The largest percentage of those who belonged to a church or synagogue was Lutheran (56 percent), with Presbyterians (8 percent) and Roman Catholics (7 percent) next. That pattern is similar to the pattern among PLU students.

While religious questions were deemed important or somewhat important by 81 percent of the faculty, they expressed less enthusiasm for the phrase in the university's statement of objectives that reads: "PLU is a community of professing Christian scholars dedicated to a philosophy of the liberal arts." Sixty-three percent of the respondents thought that phrase was either somewhat inaccurate or very inaccurate in describing PLU today, and 70 percent thought it should either be rewritten (48 percent) or removed (22 percent). Numerous suggestions about how the phrase should be rewritten were included; most wanted to preserve the liberal arts emphasis and rewrite the reference to Christian scholars, but there was no agreement as to how that should be done.

To the one question about political preference included, 74 percent of the respondents indicated they most often voted Democratic. Seventeen percent preferred to vote Republican and 9 percent selected "other" preferences. The fine arts faculty led this Democratic surge at 90 percent, and those in the humanities division ran a close second at 88 percent. Following the conservative theological, social, and political structure that dominated Lutheran colleges into the sixties and a 1972 national study that indicated Lutherans preferred the Republican party, that 74 percent figure is both striking and intriguing. It is similar to national patterns in colleges and universities, but there are too few studies of Lutheran college faculties to generalize easily. It can be said with some assurance, however, that a great distance separates 1988 and 1952, when PLU president S. C. Eastvold excoriated and threatened to fire a faculty member for campaigning for a Democratic political candidate.

Determining what all this means, and whether PLU is more or less Lutheran—and Christian—than it once was, as well as establishing the criteria to be used to make those judgments, are complicated problems that do not lend themselves to easy answers. It can be said with assurance, however, that Athens and Jerusalem are still alive in Parkland, and questions about what that means are still being asked. The institution is also academically stronger than it has ever been. Perhaps that is all one can hope for at a Lutheran university. At such institutions the intersections of Christianity and culture are elusive and indefinite, and they occur for the most part on the tangent rather than head-on. The Lutheran intellectual tradition . . . has seldom flirted with dreams of re-creation of the medieval synthesis, and it has always rejected the fundamentalist triumphalism that would "Christianize" everything it touches in society and culture.[33]

As Christians and non-Christians alike battle the complexities and contradictions of the late twentieth century and search for meaning, it is important for all the constituencies of PLU to remember that the relation between faith and learning has complicated intersections and must be constantly and critically addressed. That process and the relationship are dynamic, not static; anyone who has wrestled with the theology of Martin Luther understands that. In his *Commentary on Galatians* Luther wrote: "Do not imagine that the life of a Christian is rest and quiet; it is a passage and a progress from vices to virtue, from light to light, from virtue to virtue. And if someone is not in transit, do not think that he is a Christian." It is also important for those concerned about higher education to remember that the "Christian faith does provide one of the few secure contemporary vantage points from which to take on the prejudices of modernity."[34] That in itself may be enough to justify the existence of a church-related educational institution.

Perhaps it is best for a visitor to have the last word. In 1985 the English department began to bring a Distinguished Writer-in-Residence to the campus each spring to interact with faculty and students and stretch the imaginations of would-be writers in the burgeoning writing and publishing courses and programs that the department offers. By any measure the program has been a wonderful success; it has brought Irish poet Richard Murphy; English-Israeli psychologist, novelist, and journalist Lesley Hazelton; American novelist Stephen Becker; French children's writer Noelle de Chambrun; and American journalist and novelist Patsy Sims to the campus. Hazelton wrote about PLU and its students in the *New York Times*,[35] and Becker reflected on his experience for *Scene*. He found PLU students more innocent, curious, and courteous than students of an earlier generation, albeit less versed in English ("that is not their fault; we are now in the third generation of illiteracy as public policy"). He concluded:

And while we are all ecumenical these days, I leave with a word of thanks for the Lutheran tradition. Doctrine and ritual aside, I have become sharply aware of a respect for education in the Northwest, for literacy, that seems to descend from the fervor of men and women who valued personal freedom and associated it with a vigorous vernacular. I know that fervor in its English puritan manifestations—it is, after all, the force behind the world's greatest literature; but now when I hear praise for Luther's translation of the Bible, I think, yes, and it is still making a difference in Tacoma.[36]

Conclusion:
A Story to Live By

T HE AMERICAN THEOLOGIAN Harvey Cox has observed that "all human beings have an innate need to tell and hear stories and to have a story to live by."[1] Those stories help people, and institutions, find and ensure their identities and discover direction for the future. The past—the source of the stories—can haunt, but it can also provide liberation. The telling of the stories can give delight as well, as can all human art.[2] The author hopes that these stories about PLU have provided the reader some measure of delight as well as understanding.

The most important motif running through the stories in this book is the irrepressible Lutheran commitment to learning. That commitment gave shape to revolutionary changes in educational theory and practice in the sixteenth century, and it produced a large number of educational institutions in North America—fifty by the late twentieth century. Pacific Lutheran University is among those institutions.

Within this larger context, PLU's greatest accomplishment during the first half-century of its history was survival. Western America's relative indifference to organized religion and private education, the paucity of Lutherans in the Northwest, and the relatively modest means of most Scandinavians and Lutherans, in combination with a timetable clogged with such unpredictable and destructive events as the panic of 1893, the Great Depression, and two world wars, produced a succession of daunting situations that could have been terminal. The determined responses of the faculty, staff, and such presidents as Bjug Harstad, Nils Hong, and Oscar Tinglestad can only be described as heroic. The institution survived because of that heroism; it also grew inexorably in quality and quantity. The campus also grew: buildings were built, slowly at first, and then more rapidly, especially after World War II. The acreage provided by Ward Smith in 1890 was ultimately filled with buildings, facilities, and activity. In the second half-century of the school's history Seth Eastvold, Robert Mortvedt, Dean Buchanan, and Clayton Peterson provided especially important leadership for building activity.

Through the entire century the original parklike campus setting, dominated by towering Douglas firs, has survived. Preserving the natural beauty has required vigilance upon occasion. In the 1960s, for example, an attempt was launched to cut the trees on the hillside between upper and lower campus; it was argued that the cutting would open up the campus for building, simplify maintenance, and eliminate what some thought was an unkempt look. A few trees were cut on the hillside and around building sites—a crime political science professor Donald Farmer calls "arborcide"—but resolute pressure from numerous people saved the hillside's trees and prepared the way for the development of a more extensive natural area south of the University Center. The principal organizer of that development was chemistry professor Fred Tobiason. The area now has a recycled stream and a low-density western Washington forest, as well as frogs, ducks, other birds, dragonflies, and occasionally a fox. The Weyerhaeuser Company provided much of the plant life and a nurse log. This natural area is a wonderful reminder of the rhythms and processes of nature, and it is a model for the preservation of diverse lifeforms in an urban setting.

Both the natural area and the more formal portions of the campus have been tended with dedication and thoughtfulness by plant managers (Kenneth Jacobs in the forties and fifties and James Phillips in the seventies and eighties) and groundskeepers. The rows and clusters of flowering cherry, dogwood, honey locust, and ginkgo trees, the more than four hundred rhododendrons, and the carefully tended flowers—especially the masses of daffodils and tulips that herald the coming of spring—regularly remind one of the importance of gardens and beauty at an institution dedicated to reflection and creativity. With this parklike setting and Mt. Rainier looming in the background, PLU is certainly the loveliest of the Lutheran colleges and universities.

PLU has also maintained fidelity to mission during its first hundred years. There have been lapses of memory from time to time and some mistaken pathways followed, but the earliest institutional expression of educational philosophy still rings true and is certainly congruent with the centennial theme of "Educating for Service: Century II." In 1891 the new university announced:

> Lutheran University will give instruction on a Christian foundation. The school shall be conducted in the Christian spirit and be Evangelical Lutheran in its confession and activity.... But the school shall also give instruction in all practical courses that our young people need to have knowledge of, each in his own situation. The school will educate and bring up good Christians and good citizens.[3]

In the decades that followed the founding of the school, the faculty was not always quick to articulate or refine further what it meant to be a Lutheran institution of higher education, but the importance of teaching and the idea of service remained alive. The faculty had crushing teaching loads until well after World War II; its members had little time for such investigations. Most were Lutheran until that time, however, so an often unspoken agreement about the philosophy of education and a powerful sense of community continued to pervade the campus. By the 1950s the approach to education was sometimes more "tribal" than philosophical or theological in nature, reflecting a rather narrowly conceived institutional history and a defensive pietism. That made it less clear what difference a Christian education should make amid the agonizing intellectual, moral, and political complexities of the mid-twentieth century. PLU was without a doubt still a Christian community, but what made it a Christian intellectual community was less clear.[4] Many felt there was too much Jerusalem at PLU and not enough Athens; that issue was much discussed in the decades after 1960.

Until the 1960s, PLU was often deeply loved by those who attended it, despite its pressing academic, social, and financial problems. It must also be remembered, however, that not all who matriculated either responded affirmatively to the manners and mores of PLU or stayed; the institutional attrition rate was high, especially in the fifties and sixties, and it remained something of a problem until the late seventies. For those who stayed to graduate the situation was quite a lot like what James Nuechterlein remarked about alumni of Valparaiso University:

> Most of us, when all was said and done, loved Valparaiso with an almost uncritical passion, or better, a passion that forgave the place its faults. It gave us an experience of intimate community . . . that allowed the possibility for criticism of the world out of which we had come even while, in the larger sense, it affirmed that world. If we had not, when we were done, undergone a splendid education, we had undergone a splendid college experience. My farewell editorial in the student newspaper expressed, I'm sure, the views of many other graduates as well: "For all that Valparaiso is we are grateful; for all that it is not we are still hopeful."[5]

The activity of the thirty years since 1960 has transformed many of those hopes into realities for both PLU and Valparaiso. In 1987 *U.S. News & World Report* listed them both as among the finest small comprehensive universities in the country.

It is impossible to summarize one hundred years of history in brief compass, but perhaps some statistics will help give coherence to what has happened. Since the first commencement in 1898 PLU has graduated more than twenty-five thousand alumni, more than half of them since William Rieke became president in 1975. PLU celebrates its centennial in 1990–91, but it is in many respects still a very young institution with a very young alumni association. Of those alumni, 6,148 graduated with education degrees, 1,883 earned nursing degrees, more than 500 became pastors, 438 became medical doctors or dentists, and by 1984, 313 had received Ph.D. or Ed.D. degrees. At least a third of PLU graduates have gone into the classic "service" vocations of teaching, healing, and the ministry, and service has undoubtedly been an important component in thousands of others' lives as well. The hopes, concerns, ambitions, and sacrifices of PLU's founders have yielded a remarkably rich harvest. The stories about PLU's history are full of pain, suffering, and apparent failure, but they are also about scholarship, service, courage, and accomplishment. Many of the accomplishments have been noteworthy.

On 22 September 1967, after receiving his honorary doctorate, the archbishop of Canterbury, the Reverend Dr. Michael Ramsey, concluded his remarks by asserting that a university should be a home of freedom, truth, personality, and religion. He then offered a moving benediction that is an appropriate conclusion to this history of PLU's first hundred years as well as a guide for the future: "May God be with Pacific Lutheran University for many years, yes, for many centuries to come. May this university go on sending people out who will bring reality and faith home to the troubled world to which we belong."

Appendices

PRESIDENTS OF PACIFIC LUTHERAN UNIVERSITY

Bjug A. Harstad	1894–95, 1897–98
Ole N. Gronsberg	1895–97
Nils J. Hong	1898–1918
John U. Xavier	1920–21
Ola J. Ordal	1921–28
Oscar A. Tingelstad	1928–43
Seth C. Eastvold	1943–62
Robert A. L. Mortvedt	1962–69
Eugene W. Wiegman	1969–74
Richard P. Jungkuntz	1974–75
William O. Rieke	1975–

Presidents and Major Buildings

Bjug A. Harstad

Ole N. Gronsberg

Nils J. Hong

John U. Xavier

Ola J. Ordal

Oscar A. Tingelstad

Seth C. Eastvold

Robert A. L. Mortvedt

Eugene W. Weigman

Richard P. Jungkuntz

William O. Rieke

Harstad Hall

The Gymnasium

The Chapel

Xavier Hall

Memorial Gymnasium

Ramstad Hall

Eastvold Auditorium

Administration Building

Mortvedt Library

Olson Auditorium

The University Center

Rieke Science Center

Appendix B

ACADEMIC STATISTICS: 1920–1987

Year	Enrollment	Degrees Earned		Tuition Cost	Full-time Faculty
1920–21	87	9		$31.50 (per semester)	6
1925–26	143	9		45.00	9
1930–31	237	44		54.00	23
1935–36	348	68		78.00	22
1940–41	523	103		87.00	28
1944–45	287	66		105.00	25
1949–50	1273	268		175.00	47
1954–55	1373	180		225.00	53
1959–60	2068	214		325.00	76
1964–65	2086	328	baccalaureate	450.00	106
		11	graduate		
1969–70	2831	543	baccalaureate	865.00	145
		93	graduate		
1974–75	3367	584	baccalaureate	66.50 (per hour)	185
		263	graduate		
1979–80	3326	591	baccalaureate	111.00	217
		174	graduate		
1984–85	3674	666	baccalaureate	185.00	259
		152	graduate		
1985–86	3758	650	baccalaureate	188.00	264
		154	graduate		
1986–87	3857	715	baccalaureate	230.00	280
		142	graduate		

Appendix C

UNIVERSITY INCOME AND NET RESULTS: 1943–1988

Fiscal Year	Income	Net Results	Gifts/Grants	Endowment
1943	$90,320	$3,280	$39,017	$71,563
1944	149,274	49,126	106,476	68,626
1945	146,422	30,528	55,771	69,664
1946	171,314	22,259	49,042	72,182
1947	337,526	25,730	43,641	71,984
1948	537,854	38,333	44,584	75,608
1949	594,471	19,484	46,500	103,150
1950	647,308	28,126	52,195	115,193
1951	635,064	19,263	60,250	133,329
1952	634,564	16,055	84,140	139,299
1953	712,482	45,722	99,294	130,329
1954	787,101	62,311	113,228	141,195
1955	933,873	31,934	113,774	146,655
1956	1,161,829	87,645	125,860	269,710
1957	1,332,862	67,054	127,239	431,637
1958	1,535,014	152,434	142,783	453,882
1959	1,806,607	232,209	157,043	445,118
1960	1,913,980	154,101	163,328	459,826
1961	2,350,486	167,039	222,259	457,951
1962	2,445,469	79,056	254,118	448,337
1963	2,747,110	95,995	244,297	519,376
1964	2,947,481	41,879	294,668	549,606
1965	3,299,762	92,960	289,810	551,611
1966	3,727,181	63,449	338,024	560,134
1967	4,328,892	63,185	364,018	560,376
1968	5,378,996	112,017	512,221	710,059
1969	5,698,859	(78,114)	682,210	744,172
1970	6,189,137	(11,922)	625,325	698,073
1971	7,563,040	0	605,175	738,259
1972	7,942,110	0	661,467	1,053,325
1973	9,193,635	23,269	665,332	1,069,950
1974*	8,826,017	79,017	593,774	1,178,702
1975	10,519,634	157,430	655,046	1,178,562

Fiscal Year	*Income*	*Net Results*	*Gifts/Grants*	*Endowment*
1976	11,965,361	(143,285)	817,311	1,234,675
1977	13,422,817	119,359	1,387,503	1,295,937
1978	14,345,629	(50,520)	1,077,662	1,356,055
1979	16,724,700	226,491	1,176,001	1,472,856
1980	18,539,273	310,710	1,060,041	1,623,750
1981	21,412,466	310,710	1,726,695	1,835,211
1982	25,152,864	105,661	1,644,091	2,048,173
1983	27,593,303	145,421	2,299,412	2,544,709
1984	30,083,490	1,015	1,841,605	2,920,533
1985	32,944,757	159,909	2,106,671	2,822,692
1986	35,186,794	317,961	2,831,317	3,534,031
1987	37,331,404	10,180	2,976,045	4,303,355
1988	41,309,860	45,051	3,123,224	5,146,365

* Fiscal year changed to 1 June–31 May

Appendix D

BUILDINGS AND FACILITIES

Construction on *Harstad Hall* began in 1891. This building housed the entire institution until 1912, when the gymnasium was built. Its ground floor included the dining hall, apartments for staff and faculty, dressing rooms for sports, and work rooms. On the first floor were offices, classrooms, the library, and apartments. The second floor had classrooms in the center and dormitories for women on the north end and for men on the south end, set off by partitions in the hallways. The third floor housed men on the south wing and women on the north wing, with a partition in the center. The fourth and fifth floors were completed as dormitory wings by 1949. The cafeteria was moved to Ingram in 1955, but administrative offices remained in the building until 1960. That year the entire building became a residence hall, except for a few offices on the ground floor. Its architect was A. J. Heide.

The *Gymnasium*, built in 1912 on the site where the University Center presently stands, included a running track and stage, with science laboratories in the basement. It was destroyed by fire in June 1946.

The *Chapel*, built in 1920, was a frame structure located between the present Mortvedt Library and Harstad. Site of daily chapel services, it was also home for Trinity Lutheran Church until Trinity moved across the street to its present location in 1937. The Chapel served as the religious center for PLU and as a classroom building until 1947, when chapel services were moved to Memorial Gymnasium. The Chapel's basement was used as a commercial print shop from 1945 until 1954; the *Mooring Mast* was printed there. The building then housed the art department until 1970, when the University Center was built and art classes moved into Ingram. The Chapel was razed in 1971.

Xavier Hall, built as the library in 1937, also housed classrooms and offices on the ground floor. The entire building was renovated into an academic facility when the library was moved in 1967. It also housed Central Services from 1967 to 1982. It was named after J. U. Xavier, professor from 1902 to 1942 and acting president in 1920–21. The architect was E. J. Bressman of Heath, Cove & Bell.

The *Golf Course and Athletic Fields* were obtained by PLU in 1937 when the eighteen-hole Parkland Golf Course gave its properties to the university. Nine holes have been maintained; the other nine holes were converted into athletic fields. Prior to that the athletic fields were west of Harstad Hall where the quad is located today.

Ivy Hall, consisting of portable buildings acquired from the government after World War II, served first for student housing, then for various academic units. Ivy Hall housed the biology department until Rieke Science Center was completed in 1985. It was razed later that year.

The *Student Union Building* was completed in 1947 on the foundation of the old gymnasium. It housed classrooms and offices as well as an auditorium, stage, coffee shop, and games room. Renamed the Classroom Building in 1955 when a new college union was built, it was razed in 1969.

Memorial Gymnasium, completed in 1947, was named in honor of PLU students who served in World War II.

Ramstad Hall was completed in fall of 1947. An addition was built in 1958, and the whole building was completely renovated in 1985. Named after A. W. Ramstad, professor of chemistry from 1925 to 1961, the building was used as the science hall until Rieke Science Center was completed. Ramstad now houses the School of Nursing and various student services offices. The original architects were from the firm of Lea, Pearson, & Richards; the 1985 renovation was designed by Michael Fogde and Ted A. Werner.

Eastvold Chapel, built in 1952, features a stage and an auditorium seating twelve hundred persons, as well as facilities for the music and communication arts departments. Named after S. C. Eastvold, PLU president from 1943 to 1962, it also houses the KPLU-FM studios. It was designed by the architectural firm of Lea, Pearson, & Richards.

Hong Hall, originally called North Hall, was built in 1954. Named to honor Nils J. Hong, professor of English and president of PLU from 1897 to 1918, it is a residence hall for students. Like its neighboring buildings—Hinderlie, Ingram, and Kreidler halls—Hong Hall was designed by Lea, Pearson, & Richards.

Hinderlie Hall, built in 1954, was originally named South Hall. A student residence hall, it was later named after Mr. and Mrs. Berndt I. Hinderlie, long-time PLU staff members.

Ingram Hall, built in 1955 and originally called the College Union, at first housed the cafeteria, coffee shop, bookstore, student government and publication offices, and lounges. Chris Knutzen Fellowship Hall was added as an east wing in 1960. The building was converted into office and classroom facilities for the art department and School of Nursing in 1971 when the University Center was built. The south wing was added as a lecture-teaching facility in 1972. The building was renamed in memory of Aida Ingram, wife of Charles Ingram, a PLU benefactor.

Kreidler Hall, originally called West Hall, was built in 1957. A residence hall for students, it was later named to honor Lora B. Kreidler, dean of women and art professor from 1921 to 1943.

The *Health Center* was obtained by the university in 1956. It had been built in 1948 by Donald Eastvold, son of S. C. Eastvold. It served as the president's residence until 1961 and as the home of the vice president for development until 1966. It was converted to the Health Center in 1966. The office of LITE (Lutheran Institute for Theological Education) occupied the ground floor until 1988.

The *Hauge Administration Building*, completed in 1960, was originally called the Tacoma-Pierce Administration Building. Housing administrative and faculty offices as well as classrooms, it was renamed to honor Philip E. Hauge, who served as dean, registrar, academic vice president, and professor from 1920 to 1968 and as university archivist from 1968 to 1976. The building was designed by architects from Lea, Pearson, & Richards.

The *Nesvig Alumni Center* was obtained by the university in 1961. Originally the John Tenquist home, built in 1954, it served as the president's residence until 1970. It currently houses offices for the alumni association, church relations, development, and university relations. The building was named after Milton Nesvig, professor of English and vice president of university relations from 1947 to 1980 and archivist until 1988.

The *Columbia Center*, built in 1962 as a student cafeteria, bakery, coffee shop, and golf pro shop, was named in honor of one of PLU's predecessor institutions, Columbia College in Everett. It was designed by architects from Johnson, Austin and Associates.

Pflueger Hall, built in 1962, is a residence hall for students. Named after J. P. Pflueger, professor of religion and philosophy from 1930 to 1958, its architects were from the firm of Lea, Pearson, & Richards, who also designed Foss, Stuen, and Ordal residence halls.

Foss Hall, built in 1965 as a student residence hall, was named after H. L. Foss, bishop of the North Pacific District of the ALC from 1932 to 1965 and chair of PLU's board of regents for many years.

The *Swimming Pool* was built in 1965, funded through student pledges and assessments.

Stuen Hall was built in 1966 as a student residence hall on the site of the home of Ole J. Stuen, PLU librarian and professor from 1913 until his death in 1952.

Mortvedt Library, completed in 1967, also houses the university archives, computer center, and graphics and photo services. Named in honor of Robert A. L. Mortvedt, PLU president from 1962 to 1969, its architect was from the firm of Bindon & Wright. The third floor, added in 1986–87, was designed by architects from URS Corporation.

Tingelstad Hall, built in 1967 as a residence hall, was named after O. A. Tingelstad, PLU president from 1928 to 1943. The eight-story dormitory includes Alpine, Cascade, Evergreen, and Ivy houses.

Ordal Hall was built in 1967 as a residence hall and named to honor O. J. Ordal, PLU president from 1921 to 1928.

Olson Auditorium was built in 1969 as an athletic facility and assembly hall with faculty offices and classrooms. It was named after Clifford O. Olson, coach and athletic director from 1929 to 1948. Its architects, from the firm of Robert, Billsbrough & Price, also designed the Swimming Pool and Tingelstad Hall.

The *University Center*, built in 1970, houses the bookstore, cafeteria, coffee shop, games room, student government and publications offices, Chris Knutzen Fellowship Hall, campus ministry, and other student offices. It was designed by architects from Bindon & Wright.

The *Math Building* was built in 1979 and expanded in 1982 and 1984. It houses classrooms and offices for the mathematics and computer science department. Its architect was Ted A. Werner, who also designed the physical plant complex.

The *Physical Plant*, built in 1982, houses maintenance and printing facilities and the Elliott Press. Former physical plant facilities were razed (or moved) from the site of Rieke Science Center.

East Campus, the former Parkland School located at Pacific Avenue and South 121st Street, has been leased from the Franklin Pierce School District since 1982. It houses programs in special education and social work as well as the Center for Human Organizations in a Changing Environment (CHOICE).

The *Names Physical Fitness Center* was added to the north end of Memorial Gymnasium in 1984. The gift of the Scott Names family, it was designed by N. Arrison.

Construction of the *William O. Rieke Science Center* was completed in 1985. It contains science laboratories, classrooms, faculty offices, and the Leraas Lecture Hall. Named for PLU's president since 1975, it was designed by the architectural firm of Broome, Oringdulph, O'Toole, Rudolf, & Associates.

The Scandinavian Cultural Center was completed in 1989. Built in the northeast corner of the University Center's basement, it was funded through gifts from the Scandinavian community in the Northwest. It includes areas for lectures and concerts, a demonstration kitchen, a class-room for crafts and language instruction, and a meeting room that reflects nineteenth-century pan-Scandinavian ethnicity. The Center was designed by Tsang Partnership Inc.

AUXILIARY BUILDINGS

Delta Hall, a twenty-unit motel-type residence hall, was built in 1961.

Evergreen Court, a twenty-unit residence hall, was built in 1961.

Family Student Housing is comprised primarily of surplus government housing units.

The *Gonyea House*, the current president's residence, occupies a five-acre tract on Spanaway Loop Road, south of the campus. Constructed in 1955, the estate was given to PLU by the Gonyea family in 1971.

Park Avenue House, converted into student housing, was acquired in 1971.

The *Music Practice House*, containing piano practice rooms, was acquired in 1972. It was razed in 1989.

Ramsey House, containing faculty offices, was constructed in 1960 and purchased from the William Ramsey family in 1976.

Haavik House, which houses the Intensive English Language Institute and faculty offices, is named after former regent O. L. Haavik. It was constructed in 1945 and acquired in 1977.

The *Faculty House* is the former home of Joe and Anna Enge, who worked in PLU's maintenance department and business office, respectively. The house is owned by the University Scholars Association, a private, nonprofit corporation.

Knorr House, adapted to house faculty offices in 1980, is the former home of E. C. Knorr, professor and dean of the College of Arts and Sciences from 1949 to 1969.

The *Mailroom*, former home of M. T. Hokenstad, a PLU regent in the 1930s, was acquired in 1981.

Blomquist House has housed faculty offices since 1982. It was named to honor Grace Blomquist, professor of English from 1939 to 1976.

Dunmire House, acquired in 1985, is used for visitors' housing.

Rosso House was acquired in 1987. It was remodeled in 1989 to house the Office of Graduate Studies.

FACULTY BEGINNING SERVICE BEFORE 1965

Adams, George E.	Mathematics	1963–66
Adams, Harry S.	Physics	1947–51, 1962–
Akre, Elvin M.	History	1937–70
Alcorn, Gordon D.	Biology	1944–45
Alfsen, Theodora A.	Music	1913–17
Aller, Wayne	Psychology	1962–64
Amend, John	Education	1960–64
Amundsen, Lavina	English	1927–28
Anderson, Charles D.	Chemistry	1959–
Arbaugh, George E.	Philosophy	1959–
Arko, Dee Ann	Physical Education	1963–64
Arlton, Alexander	Biology	1942–43
Axford, Herbert M.	Economics	1954–58
Bache, Helen A.	Nursing	1960–61
Bamer, J. Lucille	English	1946–47
Bardon, Peter J.	Economics	1907–17, 1928–38
Baronhill, Eva	French, Violin, Orchestra	1921–22
Barteky, Tibor	Reference Librarian	1963–65
Bassett, Abe	Speech	1964–68
Beck, Alvar J.	History, Economics	1929–35
Beckman, Miriam	Reference Librarian	1964–73
Belcher, Victor R.	History	1959–60
Berg, Dora Almeda	Art	1940–49
Berge, Elsie Marie	Economics, Business Administration	1948–52, 1956–57
Berk, Barbara Jane	English	1958
Black, David	English	1958–61
Blomquist, Grace	English, Dean of Women	1939–76
Bolon, Victor R.	Psychology	1961–62
Bomstead, Olive E.	Shorthand, Typing	1930–32
Bondy, Elizabeth H.	German	1929–43
Botten, Mary A.	Assistant Librarian	1940–43
Brandvig, Meyer	Greek, German, English	1894–96
Briesmeister, Robert F.	English	1961–63
Broeckel, June	Education	1960–64
Buchanan, A. Dean	Business Manager	1962–73

Bull, Olof	Violin, Orchestra	1906–16
Burrell, Prudence	Nursing	1963–64
Caddey, Eugene W.	Physical Education	1941–42
Carlson, Paul R.	Geology	1961–63
Carlson, Roy E.	Physical Education	1962–83
Carlson, Vernon	Education	1955–64
Chase, Georganne	Nursing	1964–68
Chesterman, Elnora E.	English	1955–57
Chilson, Clara J.	Speech	1945–48
Christensen, Ellen K.	Music	1955–57
Christensen, Janet Sue	Nursing	1961–62
Christensen, Olive T.	English, German	1909–13
Christensen, P. Louis Kai	Music	1959–64
Christopherson, Harley J.	Music	1950–53
Christopherson, Kenneth E.	Religion	1958–
Clary, J. M.	Arithmetic, History, Greek	1906–14
Colton, Grant H.	Mathematics	1946–47
Colyar, Alice	Physical Education	1942–43
Cone, Dorothy M. Tollefson	Nursing	1961–88
Craig, W. Jeanne	Economics, Business Administration	1959–60
Creso, Irene	Biology	1950–53, 1955–71
Crosno, May Frances	Latin, English, History	1942–43
Culver, Lowell	Political Science	1964–69
Dahl, Jean E. MacGregor	Speech	1948–54
Danielson, J.E.	Director of Admissions	1960–69
Dapper, Adah H.	Physical Education	1934–38
Davenport, Grace R.	Music	1899–1900, 1907–08
DeBower, Carrol E.	Education	1964–68, 1970–
Dizmang, Oscar K.	Business Administration	1955–59
Dougherty, Edith	Dietician	1962–65
Doughty, Judd C.	Communication Arts	1962–
Drotning, Theodore M.	English, Music	1913–16
Durham, Gail	French	1964–69
Dvergsdal, Daniel K.	History	1954–55
Eastvold, S. C.	President	1943–62
Edwards, Ardie	Drama	1928–29
Edwards, J. O.	Music	1925–37
Eggan, Lawrence	Mathematics	1964–68
Ehret, Harold F.	Mathematics	1963–66
Eklund, Emmet E.	Religion	1946–82

Eklund, Leslie O.	Dean of Men, Psychology	1946–64
Elberson, Stanley D.	Speech	1953–57, 1960–64
Ellingson, E. B.	Architectural Drawing	1914–17
Ellingson, Jack A.	Geology	1963–68
Ellingson, Louise H.	Librarian	1950–51
Elliott, Madge	Bookkeeping, Arithmetic	1915–16
Ellison, Alpha	English, History	1920–21
Elvestrom, Victor A.	Development, Mathematics	1928–37
Elwell, George R.	Art	1959–85
Enger, Helen Joanne	Physical Education	1957–58
Ericson, Jon M.	Speech	1954–57
Farmer, Donald R.	Political Science	1955–
Farness, Nancy Lee	Physical Education	1963
Faulk, Carl G.	Typing	1954–59
Fletcher, M. Josephine	Nursing, Education	1961–
Ford, Lee	Biology	1956–62
Foss, Carl L.	French, Bible	1921–23, 1928–31
Foster, Daisy	Music	1905–07
Fowler, Sophia	Education	1930–33
Francis, Nelle Jo	Romance Languages	1948–49
Franck, Michel N.	Political Science	1935–51
Franck, Ruth S.	English	1935–47
Freed, William Jay	Business Administration	1926–29
Fritts, R. Byard	Music	1949–66
Fritz, Alvin E.	Psychology	1945–48
Fullilove, Emma Sue	Nursing	1964–65
Gaard, Grace O.	Mathematics	1914–15
Gabrielson, James O.	Physical Education	1958–63
Gaines, John Edward	Geology, Geography	1956–61
Gerheim, Earl B.	Biology	1962–68
Giddings, William P.	Chemistry	1962–
Giere, Arthur F.	Band, Orchestra	1911–12
Gilbertson, Gladys	English	1936–39
Gilbertson, Gordon O.	Music	1954–86
Gildseth, Wayne	Chemistry	1964–66
Govig, Stewart D.	Religion	1958–60, 1961–
Grimstead, Katherine	Acting Normal Supervisor	1939–42
Gronsberg, Ole N.	President	1895–97
Guilford, Roger K.	Biology	1962–66
Gustafson, Milton	Commercial, Arithmetic	1916–17
Haddad, Marie	Nursing	1963–64
Hagen, Arnold J.	Education	1955–71

Hageness, Mabelle Thompson	Music	1903–06
Hageness, Nils N.	Commercial	1902–06
Haley, Frank H.	Librarian	1951–76
Hansen, Alma H.	Music	1908–12
Harshman, Marvel K.	Physical Education	1945–58
Harstad, Bjug A.	President, Religion, Norwegian, German	1894–1915
Harstad, T. Amelia	English	1908–15
Hauge, Philip E.	Education, Dean	1920–68
Haydon, Charles E.	French, Spanish	1958–62
Hedahl, Beulah M.	Nursing	1948–51
Hegland, Leonard	English	1951–53
Heimdahl, Olaf Emil	Language, History, Religion	1907–09
Heinicke, Frances M.	Nursing	1960–61
Helgeson, John G.	Religion	1963–65
Hellman, Walter H.	Dean of Men, English, Christianity	1929–30
Hermann, Regina	Biology	1948–49
Highby, Paul R.	Biology	1930–35
Hilbert, Martha S.	Typing	1959–61, 1962–64
Hillger, Martin E.	English	1962–67
Hoff, Hans Jacob J.	Languages	1926–31
Holmberg, Branton	Psychology	1964–70
Holmes, F. M.	Art	1898–1901
Holum, John R.	Chemistry	1958–59
Holum, M.	Geography, Arithmetic, Norse	1921–22
Hong, Adolph	Arithmetic, Physics, Chemistry	1900–01
Hong, Inga D.	Shorthand, Typing	1906–17
Hong, Mary Wiborg	Matron	1899–1902
Hong, N. J.	English, President	1897–1918, 1928-38
Hougen Stuen, Agnes C.	Geography, Reading, Composition	1912–15
Hoverstad, Bertha	Teacher	1906–10
Huber, Curtis E.	Philosophy	1964–
Huestis, Laurence D.	Chemistry	1961–
Hundtofte, Jo Ann	Nursing	1961–63
Ilyashevich, Boris	Russian	1962–63
Jacobsen, Helen C.	Nursing	1960–63
Jacobson, Hazel	Physical Culture, German	1915–16

Jahr, Hannah	Principal, Teacher (Primary)	1896–?
Jansen, Luther T.	Sociology	1961–63
Jensen, James E.	Economics, Business Administration	1951–53
Jenson, Lars	English, Reading, German	1905–06
Jessen, Margarethe	Voice	1917–18, 1920–22
Johnson, Donna Mae	Nursing	1961–65
Johnson, Mrs. George S.	Dressmaking	1914–15
Johnson, Linka	Registrar	1960–65
Johnson, Lucille M.	English	1953–89
Johnson, Robert I.	Industrial Arts	1949–54
Johnson, Shirley R.	Nursing	1961–63
Johnson, Verner	Biology	1946–48
Johnson, Vivian	Normal Supervisor	1934–39
Johnston, Kenneth A.	Education	1964–
Jones, Albert	Education	1964–69
Jordahl, Catherine S.	French	1942–47, 1957–59
Jordahl, Olaf M.	Physics	1940–69
Julson, Mrs. I.	English	1911–12
Karl, T.O.H.	Speech	1940–42, 1948–78
Kasen, Astrid E.	Nursing	1941–43
Kempe, H.F.	Common Branches and Mathematics	1901–02
Kindley, Olga Mathilde E.	Music	1903–08
King, Gundar J.	Business Administration	1960–
Kirk, James A.	Physics	1961–62
Kittleson, Lars E.	Art	1956–
Klopsch, Raymond A.	English	1953–
Knapp, Calvin H.	Music	1960–
Knorr, Erich C.	Sociology, Dean	1949–69
Knudsen, Jens W.	Biology	1957–
Knudson, Anne E.	English	1946–70
Koppitch, Richard J.	French	1961–64
Krefting, Elsie M.	Music	1906–07
Kreidler, Lora B.	Dean of Women	1921–43
Kuethe, John G.	Philosophy	1954–64
Lane, George O.	Field Representative	1930–32
Langemo, Lillian	Assistant Librarian	1946–49
Langton, Richard	Dean of Students	1964–65
Larsen, Nettie	Shorthand, Typing, English	1923–24
Larson, E. Arthur	Swedish	1932–43

Larson, Everett M.	English	1948–51
Larson, Ludvig	Business Manager, Commercial Subjects	1917–18, 1919, 1929–37, 1943–44
Larson, Mathilda	Arithmetic, Latin	1901–02
Larson, Robert	Music	1953–54
Laursen, Carolyn	Nursing	1964–65
Lawless, Homer	Economics	1953–55
Lee, Renete William D.	Religion	1961–64
Lehman, Elsie	Nursing	1964–65
Leraas, Harold J.	Biology	1935–42, 1947–74
Little, Ottilie E.	German	1946–51, 1952–66
Loe, Emma	Music	1900–01
Loeffler, Vangie	Violin	1923–24
Lono, Mikkel	Vice President of Development	1936–43
Luciow, Theo	Russian	1961–62
Ludtke, Frederick E.	Industrial Arts	1955–56
Lundgaard, Gene C.	Physical Education	1958–
Lussky, Warren	Librarian	1948–49
MacIsaac, Shirley	German	1959–61
Mackey, Harold	Sociology	1963–66
Maier, Eugene A.	Mathematics	1955–61
Malmin, Gunnar J.	Music, Latin, Norse	1937–69
Martilla, John A.	Business Administration	1963–64, 1969–77
Mathers, Marjorie I.	Education	1964–66, 1968–
Mayfield, Doris	English	1957–58
Michaelson, Ruth J.	Education	1949–53
Moe, Ruth V.	Physical Education	1955–56, 1958–59
Monson, Melvin S.	Education	1949–51
Moore, E. Inez	Economics, Business Administration	1957–59
Moravec, Jeanine Ann	English	1957–58
Morken, Eline K.	Nursing	1953–67
Mortvedt, Robert A. L.	President	1962–69
Muyskens, Henry H.	Mathematics	1961–63
Myhre, Clara M.	Music	1928–29
Napjus, Alice J.	Education	1963–75
Nelson, Ann Carolyn	Sociology	1954–58
Nelson, Lloyd	Dean of Men	1944–45
Nelsson, F. E. Theo.	Dean of Men, Business Manager	1932–43
Nerison, George H.	Music	1908–11
Ness, Mrs. E. T.	Violin	1923–24

Nesvig, Milton L.	Journalism, Vice President for Public Relations	1947–80
Newell, Edwin R.	Mathematics	1960–63
Newnham, Frederick L.	Music	1950–69
Nielsen, Anna M.	Education	1939–64
Nielsen, Dale F.	Psychology	1962–65
Nielsen, Donna	Nursing	1962–65
Nielsen, Elizabeth	Piano, English	1920–22
Nodtvedt, Magnus	History	1947–63
Nordholm, Eric	Communication Arts	1955–
Nordquist, Philip A.	History	1963–
Nornes, Sherman B.	Physics	1959–61, 1965–
Nothstein, Donald L.	Biology	1956–57
Olafson, Robert B.	English	1959–62
Olsen, Robert C.	Chemistry	1947–73
Olson, Albert J.	Common Course	1898–1900
Olson, Clifford O.	Physical Education, Consultant	1929–48, 1962–64
Olson, Ella Lavinia	English	1929–30
Olson, Mary Annette	Nursing	1958–59
Olson, Roy	Public Relations	1951–65
Olson, Viola	Home Economics	1951–55
Oman, Sylvia	Spanish, French	1962–63
Ordal, O. J.	President	1921–28
Ostenson, Burton T.	Biology	1947–77
Parr, Sarah	Education	1927–28
Patrick, James G.	Business Administration	1946–51
Pattie, Donald L.	Biology	1964–69
Payne, Dorothy K.	Music	1959–65
Peck, Anilaura F.	Business Administration	1946–48
Peckman, Glen G.	Librarian	1942–43
Pederson, Arne K.	Education	1956–89
Pellet, Claude	Orchestra	1923–24
Peterson, Clayton	Vice President for Development	1960–74
Peterson, Freda A.	Nursing	1951–53
Peterson, Helmer S.	Mathematics, Natural Sciences	1907–10
Peterson, Joseph M.	Arithmetic, German, Latin, Principal	1898–1900
Peterson, Sophie	English, Mathematics, Art	1894–1907
Pflueger, J. P.	Philosophy, Religion	1930–58

Pierson, Robert	Economics, Business Administration	1959–69
Potratz, Clarence J.	Mathematics	1959–61
Poulsen, Dee Ann Arko	Health & Physical Education	1963–66
Preus, Paul A.	Field Representative	1931–39
Pritchard, Martha E. Huber	Nursing	1962–63, 1965–67
Purvis, Howard W.	German	1963–65
Quast, Florence	Dietician	1955–62
Ramer, Leah Sonya Byles	Nursing	1961–63
Ramstad, Anders W.	Chemistry	1925–61
Ranson, Herbert R.	English	1940–68
Raun, Alo	Romance Languages	1949–51
Reeves, Thomas C.	History	1962–63
Reid, W. D. Keith	Business Administration	1932–45
Reigstad, Paul M.	English	1947–48, 1958–
Reitz, Karl P.	Mathematics	1963–65
Reneau, George	History, Sociology	1933–52
Reynolds, Betty B.	English	1961–66
Reynolds, Donald L., Jr.	English	1961–68
Reynolds, Phyllis Holum	English	1964–66
Ringstad, M.	Physical Education	1921–22
Ristuben, Peter John	History	1960–66, 1968–69
Roe, Kelmer N.	Religion, Greek	1947–67
Ronning, Harold G.	Education, Dean	1940–53
Roskos, George	Art	1950–89
Runbeck, Junet E.	Education	1955–62
Running, Josef E.	Mathematics	1948–61
Ruth, June	Nursing	1964–66
Ryder, Maude	History, English	1925–26
Rynning, Johan L.	History, Physiology, College Physician	1896–1917
Salzman, H. Mark	Physical Education	1951–68
Sannerud, Arling	Principal, History	1939–42
Sarsland, Ambrose G.	Band, Orchestra	1904–05
Satre, Lowell J.	Latin, Greek	1941–42, 1945–47
Sawhill, William A.	English	1947–48
Schamberger, Melvin	Biology	1964–65
Schiller, John A.	Sociology	1958–
Schmieder, Lucille Anne	Biology	1953–55
Schnackenberg, Walter	History	1942–44, 1952–73
Schwarz, Frederick E.	Chemistry	1961–62
Scott, Richard T.	Psychology	1958–61

Seger, Katharine	Business Administration	1965–70
Shahan, W.	Teacher	1894–95
Sherman, W. J.	Arithmetic, Commercial	1910–11
Sihler, K. Elizabeth	Teacher, Preceptress	1902–03
Sjoding, Theodore	Education	1951–68
Skones, Maurice	Music	1964–83
Smith, Ann S.	Nursing	1960–61
Smith, Jane	Speech	1957–60
Solberg, Kristen B.	Psychology, Dean	1953–64
Solling-Fynboe, Carl	Field Representative	1938–40
Spangler, Carl D.	Languages	1961–62, 1963–88
Sperati, Carlo A.	Music	1894–1905
Stampolis, Anthony	Economics	1953–57
Steen, Paul	Speech	1960–67
Stein, Lynn S.	Education	1961–81
Stenson, Pauline M.	Education	1960–63
Stintzi, Vernon	Business Administration	1964–77
Strombo, P. G.	Physical Education	1942–43
Strunk, William L.	Biology	1948–61
Stuen, Ole J.	Mathematics, Norse, Librarian	1913–18, 1921–52
Svare, Trygve O.	Religion	1924–39, 1949–57, 1959–60
Takei, Kazuye	Economics, Business Administration	1952–53
Tandberg, Carl	History, Political Science	1952–53
Taylor, Louise Stixrud	Education	1927–29, 1930–35
Templin, Phyllis	Physical Education	1958–63
Tenwick Sovik, Anna M.	Latin, Mathematics, English	1901–13
Tetlie, Harold M.	Sociology	1957–59
Thiessen, Alvin D.	Librarian	1964–65
Thompson, Patricia	Nursing	1957–59
Thompson, Robert J.	Business Administration	1953–1954
Thorson, Alice	Music, Art	1901–02
Thorson, O. L.	History, English	1924–25
Thuesen, Theodore	Sociology	1963–68
Tingelstad, Edvin	Principal, Field Representative	1931–45
Tingelstad, Gertrude B.	Librarian	1940–53
Tingelstad, O. A.	President	1928–43
Tommervik, Marvin S.	Physical Education	1946–51

Tye, Velmont M.	Psychology	1962–64
Ulleland Labes, Janet M.	Nursing	1961–65
Utzinger, Vernon A.	Speech	1950–53, 1957–69
Veldey, Selmer	French, Bible	1920–21
Vigness, Paul G.	History	1956–65
Wagness, Berna	Piano	1923–24
Wagner, Doris L.	Nursing	1960–63
Weber, Robert B.	German	1961–64
Weiss, Karl E.	Music	1941–57
Wickstrom, Margaret	Dean of Women	1951–78
Williamson, E. Jane	Education	1964–
Winther, Sven	Psychology	1960–61, 1964–67
Workman, Eugenia	Nursing	1963–64
Wylie, J. H.	Commercial, Arithmetic	1897–98
Xavier, Anna Charlotte	Needlework, Embroidery	1903–34
Xavier, J. U.	Acting President, Librarian, Religion	1908–16, 1920–42
Xavier, Signe Skattlebol	Reading, Grammar, Basketball	1912–17
Yaley, Janet	Nursing	1963–65
Young, Rhoda Hokenstad	Physical Education	1938–42, 1943–69
Ziemke, Donald C.	Religion	1960–61
Zulauf, Dwight	Business Administration	1949–52, 1959–85

FACULTY BEGINNING SERVICE IN OR AFTER 1965

Aaby, Nils-Erik	Business Administration	1977–79
Achepohl, Keith	Art	1969–73
Acuff, Mathilde	Nursing	1974–78
Adachi, Seichi	Counseling, Psychology	1967–
Adams, Rebecca	Communication Arts	1988–89
Adams, Virginia D.	Biology	1981–82
Aikin, Shirley	Nursing	1974–
Alcantara, Amelia	Nursing	1965–72
Alexander, Angelia	Biology	1971–
Alford, Garth	Languages	1987–88
Allen, Merrily	Nursing	1982–88
Alseth, Richard	Physical Education	1965–69
Alvin, Barbara	Mathematics	1982–83
Anderson, Bonnie	Nursing	1968–70
Anderson, Dana D.	Psychology	1984–
Anderson, Edward W.	Physical Education	1975–83
Anderson, Gary	Mathematics, Computer Science	1979–80
Anderson, Joseph	Religion	1966–69
Ankrim, Ernest	Economics	1976–
Arndt, Michael	Communication Arts	1981–82
Arnold, Jeffrey	Communication Arts	1988–89
Arnold, Richard	Speech	1968–70
Ash, Phillip	Chemistry	1986–87
Atkinson, David M.	Political Science	1976–
Auping, Carol	Physical Education	1974–80
Baird, Brian	Psychology	1986–87, 1988–
Bakken, Richard M.	English	1965–66
Bancroft, D. Stuart	Business Administration	1967–68, 1971–
Bandy, Howard B.	Computer Science, Dean for Computing	1984–88
Barndt, Stephen E.	Business Administration	1978–
Barnowe, J. Thaddeus	Business Administration	1977–
Bartenen, Michael D.	Communication Arts	1979–
Batker, Kenneth E.	Mathematics	1966–
Baty, Daniel	Business Administration	1968–71

Baughman, Myra J.	Education	1970–
Baumann, Joanruth	Business Administration	1986–88
Beal, Philip	Vice President for Student Life	1968–76
Bearse, Arthur	Business Administration	1974–75
Beaty, Kathleen A.	Nursing	1973–74
Beaulieu, John E.	Mathematics, Computer Science	1985–
Beckman, Katherine Iverson	Physical Education	1972–80
Becvar, William	Communication Arts	1973–
Bekemeier, Luther W.	Vice President for Development	1976–
Benham, Steven R.	Earth Sciences	1982–
Benkhalti, Rachid	Mathematics, Computer Science	1987–
Benson, Keith	Earth Sciences	1979–81
Benton, Megan	English	1986–
Benton, Paul F.	English	1969–
Berg, Marta	Physical Education	1967–68
Bergeson, Lois	Nursing	1970–77
Bergman, Charles A.	English	1977–
Bermingham, Jack R.	History	1983–
Berniker, Eli	Business Administration	1982–
Bettridge, Fern	Nursing	1975–76
Bexton, W. Harold	Psychology	1965–76
Biblarz, Arturo	Sociology	1977–
Bisnett, Russell F.	Languages	1966–67
Blomgren, Robert	Mathematics	1978–79
Blomme, Gayle	English	1975–78
Blubaugh, Glen	German	1969–73
Bohannon, Randolph	Biology	1969–77
Boots, Susan	Nursing	1979–82
Bowen, Florence	Nursing	1976–77
Bowers, Mark	Physics	1986–88
Bradford, Esther	Nursing	1972–74, 1978–81
Briar, Katharine	Social Welfare	1976–81
Brink, James E.	Mathematics, Computer Science	1970–
Brochtrup, William A.	Education	1975–88
Broeker, Herman	Physical Education	1966–78
Brown, Cara	Nursing	1986–87
Brown, Carolyn	Sociology	1977–79
Brown, Joanne E. C.	Religion	1983–88

Brown, R. Michael	Psychology	1982–
Brown, Richard L.	Art	1986–
Brown, Roberta S.	French	1979–
Browning, Christopher	History	1974–
Brue, Stanley L.	Economics	1970–
Brunner, Charles	Business Administration	1977–79
Buckham, Richard	Psychology	1981–82
Brusco, Elizabeth	Anthropology	1988–
Burk, Robert	Nursing	1973–77
Burke, Barbara	Business Administration	1987–
Burke, David	Legal Studies	1987–88
Cady, Jack	English	1987–
Campbell, Thomas J.	English	1984–
Candiotti, Joseph	History	1980–82
Capp, Glenn R.	Communication Arts	1970–73
Carey, Andrew	Education	1988–
Carleton, Samuel B. B.	Classics	1969–81
Carlson, John T.	Biology	1975–
Carp, E. Wayne	History	1986–
Carpenter, Maryiva	Nursing	1974–
Carper, Clara	Nursing	1972–83
Carr, Judith W.	Dean of Special Academic Programs	1979–
Carter, Barbara J.	Nursing	1977–80
Carvey, Davis W.	Business Administration	1971–89
Cather, Melba	Nursing	1966–69
Catlett, Duane	Chemistry	1968–70
Catlin, R. William	Biology	1968–69
Chambers, Alice-Marie	Education	1966–68
Chang, Taiping	Chinese	1986–88
Chang, Wei	Computer Engineering	1987–88
Chen, Jiabo	Chinese	1985–86
Chase, Gary A.	Physical Education	1970–
Chauff, Karl	Earth Sciences	1978–80
Choi, Byang-Ho	Physics	1973–74
Christopher, Stefan C.	Sociology	1975–77
Churney, Marie	Education	1974–
Clark, Roy W.	Engineering	1977–86
Clark, Thomas	Music	1973–74
Clarke, Andrew	Engineering	1987–
Clarke, Anthony	Sociology	1973–78
Clausen, Edwin G.	History	1983–
Coats, Gary	Mathematics	1968–71

Collinge, Francis	Political Science	1971–75
Comsia, Diane E.	Mathematics	1976–78
Comte, Michael	Sociology	1973–77
Connolly, Linda	Mathematics	1966–69
Conway, Steven	History	1980–81
Cook, Anne K.	Mathematics	1983–88
Coombe, Evelyn	Nursing	1981–86
Cooper, Keith J.	Philosophy	1984–
Cooper, Stanley	Education	1968–69
Coutu, Margaret	Nursing	1969–73
Cox, Dennis	Art	1972–
Cox, Linda	Education	1975–80
Crayton, Michele A.	Biology	1977–
Crockett, Marilyn	Art	1969–70
Crockett, Richard	Political Science	1970–75
Croes, Dale	Anthropology	1982–84
Crooks, William	Business Administration	1976–80
Cubbage, Kenneth	Business Administration	1968–70, 1980–86
Dahl, Alison	Physical Education	1978–80
Dahl, David P.	Music	1969–
Daines, Gary S.	Communication Arts	1978–79
Danielson, Barbara	Physical Education	1971–72
Davis, James E.	Economics	1965–68
Davis, Kenneth	Engineering	1981–83
De Sherlia, Janet	Sign Language	1982–
Dickman, Alan W.	Biology	1984–87
Dirksen, Charles	Business Administration	1970–74
Dorner, Bryan C.	Mathematics, Computer Science	1978–
Dorner, Celine	Mathematics, Computer Science	1984–
Drake, H. Max	Sociology	1973–76
Dumor, Ernest	Sociology	1973–79
Dunn, Robert	Business Administration	1975–79
Durham, Karin	German	1966–69
Dwyer-Shick, Susan	Legal Studies	1984–
Easterwood, Beverly	Nursing	1969–70
Edison, Larry A.	Mathematics, Computer Science	1982–
Egan, Maura G.	Nursing	1983–
Eman, Virginia	Communication Arts	1971–77
Enderby, Marshall	Economics	1969–70
Engelhardt, Elizabeth	Mathematics	1987–89

Engh, Michael	Computer Science	1985–86
Erickson, Robert	History	1984–85
Erwin, Janet	English	1967–69
Espeseth, Loleta	Associate Registrar	1965–89
Espeseth, Rolf	Music	1966–68
Evans, Anthony	Physical Education	1988–
Eyler, Audrey	English	1981–
Fanslow, Julia E.	Nursing	1985–
Farner, Kathleen A. Vaught	Music	1978–
Farner, Richard A.	Music	1976–
Fatland, Dennis	Mathematics	1984–85
Faye, Louise Sand	Spanish	1969–
Fenili, Mary Lou	Vice President, Dean of Student Life	1982–87
Feucht, Robert	Religion	1987–88
Fiedler, Phyllis	Psychology	1975–83
Fisher, Winnifred	Languages	1966–69
Fisk, Robert	Mathematics	1968–79
Foley, Duncan	Earth Sciences	1986–
Forster, Mary	Biology	1973–75
Freeman, Scott A.	Business Administration	1975–79, 1986–89
Frohnmayer, Mira J.	Music	1980–
Frolich, Reba	Nursing	1973–74
Fryhle, Craig B.	Chemistry	1986–
Gabel, Helen	Nursing	1987–88
Garcia, Kay Sauer	Spanish	1986–88
Gard, Roger	Music	1974–
Gaspar, Patricia	Nursing	1987–88
Gaustad, Mary	Physical Education	1965–67
Gary, Anne Bridget	Art	1984–85
Gee, Arthur	Biology	1968–
Gehrke, Ralph D.	Religion	1975–
Geller, Beatrice	Art	1984–
Genda, Ronald	Economics	1967–72
Gerlach, Kent P.	Education	1980–
Gilbert, Robert	Communication Arts	1986–87
Gilbertson, William H.	Social Work	1968–
Gilchrist, Debra	Reference Librarian	1987–
Gillett, Patricia A.	Nursing	1977–80
Gillette, Gregory	Communication Arts	1982–85
Gilmour, David	Classics	1983–86
Gintz, Ingrid	Mathematics	1971–72, 1978–79

Glaser, Nicola	Mathematics, Computer Science	1983–85
Gold, Lawrence B.	Art	1984–
Goodwin, Sheila	Nursing	1987–
Gough, Fern A.	Nursing	1971–
Graham, James E.	Business Administration	1970–71
Greenwood, William G.	Physics	1981–
Grefrath, Richard W.	Reference Librarian	1973–78
Grieshaber, Kate	Music	1984–
Grochulski, Andrzej	Economics	1985–87
Grochulski, Maria	Languages	1986–87
Guldin, Gregory E.	Anthropology	1979–
Gutmann, Robert L.	Chemistry	1984–88
Hacker, Colleen M.	Physical Education	1979–
Hagerott, R. Jalane	Nursing	1981–83
Halseth, James A.	History	1966–68, 1970–80
Hanna, J. Ray	Mathematics	1981–82
Hansen, Constance H.	Nursing	1980–
Hansen, David H.	Biology	1974–
Hanson, Katherine	Norwegian	1983–84
Hanson, Marlis	Education	1971–
Hanson, Vernon R.	Social Work	1970–
Hansvick, Christine L.	Psychology	1979–
Hanthorn, Dennis	Music	1977–78
Harmic, Edward R.	Music	1971–
Harris, Peter	Sociology	1980–83
Harter, Edward	Mathematics, Computer Science	1985–87
Hartman, Paul	Speech	1967–69
Haueisen, Donald	Physics	1977–87
Haueisen, William	Business Administration	1977–78
Hauser, George, Jr.	Computer Science	1987–
Heeren, Robert	Engineering	1973–83
Hefty, Luella V.	Nursing	1973–
Hegstad, Larry P.	Business Administration	1979–
Hemion, Katharine	Physical Education	1979–84
Hendricks, Perry B., Jr.	Vice President for Finance and Operations	1973–87
Herman-Bertsch, Janet L.	Nursing	1984–
Herzog, John O.	Mathematics	1967–
Herzog, Margaret	Mathematics	1980–
Heussman, John W.	Director of the Library	1976–
Heyer, William R.	Biology	1970–73

Hildahl, Richard	Business Administration	1967–68
Hill, D. Sharon	Education	1975–77
Hinchee, Alvin	Biology	1977–78
Hirsch, Anne M.	Nursing	1983–
Hoffman, David	Music	1975–
Holden, Lavon	Speech	1967–68
Holman, Gary	Economics	1967–80
Hoseth, Paul E.	Health and Physical Education	1968–
Hostetter, Thelma	Nursing	1971–81
Houk, Theodore	Physics	1975–76
Hoxit, Kathy	Mathematics, Computer Science	1985–87
Hua, Wei	Chinese	1988–
Huck, Wilbur	English	1968–69
Huggins-McLean, Yvonne	Political Science	1982–84
Hulen, Myron	Business Administration	1988–89
Hutcheon, William J.	Business Administration	1967–73
Inch, Edward S.	Communication Arts	1986–
Ingram, Paul O.	Religion	1975–
Irvine, William	Philosophy	1981–82
Irwin-Brandon, Margaret	Music	1975–77
Jacobs, Clarence	Physics	1969–77
Jacobson, Lois Elam	Nursing	1966–81
Jansen, Sharon	English	1980–
Jensen, Jo Ann S.	Biology	1967–
Jensen, Robert J.	Economics	1968–
Jenseth, Richard H.	English	1985–89
Jerke, Donald	University Minister, Vice President for Student Life	1975–81
Jewell, Joann	Nursing	1969–70
Jobst, Richard J.	Sociology	1967–
Johnson, David	History	1970–78
Johnson, Deborah	Nursing	1982–86
Johnson, Edith	Nursing	1974–81
Johnson, Gregory A.	English	1984–
Johnson, H. Thomas	Business Administration	1986–88
Johnson, Roosevelt	Biology	1973–75
Johnson, William L.	Mathematics	1969–70
Jones, Richard P.	English	1969–
Jorgenson, Ronald	Education	1968–75
Jungkuntz, Richard P.	Provost, Religion	1970–89
Kamath, Rajan	Business Administration	1987–89

Kazzimer, Edward	Catalog Librarian	1988–89
Kelleher, Ann	Political Science	1981–
Keller, Kathryn J.	English	1977–78
Kelly, Timothy	Chemistry	1981–83
Kendall, Nancy J.	Reference Librarian	1985–89
Kerk, David K.	Biology	1986–
Keyes, David T.	Art	1969–
Kibbey, Richard	Business Administration	1988–
King, Vivian	Music	1969–74
Kirkpatrick, Constance S.	Nursing	1980–
Kitzman, Marion	Art	1966–68
Klein, Alan	Sociology	1975–77
Klein, Colleen	Nursing	1978–83
Klein, Laura F.	Anthropology	1979–
Kliewer, Pauline	Nursing	1986–87
Klisch, Mary Lou	Nursing	1986–
Klopfenstein, William	Chemistry	1986–87
Klug, Malcolm	Engineering	1983–84
Kluge, Mary Ann	Physical Education	1985–
Knutson, David R.	Religion	1969–
Kohl, Jeanne E.	Sociology	1986–88
Kollock, Maria	Spanish	1988–89
Kossova, Edward	Language	1965–66
Kottal, Terri	Nursing	1987–
Kracht, Jerry	Music	1967–68, 1969–
Kramer, Elizabeth	Nursing	1983–85
Kruse, Thomas	Economics, Institutional Research	1971–72
Kuhlman, Henry	Business Administration	1973–74
Lamb, Jeannine E.	Physical Education	1986–87
Lambert, Elaine	Nursing	1987–88
Landau, Edith	Library, Technical Services	1982–89
Lange, Karen	Languages	1966–67
Langevin, Thomas	Academic Vice President, History	1965–69
Larsgaard, John O.	Psychology	1970–81
Larson, Dale	English	1971–77
Lauer, Anthony J.	Business Administration	1969–
Lavik, Diane	Nursing	1970–71
Lawrence, Allyn E.	Education	1981–84
Lawrence, Cora	Nursing	1973–78
Layman, Lawrence	Chemistry	1974–78

Leake, Penny	Nursing	1969–73
Leasure, Daniel	Vice President for Student Affairs, Education	1966–73
Lee, Ann	Nursing	1969–71
Lee, Donald G.	Chemistry	1966–67
Leister, Douglas	Business Administration	1973–76
LeJeune, Jerome P.	Psychology	1972–
Lemieux, Nona	Nursing	1970–73
Lerum, Jerrold	Biology	1973–
Levy, Paul	Biology	1975–77
Liebelt, Paul	Mathematics	1970–84
Ling, Nancy	Nursing	1970–71
Lingenfelter, Janet	Nursing	1981–87
Lonborg, Richard	Sociology	1969–70
Long, Grace	Religion	1987–89
Loscutoff, Susan	Nursing	1983–84
Lovell, David	Philosophy	1974–77
Lowe, Joseph	Political Science	1968–70
Lowes, Brian E.	Earth Sciences	1968–
Lueder, Kenneth	Mathematics	1967–68
Lundeen, Lyman	Religion	1989–
MacDonald, Diane	Business Administration	1987–
Maier, Eugene A.	Mathematics	1967–68
Main, John L.	Biology	1971–
Malan, Roland, Jr.	Business Administration	1980–82
Malone, Kathryn	History	1981–86
Mallon, Ann Adele	Education	1987–
Manber, Michele	Psychology	1985–86
Mansell, D. Moira	Dean of Nursing	1982–
Marchetti, Veeda	Anthropology	1985–87
Marek, Jayne	English	1988–
Marsh, Carolyn	Political Science	1980–82
Martin, Dennis J.	Biology	1975–
Martin, Dennis M.	English	1976–
Martin, Gloria	English	1984–
Martin, Marilyn	Reference Librarian	1979–84
Martinson, Arthur D.	History	1966–
Mason, Celestine	Nursing	1973–86
Matthaei, C. Frederick	Business Administration	1987–89
Matthias, Dixie	Biology	1975–
Mattson, Philip	Music	1987–89
Mays, Thomas	Physical Education	1970–71
McBride, Dennis	Sociology	1980–83

McBride, Margy	Mathematics	1984–86
McCarthy, Franklin L.	Business Administration	1975–78
McDonald, Susan J.	Reference Librarian	1975–
McGear, Reba	Nursing	1985–86
McGinnis, Richard	Biology	1972–
McKain, Jerry	Social Work	1979–83
McKay, Thomas A.	Philosophy	1967–68
McKim, Lester W.	French	1983–89
McMaster, Keith	Business Administration	1967–74
McNabb, David E.	Business Administration	1979–
McTee, Cindy	Music	1981–83
Medlin, Susan	Economics	1987–88
Meehan, Elizabeth	Nursing	1980–85
Meehan, John	Business Administration	1980–83
Mellquist, Mary	Nursing	1972–75
Menzel, Barbara	Nursing	1971–73
Menzel, Paul T.	Philosophy	1971–
Menzel, Robert	Director, CHOICE	1969–86
Meyer, Lawrence J.	Music	1969–
Meyer, N. Christian, Jr.	Mathematics	1970–
Milham, Lorna	English	1968–69
Miller, Christine	Nursing	1971–73
Miller, Marlen E.	Economics	1970–
Minas, Barbara	Art	1984–86
Minetti, Gary L.	Education, Counseling and Testing	1970–
Mobley, Curtis D.	Physics	1987–89
Moe, Richard D.	Education; Dean of the Arts and Summer Studies	1965–
Monroe, Katharine	French	1967–76
Moon, Victor	Political Science	1966–67
Moore, Bradford L.	Physical Education	1980–
Moritsugu, John N.	Psychology	1975–
Mork, Erling	Political Science	1970–71
Mucci, Joan	Spanish	1968–69
Mulder, Robert	Education	1987–
Myers, Gerald M.	Business Administration	1982–
Myrabo, Jessica	Nursing	1975–78
Myrbo, Gunnulf	Philosophy	1970–
Nelson, C. Lennard	Mathematics	1984–
Nelson, Charles T.	Registrar	1967–
Nelson, Neale	Sociology	1970–75
Nesset, Burton L.	Chemistry	1967–

Neufeld, Harvey J.	Director of Church Relations	1965–
Nibler, Roger	Business Administration	1974–78
Nolph, Jesse D.	Psychology	1968–
Nordby, Jon J.	Philosophy	1977–
Novak, Sylvia	Nursing	1979–82
Nunes, Kimberly	Business Administration	1986–87
Oakman, Douglas	Religion	1988–
Oberholtzer, W. Dwight	Sociology	1969–
O'Connor, Kathleen	Sociology	1977–86
O'Donnell, Michael J.	Communication Arts	1986–89
O'Dor, Richard	Communication Arts	1977–79
Officer, Sara A.	Physical Education	1967–
Offutt, William, Jr.	History	1987–88
Ohanian, Nancy	Art	1973–74
Olson, Carol	Business Administration	1980–84
Olson, David M.	Physical Education	1968–
Olson, Franklin C.	Education	1971–
Olson, Linda	Nursing	1967–
Olson, Lise	Communiction Arts	1980–81
Olson, Paul	Music	1983–84
Olufs, Dick W.	Political Science	1982–
O'Neal, Thomas	Music	1988–
O'Neill, Michael	Business Administration	1975–79
Orvik, Florence	Education	1967–73
Osborne, Joseph	Chemistry	1985–86
Owens, Helmi C.	Education	1985–
Page, Phyllis A.	Nursing	1976–
Parker, Robert	Physics and Engineering	1987–
Parker, William E.	Communication Arts	1970–
Paterson, Robert	Dean for Computing	1989–
Payne, Beverly	French	1975–80
Payne, Thelma	Social Work	1978–83
Petersen, John E.	Religion	1967–
Peterson, Gary D.	Mathematics	1967–
Peterson, Lois	Art	1987–89
Peterson, Norris A.	Economics	1981–
Peterson, Wilma E.	Nursing	1965–75
Petrulis, Stanley D.	Music	1965–67
Petty, Rodney	Education	1969–73
Phillips, Carolyn	Physical Education	1968–74
Pierce, Douglas	Business Administration	1975–76
Pilgrim, Walter E.	Religion, Director of LITE	1971–

Poellet, Michael	Religion	1983–86
Ponto, Robert D.	Music	1985–88
Poulshock, Barbara	Music	1976–
Predmore, James R.	Spanish	1977–
Preiss, Raymond	Communication Arts	1981–82
Pritsker, Kenneth	Business Administration	1986–87
Purdy, Charles	Business Administration	1981–82
Rahn, Suzanne	English	1981–
Ramaglia, Judith	Business Administration	1982–
Ramey, B. Jean	Nursing	1971–73
Randall, Susan	History	1979–83
Rasmussen, Janet E.	Norwegian	1977–
Rasmussen, Wolfgang	Physics and Engineering	1985–86
Rasson, Judith	Anthropology	1984–89
Raymond, Mary Anne	Business Administration	1986–
Reiman, Mark	Economics	1988–
Reisberg, Leon E.	Education	1981–
Reisman, Jane	Sociology	1984–89
Revis, Mickey	Speech	1968–71
Rhoades, Lois	Nursing	1980–
Rickabaugh, Karl R.	Education	1975–
Rieke, William O.	President	1975–
Riemer, Milton	English	1970–71
Rimer, Lois M.	Nursing	1965–69
Ringe, Louis	Geology	1966–68
Robbins, David P.	Music	1969–
Robinson, G.A. St. John	Spanish	1970–77
Roediger, Jeanette	Nursing	1975–79
Rosenfeld, Moshe	Mathematics, Computer Science	1986–
Rowe, Clifford G.	Communication Arts	1980–
Royce, Joan	Nursing	1970–74
Rozanski, Mordechai	History	1975–82
Ruble, Jeffrey C.	Mathematics, Computer Science	1985–88
Ruidl, Richard	Communication Arts	1981–84
Sandler, William	Education, Dean of Men	1967–68
Sare, William	Music	1968–74
Savarino, James E.	Business Administration	1984–89
Sawrey, Susana	Spanish	1985--86
Saxby, Douglas	Religion	1988–89
Schafer, Eldon L.	Business Administration	1974–
Scharnberg, William	Music	1975–77

Scharnweber, William	History	1970–71
Scherwood, Karen	Physical Education	1985–86
Schmitt, Susan	Nursing	1980–81
Schmutte, Denise	Psychology	1982–86
Schultz, Carolyn W.	Nursing	1974–79, 1982–
Schwanter, Joseph	Music	1968–69
Schwidder, Ernst C.	Art	1967–
Scott, Damon A.	Mathematics	1986–
Seal, David O.	English	1977–
Seal, Maureen E. McGill	Physical Education	1977–
Seeger, Richard A.	Director of Academic Advising	1973–
Seger, Katherine	Business Administration	1965–70
Sepic, F. Thomas	Business Administration	1979–
Seulean, Kathryn A.	Music	1965–67
Severtson, S. Erving	Psychology, Vice President for Student Life	1966–83; 1986–
Sevin, Dieter	German	1967–68
Sherwin, Constance	Nursing	1980–81
Shumaker, Susan E.	Nursing	1980–83, 1984–86
Siegelman, Linda	Education	1982–84
Simon, Caroline J.	Philosophy	1986–87
Simmonds, Kent	Philosophy	1968–71
Smith, Elaine C.	Nursing	1986–89
Smith, Judy	Education	1975–80
Smith, Ronald	Biology	1979–80
Snee, Rochelle E.	Classics	1981–
Soden, Dale	History	1977–78
Sole, Jimmie	English	1967–69
Sorenson, Ruth M.	Biology	1968–74
Sparks, Richard A.	Music	1983–
Spencer, Wallace H.	Political Science	1974–
Spicer, Christopher H.	Communication Arts	1978–
Spillman, Richard J.	Computer Science	1981–
Stave, Douglas	Education	1968–69
Stavig, Maren C.	Nursing	1979–87
Steege, Esther	Nursing	1981–83
Stephany, Theresa M.	Nursing	1981–82
Stiggelbout, Joan D.	Nursing	1973–
Stivers, Robert L.	Religion	1973–
Stoffer, Gerald	Psychology	1973–78
Storlie, Frances	Nursing	1977–79
Storm, Cheryl Lee	Social Work	1985–

Strickland, Kathryn	Music	1968–69
Stringer, Jeremy	Residential Life	1973–77
Struxness, Miles	Art	1977–78
Stucke, Doris	Nursing	1967–83
Sturgill, Donald	Vice President of Finance and Operations	1987–
Sudermann, David	German	1973–83
Sullivan, Valerie	Health and Physical Education	1972–73
Sundberg, Roger	Norwegian	1975–78
Suter, David	Religion	1981–83
Swank, Duane D.	Chemistry	1970–
Swanson, David	Sociology	1987–
Swenson, Marvin	Director, University Center	1969–
Swenson, Rodney N.	German	1968–
Sydnor, Darlean A.	Education	1984–
Tang, Kwong-Tin	Physics	1967–
Taylor, Charles	Physics	1987–
Templin, Phyllis Pederson	Physical Education	1958–63, 1970–71
Thieman, Jon	Physical Education	1977–79
Thompson, Beti	Sociology	1981–83
Thornton, Seabe, III	Social Work	1981–83
Thorson, Eleanor	Nursing	1973–74
Thrasher, Steven D.	Business Administration	1980–
Tobiason, Frederick L.	Chemistry	1966–
Tomsic, Walter L.	Art	1970–
Tonn, Sheri J.	Chemistry	1979–
Torrens, Thomas N.	Art	1974–
Toven, Audun T.	Norwegian	1967–
Tremaine, Ann K.	Music	1972–
Turner, Andrew	Business Administration	1976–83
Turnpaugh, Sharan	Education	1986–89
Ulbricht, Paul	Political Science	1967–89
Upton, Joseph, II	Physics and Engineering	1988–
Urness, David	Music	1967–69
Van Beek, M. James	Admissions and Financial Aid	1963–
Vancil, Gregory	Music	1988–89
Van Druff, John C.	Mathematics	1966–68
Van Tassel, Daniel	English	1970–81
Van Whye, Glen A.	Business Administration	1979–
Vice, Roy	History	1986–87
Vinje, David L.	Economics	1970–

Voisin, Carol	Religion	1981–82
Wahlen, James	Business Administration	1983–86
Walters, Clarence	Psychology	1968–69
Walton, Ann	Business Administration	1973–78
Walter, George	Anthropology	1970–79
Watkinson, Grant	Business Administration	1970–73
Watson, Anne Thaxter	Communication Arts	1986–89
Webster, Mary M.	Psychology	1970–73
Webster, Paul M.	German	1969–
Weirick, Lenora	Nursing	1975–80, 1982–86
Weisbrod, Rita	Sociology	1975–76
Wells, Judee	Business Administration	1978–79
Wells, Richard	Communication Arts	1975–80
Wentworth, Donald R.	Economics, Education	1972–
Westering, Forrest	Physical Education	1972–
White, Eleanor McNeely	Nursing	1967–68
Whitman, Jill	Earth Sciences	1988–
Wiegman, Eugene	President	1969–75
Wiles, Jeff	Communication Arts	1975–77
Wilhelm, Wera	German	1973–74
Willhite, Margaret	Sociology	1973–80
Williams, Gregory J.	Education	1985–
Willis, Margaret	Sociology	1976–80
Wilson, Gary B.	Communication Arts	1975–
Wilson, Margaret	Nursing	1981–83
Woehrle, Margaret	Nursing	1971–73
Wolter, Mary	French	1969–70
Woo, Hokwai	Computer Engineering	1988–
Woolley, Kenneth	Business Administration	1974–81
Wrigley, John	Physics	1987–
Yagow, David C.	Deputy Provost	1976–
Yang, Jefferson Yuan-Sheng	Engineering	1970–74
Yetter, Cathleen	Education	1986–
Yiu, Chang-Li	Mathematics	1973–
Youngquist, Walter	Earth Sciences	1976–78
York, Charles D.	Social Work	1981–
Youtz, Gregory L.	Music	1984–
Yumibe, Yukie	Nursing	1980–
Zabriskie, Felistis	Nursing	1966–67
Zernel, John	Physics	1985–87
Zerwekh, Joyce	Nursing	1975–77
Ziebarth, Charles	Business Administration	1966–67
Zierath, Marilyn	Nursing	1977–79

NOTES

CHAPTER ONE
ATHENS AND JERUSALEM

1. Quoted in E. Harris Harbison, *The Christian Scholar in the Age of the Reformation* (New York, 1956), 1.

2. Gordon Rupp, "Christian Learning—The Great Tradition," in F. H. Hilliard, Desmond Lee, Gordon Rupp, and W. R. Niblett, *Christianity in Education*, The Hibbert Lectures for 1965 (London, 1966), 70.

3. Theodore G. Tappert, "Luther in His Academic Role," *The Mature Luther*, Martin Luther Lectures, vol. 3 (Decorah, Iowa, 1959), 17. The next several quotations are from this source.

4. J. S. Whale, *The Protestant Tradition* (Cambridge, 1959), 21ff., provides a brilliant discussion of Luther's paradoxical theology.

5. Heinrich Bornkamm, *Luther's Doctrine of the Two Kingdoms* (Philadelphia, 1966), 18.

6. In the preceding explanation, I am heavily indebted to an unpublished paper by Herman Diers, "Implications of Luther's Dialectical Theology for a College Curriculum," delivered at the Theological Development of College Faculties Conference, St. Paul, Minn., 30 May–2 June 1978. See also W.D.J. Cargill Thompson, "The 'Two Kingdoms' and the 'Two Regiments': Some Problems of Luther's ZWEIREICHE LEHRE," *Journal of Theological Studies* 20 (1967): 164–85.

7. *A Statement of the Lutheran Church in America: The Basis for Partnership between Church and College*, adopted by the Eighth Biennial Convention of the Lutheran Church of America, Boston, Mass. (New York, 1976), 2–3.

8. Franklin D. Fry, "The Basis for Partnership between Church and College" (paper delivered at the regional Conference on Church-Related Higher Education, Thousand Oaks, Calif., 11–12 October 1979), 3.

9. David W. Lotz, "Education for Citizenship in the Two Kingdoms: Reflections on the Theological Foundations of Lutheran Higher Education," in *Institutional Mission and Identity in Lutheran Higher Education: Papers and Proceedings, Lutheran Educational Conference of North America, 1979* (Washington, D.C., 1979), 8.

10. Helmut T. Lehman, ed., *Luther's Works* (Philadelphia, 1962), 45:350.

11. Ibid., 360.

12. Lotz, "Education for Citizenship," 10.

13. Lehman, ed., *Luther's Works*, 45:367.

14. Lotz, "Education for Citizenship," 11.

15. See Richard W. Solberg, *Lutheran Higher Education in North America* (Minneapolis, 1985).

16. Lotz, "Education for Citizenship," 18–19.

17. Sydney E. Ahlstrom, "What's Lutheran about Higher Education?—A Critique," in *What's Lutheran about Higher Education? Papers and Proceedings, Lutheran Education Conference of North America, 1974* (Washington, D.C., 1974), 8.

18. Ibid., 9.

19. Ibid., 10.

20. Ibid., 11.

21. Ibid., 12.

CHAPTER TWO
ETHNICITY, THEOLOGY, AND EDUCATION

1. E. Clifford Nelson, ed., *The Lutherans in North America* (Philadelphia, 1975), 351.

2. E. Clifford Nelson and Eugene L. Fevold, *The Lutheran Church among Norwegian-Americans* (Minneapolis, 1960), 1:35.

3. Odd S. Lovoll, *The Promise of America* (Minneapolis, 1984), 59.

4. Nelson and Fevold, *Lutheran Church*, 1:81.

5. Ibid., 150.

6. Ibid., 161.

7. Ibid., 155.

8. Lovoll, *Promise of America*, 59.

9. Nelson and Fevold, *Lutheran Church*, 1:188.

10. Nelson, ed., *Lutherans in North America*, 188.

11. Leigh D. Jordahl, "The Gentry Tradition—Men and Women of Leadership Class: How Shall the Faith and Human Culture Interrelate?" in Charles P. Lutz, ed., *Church Roots* (Minneapolis, 1985), 116.

12. Ibid.

13. Ibid, 110.

14. Nelson, ed., *Lutherans in North America*, 190.

15. There were 152,220 baptized members in the United Church, 94,166 in the Norwegian Synod, and 22,279 in the Hauge Synod (ibid., 340).

16. S. C. Eastvold, ed., *Rev. C. J. Eastvold, D.D., 1863–1929: His Life and Work* (Minneapolis, 1930), 171.

17. Nelson, ed., *Lutherans in North America*, 372.

18. Ibid., 373.

19. For this story, see Philip A. Nordquist, "Lutherans in the West and Northwest," in Heidi Emerson, Milton Nesvig, Philip Nordquist, and Roland Swanson, eds., *New Partners, Old Roots* (Tacoma, Wash., 1986), 7–12.

20. Toivo Harjunpaa, "The Lutherans in Russian Alaska," *Pacific Historical Review* (May 1968): 132.

21. Nordquist, "Lutherans," 11.

22. For Lutheran educational activity on the Pacific Coast, see Philip A. Nordquist, "You Must Raise Your Own Crop: Lutheran Higher Education on the Pacific Coast," *The Lutheran Historical Conference: Essays and Reports*, 12 (1988).

CHAPTER THREE
THE FOUNDING OF PACIFIC LUTHERAN UNIVERSITY

1.   Solberg, *Lutheran Higher Education*, 224.

2.   Ibid., 228.

3.   "Memories from before the Placement of Lutheran University in Parkland," *Pacific Herold*, 14 July 1916. This is also discussed in Walter C. Schnackenberg, "The Development of Norwegian-Lutheran Schools in the Pacific Northwest from 1890 to 1920" (Ph.D. diss., Washington State University, 1950), 21–27.

4.   Quoted in Schnackenberg, "Development of Norwegian-Lutheran Schools," 21.

5.   Bjug Harstad, "Early Family History and Reminiscences," trans. Oliver B. Harstad and Adolph M. Harstad (typescript, n.p., n.d.), 11.

6.   Ibid., 4.

7.   Adolph M. Harstad, *A Brief Record of the Lives of the Reverend and Mrs. Bjug Harstad and Their Descendents* (Madison, Wisc., 1977), 12.

8.   Harstad was especially concerned about the problems that science and the higher biblical criticism provided. He systematically attacked them in a 1929 publication: *Is the Bible Reliable?* (Parkland, Wash., 1929). His answer was a resounding "yes" (see pp. 9, 16, 30, 57, 71, 85, and *passim*).

9.   Richard Osness, *From Wilderness to Suburbia: An Illustrated History of Parkland, Washington* (Tacoma, Wash., 1986), 13.

10. Ibid., 3.

11. James H. Hitchman, *Liberal Arts Colleges in Oregon and Washington, 1842–1980* (Bellingham, Wash., 1981), 217.

12. *The Pacific Lutheran University Catalog: 1894* (Parkland, Wash.).

13. Walter C. Schnackenberg, *The Lamp and the Cross: Sagas of Pacific Lutheran University from 1890 to 1965* (Tacoma, Wash., 1965), 16.

14. *Lutheran University Herald* 1 (April 1891).

15. Resolution in box labeled "Early History of PLU," PLU Archives, Tacoma, Wash.

16. Schnackenberg, "Development of Norwegian-Lutheran Schools," 40–42.

17. Osness, *Wilderness to Suburbia*, 14–17.

18. *Lutheran University Herald* 2 (October 1892).

19. Ibid. 3 (January 1893).

20. Ibid. 3 (June 1893).

21. Ibid. 2 (June 1892).

22. Ibid. 4 (April 1894).

23. Kenneth O. Bjork, *West of the Great Divide: Norwegian Migration to the Pacific Coast, 1847–1893* (Northfield, Minn., 1958), 500.

24. J. Russell Hale, *Who Are the Unchurched?* (Washington, D. C., 1977), 97–99.

25. Charles M. Gates, *The First Century at the University of Washington, 1861–1961* (Seattle, 1961), 46.

26. *Lutheran University Herald* 4 (October 1894).

27. *Pacific Lutheran University Catalog: 1894.*

28. *Pacific Herold*, 21 January 1931.

29. For information on Sperati, see Camilla Sperati Strom, "Carlo A. Sperati: "Grand Old Maestro" (typescript, n.p., n.d.); for his impact on Luther College, see David T. Nelson, *Luther College, 1861–1961* (Decorah, Iowa, 1961), 190.

30. *Records of the Proceedings of the Faculty of the Pacific Lutheran University by the Secretary* (23 October 1894–22 February 1910), PLU Archives.

31. *Pacific Herold*, 8 October 1895.

32. *Pacific Lutheran University Announcement: 1896–97.*

33. Quoted in Schnackenberg, *Lamp and the Cross*, 38.

34. Ibid., 39.

35. *Pacific Herold*, 14 June 1897.

CHAPTER FOUR
PACIFIC LUTHERAN ACADEMY AND BUSINESS COLLEGE

1. Hong to M. A. Brattland, September 1901, Hong Papers, PLU Archives. All subsequent references to Hong's correspondence are from this collection.

2. *Hurricane*, June 1912.

3. Hong to John Xavier, 9 February 1902.

4. Bjug Harstad, "Letter and Articles on a Trip into the Yukon Region: Published in *Pacific Herold*, 1898 and 1899," trans. Oliver Harstad (typescript, n.p., 1973), 17. All quotations in the following three paragraphs are from this collection.

5. The horns can still be viewed in the PLU Archives.

6. *Pacific Herold*, 4 March 1898.

7. *Pacific Lutheran Academy and Business College: Sixth Annual Announcement: 1899–1900*, 19.

8. *Eighth Annual of the Pacific Lutheran Academy and Business College: 1901–02.*

9. Ibid.

10. *Ninth Annual of the Pacific Lutheran Academy and Business College: 1902–03.*

11. Ibid.

12. Hong to O. M. Holden, 28 January 1902.

13. J. U. Xavier, "PLA, PLC, PLU: My First Impressions of Parkland and the School" (1962), Xavier Papers, PLU Archives; Xavier, "Miracles," Xavier Papers.

14. Agnes Hougen to Hong, 1 July 1914.

15. Hong to H. A. Nelson, 9 September 1901.

16. Hong to N. K. Tvete, 11 September 1901.

17. *Hurricane*, 30 November 1901. Quotations in the remainder of this section are from *Hurricane* issues published between 1901 and 1915.

18. Hong to A. K. Batson, 7 July 1908.

19. Resolution to board of trustees, 14 April 1909, Hong Papers.

20. *Tenth Annual of the Pacific Lutheran Academy and Business College:*

1903–04.

21. Xavier, "PLA, PLC, PLU."

22. Oscar A. Tingelstad, "The Academy Graduate" (14 June 1907), Hong Papers.

23. Frederick E. Bolton to Hong, 25 May 1914.

24. C. K. Preus to Hong, 3 September 1909.

25. *Twenty-Second Annual of the Pacific Lutheran Academy and Business College: 1915.*

26. *Twenty-First Annual of the Pacific Lutheran Academy and Business College: 1914.*

27. Ibid.

28. Hong to S. J. Ylvisaker, 7 May 1917.

29. The definitive study of the topic up to 1920 is Schnackenberg, "Development of Norwegian-Lutheran Schools in the Pacific Northwest," chaps. 8, 9.

30. Schnackenberg, *Lamp and the Cross*, 65.

31. Ibid., 70.

32. Ibid., 74.

33. Quoted in ibid., 76.

CHAPTER FIVE
PACIFIC LUTHERAN COLLEGE

1. Hong to S.J.N. Ylvisaker, 7 May 1917, Hong Papers.

2. Ernest Wheeler to Hong, 1 June 1917.

3. S.J.N. Ylvisaker to Hong, 14 July 1917.

4. Hong to L. W. Boe, 13 August 1917.

5. L. W. Boe to Hong, 21 August 1917.

6. Hong to Boe, 10 September 1917.

7. Boe to Hong, 8 December 1917.

8. Hong to Boe, 16 December 1917.

9. Ibid.

10. Hong to Boe, 11 February 1918.

11. "A Congregational Meeting Held in Parkland Lutheran Church, Parkland, Washington: A Stenographic Report," 23 January 1918, Harstad Papers, PLU Archives.

12. Hong to Bertha Hoverstad, 16 April 1918.

13. Hong to board of trustees, 28 May 1918.

14. Hong to L. C. Foss, 10 September 1918.

15. "Memorial to the School Committee of the Norwegian Lutheran Church of America from the P.L.A.A.A." (n.p., n.d.).

16. Schnackenberg, *Lamp and the Cross*, 85-86.

17. Nelson, ed., *Lutherans in North America*, 498.

18. Solberg, *Lutheran Higher Education*, 285.

19. Ibid., 285–91.

20. Washington State *Documents*, 16 November 1920.

21. Xavier, "PLA, PLC, PLU."

22. *Pacific Lutheran College Bulletin: June 1921.*

23. Ibid., September 1921.

24. Ibid., 1922.

25. *Mooring Mast*, 29 October 1924.

26. Solberg, *Lutheran Higher Education*, 287.

27.   Donald Coltom was twice a second-team NAIA all-American, and David Coltom received all-Northwest Conference mention. Ronald Coltom was a long-time alumni secretary at PLU.

28.   Emma Kvindlog Ramstad, *Memories That Cast a Glow over Retirement* (n.p., 1973).

29. Nelson, ed., *Lutherans in North America*, 430.

30. Solberg, *Lutheran Higher Education*, 288.

31.   O. H. Pankoke, *A Great Church Finds Itself: The Lutheran Church between the Wars* (Quitman, Ga., 1966).

32. Ibid., 183.

33. *Pacific Lutheran College Bulletin: August 1927.*

34. Pankoke, *Great Church*, 183.

35. Quoted in *Mooring Mast*, 22 March 1928.

CHAPTER SIX
DEPRESSION AND WAR

1 .   O. L. Haavik to Tingelstad, 21 January 1928, O. A. Tinglestad Papers, Norwegian American Historical Association Papers, Northfield, Minn. All of Tingelstad's papers cited in this chapter are from this collection unless otherwise noted.

2. Carl Foss to Tingelstad, 21 January 1928.

3. *Luther College Chips*, 10 February 1950.

4. Nelson, *Luther College*, 191.

5.   Oscar Ludwig Olson,"A History of My Administration of Luther College, Decorah, Iowa" (typescript, Decorah, Iowa, 1952), 3.

6.   O. A. Tingelstad, "The Doctrinal Value of the First Chapter of Genesis" (typescript, n.p., 1935).

7. *College Chips*, 10 February 1950.

8. Tingelstad to Charles Howard Judd, 27 December 1928.

9. *Mooring Mast*, 19 December 1928.

10. L. W. Boe to Tingelstad, 19 December 1928.

11. *PLC Bulletin* (August 1928).

12. Ibid. (February 1929).

13. Ibid. (August 1929).

14. Tingelstad to Nelson B. Fosmark, 21 February 1929.

15. Tingelstad to O. M. Norlie, 7 June 1929.

16. See fundraising letters in the Tingelstad Papers.

17. L. Ludwig to Tingelstad, 12 August 1929.

18.   Clifford Olson to Tingelstad, 23 July 1929.

19.   Quoted in Earl Pomeroy, *The Pacific Slope* (New York, 1985), 294.

20.   *PLC Bulletin* (August 1933).

21.   *Memories That Cast a Glow over Retirement*, 28.

22.   "The Future Scope, Policy, and Financial Support of Pacific Lutheran College," *Pacific Lutheran College Bulletin* (November 1931).

23.   Tingelstad to Paul Preus, 11 September 1930.

24.   Walter H. Hellman, ed., *The Story of the Northwestern District of the American Lutheran Church* (Portland, Ore., 1941), 35.

25.   Nelson, ed., *Lutherans in North America*, 444.

26.   *PLC Bulletin* (May 1932).

27.   Tingelstad to J. A. Aasgaard, Paul Preus, and Victor Elvestrom, 2 November 1932.

28.   *Memories That Cast a Glow over Retirement*, 18.

29.   *PLC Bulletin* (August 1935).

30.   Tingelstad to Paul Preus, 20 February 1932.

31.   *Mooring Mast*, 8 March 1933.

32.   Tingelstad to Victor Elvestrom, 22 January 1934.

33.   Joseph Edwards to Tingelstad, 10 June 1928.

34.   *PLC Bulletin* (August 1929).

35.   *Mooring Mast*, 25 April 1934.

36.   Ibid., 9 May 1934.

37.   Mrs. O. A. Sandwick to Faculty, 23 January 1929.

38.   J. T. Norby to Tingelstad, 25 August 1934.

39.   Norby to Tingelstad, 31 October 1934.

40.   Nelson, ed., *Lutherans in North America*, 466.

41.   P. J. Bardon, "A Brief Statement of My Classroom Creed and My Social-Economic-Political-Philosopy Views" (typescript, n. p., 1936).

42.   H. L. Foss to Tingelstad, 4 January 1935.

43.   P. J. Bardon to Tingelstad, 6 August 1938.

44.   *PLC Bulletin* (August 1936).

45.   (Tacoma, Wash., 1972).

46.   Quoted in ibid., 40.

47.   Clifford Olson, interview with author, 16 September 1986. Unless otherwise noted, tapes of all interviews are in the PLU Archives.

48.   *Mooring Mast*, 14 December 1939.

49.   Gunnar J. Malmin, interview with author, 3 July 1986. See also the Malmin Papers, PLU Archives.

50.   Grace Blomquist, interview with author, 3 April 1987.

51.   Herbert Ranson to Charles Anderson, 21 January 1967, Ranson Papers, PLU Archives.

52.   *PLC Bulletin* (July, August, September 1941).

53.   H. J. Glenn, *Report on Pacific Lutheran College Inspection* (n.p., n.d.), Tingelstad Papers, PLU Archives.

54.   Alf Kraabel to Tingelstad, 27 April 1938; J.C.K. Preus to Tingelstad, 4 May 1938.

55. L. W. Boe to Tingelstad, 13 March 1941.
56. Tingelstad to Boe, 21 March 1941.
57. H. L. Foss to Tingelstad, 2 November 1942.
58. J. A. Aasgaard to Tingelstad, 4 November 1943.
59. For the five letters, see box 19, file 5, of the Tingelstad Papers.
60. Tingelstad to Aasgaard, 22 January 1943.
61. T. O. Svare to Tingelstad, 15 April 1943.
62. S. C. Eastvold to Tingelstad, 28 January 1944.

CHAPTER SEVEN
POSTWAR EXPANSION

1. S. C. Eastvold, ed., *Rev. C. J. Eastvold, D.D., 1863–1929: His Life and Work* (Minneapolis, 1930), 339. See also 345, 355.
2. Schnackenberg, *Lamp and the Cross*, 113.
3. S. C. Eastvold, *Immortality, the Intermediate State and the Final Issue* (Madison, S.D., 1930), preface and *passim*. See also Eastvold's *Beyond the Grave* (Eau Claire, Wisc., 1942). Both books are full of themes about death and premillenialism. The quotations are from these volumes.
4. F. L. Cross, ed., *The Oxford Dictionary of the Christian Church* (Oxford, 1978), 916.
5. *PLC Bulletin* (September 1943).
6. Eastvold Papers, PLU Archives.
7. Hitchman, *Liberal Arts Colleges*, 7.
8. Ibid. Hitchman mentions G. Herbert Smith at Willamette, 1942–68; Harry Dillin at Linfield, 1943–68; Morgan Odell at Lewis & Clark, 1941–60; C. C. Maxey at Whitman, 1948–59; R. F. Thompson at the University of Puget Sound, 1942-73; Frank Warren at Whitworth, 1940–63; and S. C. Eastvold at Pacific Lutheran University, 1943–62. A similar list could be made of Lutheran college presidents.
9. *Mooring Mast*, 2 May 1947.
10. Ibid., 22 March 1945.
11. Ibid., 28 February 1947.
12. Solberg, *Lutheran Higher Education*, 306.
13. Minutes, board of trustees meeting, 19 April 1949.
14. Milton Nesvig, "Oral History of PLU: The Campus," audiotape, PLU Archives.
15. *Mooring Mast*, 14 December 1945.
16. Eastvold to Philip E. Hauge, 13 November 1947, Eastvold Papers.
17. Paul Wangsmo, interview with author, 16 May 1988.
18. Minutes, board of trustees meeting, 19 May 1949.
19. John McCallum, *The Gladiators* (Tacoma, 1972), chap. 8.
20. Ibid., 169–79, 194.
21. *Mooring Mast*, 9 April 1948.
22. Minutes, board of trustees meeting, 19 November 1953.

23. S. C. Eastvold, *Let Us Go to Chapel* (Minneapolis, 1952), 10.

24. Ibid., 12–13.

25. *Annual Report of the Evangelical Lutheran Church* (Minneapolis, 1954), 99.

26. Minutes, board of trustees meeting, 13 October 1949.

27. Ibid., 27 March 1953.

28. S. C. Eastvold, "Adequate Leadership for Church and State" (paper delivered at the American Lutheran Conference convention, Detroit, Mich., 10–12 November, year unknown).

29. Erich Knorr, interview with Milt Nesvig, 21 December 1977; Milton Nesvig, "Oral History of PLU: The Presidents" (February-March 1975); Kelmer Roe, interview with author, 29 July 1986; Clayton Peterson, interview with author, 30 July 1986; Kenneth Christopherson, interview with author, 19 September 1986; Donald Farmer, interview with author, 24 September 1986, Roy Olson to author, 2 November 1987.

30. Schnackenberg, *Lamp and the Cross*, 124.

31. Kelmer Roe, interview with author, 29 July 1986.

32. See Jackie Jensen Clark, *Remembering, Celebrating and Hoping: A History of Pacific Lutheran University Congregation, 1955–1985* (Tacoma, Wash., 1985). See also *The Thinker*, 17 December 1954.

33. Sydney E. Ahlstrom, "The Radical Turn in Theology and Ethics: Why It Occurred in the 1960s," in John M. Mulder and John F. Wilson, eds., *Religion in American History* (Englewood Cliffs, N.J., 1978), 450.

34. See McCallum, *Gladiators*, chap. 9, 191–99.

35. *Mooring Mast*, 28 February 1958.

36. Telegram, S. C. Eastvold to Marv Harshman, Harshman Papers, PLU Archives.

37. Clayton Peterson, interview with author, 30 July 1986.

38. *PLC Bulletin* (November 1957).

39. Minutes, board of trustees meeting, 3 September 1957.

40. S. C. Eastvold, *Around the World in 180 Days* (n.p., 1959), 58, 59.

41. Ibid., 106.

42. Herbert Schaefer, interview with author, 10 August 1986.

43. S. C. Eastvold, "Some Musts in Christian Higher Education" (10 September 1959), Eastvold Papers.

CHAPTER EIGHT
COMING OF AGE

1. Minutes, board of trustees meeting, 17 March 1960.

2. "Dr. Eastvold Chooses Not to Run for the Office of Governor of the State of Washington," press release, 23 May 1960, Schnackenberg Papers, PLU Archives.

3. Minutes, board of trustees meeting, 15 March 1960.

4. H. H. Ditmanson et al., eds., *The Christian Faith and the Liberal Arts*

(Minneapolis, 1960). Schnackenberg's review is included in the university's "Finance: 1960, Eastvold," vol. 19, PLU Archives.

5.　(Tacoma, Wash., 1961).

6.　Minutes, board of trustees meeting, 7 November 1960.

7.　Clayton Peterson, interview with author, 30 July 1986.

8.　Minutes, board of trustees meetings, 3 March, 15–16 March, 2 June, 5 June, and 18 August 1961.

9.　Charles A. Nelson to H. L. Foss, n.d., Eastvold Papers.

10.　Fund Fulfillment Corporation, *The Policy-Making and Administrative Structure of Pacific Lutheran University* (Chicago, October 1961).

11.　Fund Fulfillment Corporation, *A Public-Opinion Study of the Public Relations of Pacific Lutheran University* (Chicago, November 1961).

12.　Ibid., 23.

13.　Minutes, board of regents meeting, 1–2 November 1961.

14.　Ibid., 11 December 1961.

15.　*Mooring Mast*, 16 February 1962.

16.　Ibid., 23 February 1962. For a discussion of the administrative and theological struggles at Luther College, see Leigh D. Jordahl and Harris E. Kaasa, *Stability and Change* (Decorah, Iowa, 1986), chap. 3. There was an attempt to hire Belghum at PLU that spring.

17.　Charles Mays, interview with author, 17 July 1986.

18.　"In der Name des Freiheit" to Charles May, 14 February 1962. Copy of letter in possession of author.

19.　*Mooring Mast*, 2 March 1962.

20.　Fund Fulfillment Corporation, *The Development Program for Pacific Lutheran University; Manual for Regents: Pacific Lutheran University; Fiscal Analysis: Pacific Lutheran University; Organization and Management: Pacific Lutheran University* (Chicago, March 1962). See also minutes, board of regents meeting, 5–6 March 1962.

21.　Eastvold to Faculty, 10 March 1962, Eastvold Papers.

22.　Eastvold to Earl Eckstrom, 14 March 1962, Schnackenberg Papers.

23.　Nelson, ed., *Lutherans in North America*, 497.

24.　Kelmer Roe, Paul Vigness, Knute Lee to objectives committee (n.d.), memorandum in the possession of George Arbaugh.

25.　Letters were received from professors Roland Bainton of Yale University, Harold Grimm of Ohio State University, Jaroslav Pelikan of Yale University, and George Forell of the University of Iowa; the letters are in the possession of George Arbaugh.

26.　Ibid.

27.　Erich Knorr to pastors, 29 May 1962.

28.　John Amend, T.O.H. Karl, John Kuethe, and Kristen Solberg to pastors of North Pacific District, 6 June 1962.

29.　Kenneth Christopherson, interview with author, 19 September 1986. See also Schnackenberg diary, May and June 1962, Schnackenberg Papers.

30.　*Mooring Mast*, 1 June 1962.

31.　Eastvold to O. K. Davidson, 30 July 1962, Eastvold Papers.

CHAPTER NINE
THE NEW UNIVERSITY

1.   Robert A. L. Mortvedt, *Part of a Family Story for Our Grandchildren* (n.p., n.d.), 47.

2.   Robert Mortvedt, interview with author, 15 September 1986.

3.   Mortvedt, *Family Story*, 53.

4.   For the speeches, see the Mortvedt Papers, PLU Archives, where they are chronologically cataloged.

5.   Ibid.

6.   Robert Mortvedt to Walter Schnackenberg, 1 July 1965, Schnackenberg Papers.

7.   Mortvedt, *Family Story*, 53

8.   Robert Mortvedt, interview with author, 22 September 1986.

9.   Robert A. L. Mortvedt, *Mission Fields in the Continent of Learning* (Chicago, 1958).

10.   Sydney Ahlstrom, *A Religious History of the American People* (Garden City, N.Y., 1975), 600.

11   *Mooring Mast*, 5 October 1962.

12.   Minutes, board of regents meetings, 26, 27, 28 May 1963.

13.   Robert Mortvedt, "Report to Pacific Lutheran University, Inc." (8 June 1964), Mortvedt Papers.

14.   Ibid.

15.   Dean Buchanan, interview with author, 16 July 1986.

16.   *Mooring Mast*, 26 March 1966.

17.   Robert Mortvedt, interview with author, 22 September 1986.

18.   Minutes, board of regents meeting, 3 May 1965.

19.   Ibid., 16–17 November 1966.

20.   *Mooring Mast*, 3 February 1966.

21.   Ibid., 29 April 1966.

22.   Neil Waters to author, 16 October 1987. The *Mooring Mast* editor was Neil Waters, the editorialist was Christopher Howell, and the columnist was Lewis Giovine. The faculty advisor was Philip Nordquist.

23.   *Reflections*, (July 1966).

24.   *Mooring Mast*, 27 October 1967.

25.   Steven Morrison to author, 7 October 1987.

26.   *Reflections* (January 1968).

27.   Faculty Constitution and By-Laws (25 April 1968).

28.   Earl Eckstrom to Carl Fynboe, 19 April 1968.

29.   Minutes, board of regents meeting, 10 June 1968.

30.   Robert Mortvedt, interview with author, 22 September 1986.

31.   Donald Farmer, interview with author, 24 September 1986.

32.   Quoted in Lucille Giroux, "Memories of PLU" (typescript, n.p., 1979).

33.   *Reflections* (May 1968).

34.   The three speeches are in the PLU Archives.

35.   Quoted in Lowell W. Culver, ed., *Adapting Local Government to Urban*

Problems, Proceedings of the Conferences on Community Planning (Tacoma, Wash., 1967–68), vii.

36. Minutes, board of regents meeting, 10 September 1968.
37. Ibid., 2 June 1969.
38. Ibid., 10–11 February 1969.

Chapter Ten
The Wiegman Interlude

1. "University Relations to All Hands" (11 February 1969), Wiegman Papers, PLU Archives.
2. Minutes, board of regents meetings, 5 June 1969, 2 July 1969.
3. *Mooring Mast*, 10 September 1969.
4. Ibid., 24 September 1969.
5. *Reflections* (May 1970).
6. "Inauguration of President Wiegman," Schnackenberg Papers.
7. *Mooring Mast*, 15 October 1969.
8. Ibid., 22 October 1969.
9. Minutes, board of regents meeting, 9 February 1970.
10. *Mooring Mast*, 11 February 1970.
11. Ibid., 13 May 1970.
12. *Reflections* (November 1970).
13. James E. Adams, *Preus of Missouri* (New York, 1977), 150.
14. Ibid., 196.
15. Richard Jungkuntz to Melvin R. Knudson, 13 December 1974, Presidential Search Committee Papers, PLU Archives.
16. Robert Mortvedt to Eugene Wiegman, 13 October 1970, Wiegman Papers.
17. *Mooring Mast*, 9 December 1970.
18. Ibid., 10 March 1971.
19. Gundar King to educational policies committee, 6 November 1969.
20. "Presidential Report to Regents," minutes, board of regents meeting, 29 January 1971.
21. *Mooring Mast*, 22 October 1971.
22. Minutes, board of regents meeting, 28 February 1972.
23. Ibid.
24. "Report from the Commission on Academic Excellence" (9 May 1973).
25. *Mooring Mast*, 10 May 1974.
26. Ibid., 24 September 1969.
27. A. Dean Buchanan, interview with author, 16 July 1986.
28. Nesvig, "Oral History: Presidents."
29. Boxes 13 and 16, Wiegman Papers, PLU Archives.
30. M. Roy Schwarz to Michael Dederer, 1 December 1970.
31. "Crisis of 1971," Clarence Solberg Papers, PLU Archives; see also *Mooring Mast*, 9 March 1973.

32. Lowell Culver, interview with author, 5 November 1987; Donald Farmer, interview with author, 24 September 1986; *Mooring Mast*, 1 March 1973.

33. K. E. Christopherson to Clarence Solberg, 19 October 1972; Stewart Govig to Paul Braafladt, 16 October 1972, Clarence Solberg Papers.

34. A. Dean Buchanan to Clarence Solberg, 1 December 1972.

35. *Mooring Mast*, 1 March 1973.

36. Ibid., 22 September 1972.

37. Nesvig, "Oral History: Presidents." See also Clark, *Remembering, Celebrating and Hoping*, 30–34, and Donald Taylor to author, 23 September 1988.

38. Eugene Wiegman to Kern Devin, 13 August 1970, Wiegman Papers.

39. Jon B. Olson to author, 21 July 1988.

40. "Request for Faculty Opinion" (12 January 1973); "Results of Questionnaire of 12 January 1973" (23 January 1973), Schackenberg Papers.

41. A. Dean Buchanan, interview with author, 16 July 1986.

42. Minutes, faculty meeting, 9 February 1973, PLU Archives.

43. *Tacoma News Tribune*, 10 February 1973.

44. Ibid., 11 February 1973.

45. Ibid.

46. *Mooring Mast*, 16 February 1973.

47. Clarence Solberg to North Pacific District pastors, 27 March 1973, PLU Communication Liaison Committee Papers, PLU Archives.

48. Ibid.

49. *Mooring Mast*, 1 March 1973.

50. Schnackenberg would die of a heart attack the following December, before the last act of the "no confidence" drama was played out. He was involved in more aspects of university life and was more influential in shaping institutional identity and direction than any faculty member in the second half-century of its history.

51. Communication Liaison Committee Papers.

52. Summaries of divisional and school meetings with President Eugene Wiegman, ibid.

53. Natalie Brown to "Whom it May Concern," 15 February 1973, Michael Dederer Papers, PLU Archives.

54. M. R. Stuen to Dederer, 1 May 1973, ibid.

55. Eugene Wiegman to Dederer, 1 May 1973, ibid.

56. Report of the Liaison Committee of the Faculty to the Liaison Committee of the Regents (n.d.), Communication Liaison Committee Papers.

57. Robert Mortvedt to Eugene Wiegman, 5 May 1973, Wiegman Papers. See also Emmet Eklund to Clarence Solberg, 21 April 1973, Solberg Papers.

58. Richard D. Moe to faculty liaison committee, 14 May 1973, Communication Liaison Committee Papers.

59. Michael Dederer to Esther Aus, 27 June 1973, Dederer Papers.

60. Dederer to Melvin Knudson, 10 June 1974, ibid.

61. "Discussion with Dr. Wiegman about Situation at PLU" (19 April 1973), Melvin Knudson Summary, Communication Liaison Committee Papers.

62. Minutes, board of regents meeting, 18 October 1973.

63. Eugene Wiegman to executive committee of the board of regents, 27 December 1973, Clayton Peterson file, Wiegman Papers.

64. Ibid.

65. Nesvig, "Oral History: Presidents"; Clayton Peterson, interview with author, 30 July 1986.

66. *Mooring Mast*, 22 March 1974.

67. Ibid., 29 March 1974.

68. Joann Jensen to author, 28 September 1988.

69. Hitchman, *Liberal Arts Colleges*, 215.

70. *Mooring Mast*, 16 September 1983, 2 March 1984.

71. Ibid., 10 May 1974.

72. Meeting minutes, 16 February 1975, Presidential Search Committee Papers.

CHAPTER ELEVEN
STABILITY AND CHANGE

1. James A. Clifton to Melvin Knudson, 25 October 1974, Presidential Search Committee Papers.

2. Ibid.

3. R. J. Blandau to Melvin Knudson, 30 October 1974, ibid.

4. William O. Rieke to Melvin Knudson, 12 December 1974, ibid.

5. Article reprinted in *Scene* (October 1975).

6. Ibid.

7. Minutes, board of regents meeting, 11 September 1975.

8. Reprinted in *Scene* (October 1977).

9. Ibid.

10. Reprinted in "President's Newsletter to Regents" (February 1979), Board of Regents Papers, PLU Archives.

11. *Scene* (February 1980).

12. Ibid. (June 1986).

13. Quoted in ibid. (June 1987).

14. *Mooring Mast*, 10 December 1976. For the controversy over FCA involvement in the football program see ibid., 15 October 1976, 29 October 1976.

15. Ibid., 9 September 1986.

16. *Mooring Mast*, 13 February 1976.

17. *Scene* (February 1979).

18. Ibid. (October 1987).

19. Ibid. (December 1980).

20. Rodney Swenson, "International Students among Us" (PLU Humanities Division) *Prism* (Spring 1988).

21. *Mooring Mast*, 24 October 1975.

22. *Scene* (October 1980).

23. "PLU Baccalaureate Alumni Survey" (1981, 1986).

24. *Mooring Mast*, 6 November 1987.

25. "Interview with Robert Bellah," *Trinity News* (August 1986).

26. Warren Bryan Martin, "Where Is Christian Higher Education Going?" *Faculty Dialogue* (Spring-Summer 1986), 17.

27. *Scene* (February 1975).

28. Joseph M. Shaw, *History of St. Olaf College, 1874–1974* (Northfield, Minn., 1974), 606.

29. *Mooring Mast*, 23 March 1979.

30. W. O. Rieke to author, 12 January 1981.

31. *Mooring Mast*, 19 November 1982.

32. *Scene* (October 1985).

33. James Nuechterlein, "Athens and Jerusalem in Indiana," *American Scholar* (Summer 1988), 367.

34. Ibid., 368.

35. Lesley Hazelton, "Hers," *New York Times*, 24 April 1986.

36. *Scene* (June 1987).

Conclusion
A Story to Live By

1. Harvey Cox, *The Seduction of the Spirit* (New York, 1973), 9.

2. Martin Marty, "A Curious People—A Usable Past," *Concordia Historical Institute Quarterly* (Fall 1985): 102.

3. *Lutheran University Herald* (April 1891).

4. James Nuechterlein, "Athens and Jerusalem in Indiana," 357.

5. Ibid., 359.

INDEX

Educating for Service
was designed by Megan Benton & Paul Porter.
It was composed in Stempel Garamond,
a typeface adapted for computer composition
from the sixteenth-century type designs
of Claude Garamond.
The book was printed on acidfree 60-lb. Warren's Sebago
and bound in Iris cloth, imported from West Germany,
by Thomson-Shore, Inc., Dexter, Michigan.
The endsheets are Passport, an acidfree recycled paper that,
like all materials used in this book,
was selected for durability and permanence.